Introduction to the Sociology of Development

Also by Andrew Webster

INTRODUCTORY SOCIOLOGY (*co-author*)

Introduction to the Sociology of Development

Second Edition

Andrew Webster

palgrave
macmillan

Published by
PALGRAVE
Houndmills, Basingstoke, Hampshire RG21 6XS and
175 Fifth Avenue, New York, N.Y. 10010
Companies and representatives throughout the world

PALGRAVE is the new global academic imprint of
St. Martin's Press LLC Scholarly and Reference Division and
Palgrave Publishers Ltd (formerly Macmillan Press Ltd).

ISBN 0–333–49507–1 hardcover
ISBN 0–333–49508–X paperback

This book is printed on paper suitable for recycling and made from fully managed and sustained forest sources.

A catalogue record for this book is available from the British Library.

Transferred to digital printing 2006

For Helen, Matthew and Nick

Contents

List of Maps

List of Illustrations

List of Figures

List of Tables

Acknowledgements

It is five years since the publication of the first edition of this text, a period in which the sociology of development has itself experienced change, happily of a generally progressive nature. This new edition tries to capture the flavour of some of these new debates while still retaining its broadly introductory nature.

The revision has been helped by sustained debate within the School of Sociology at Cambridge as well as by wider opportunities I have had elsewhere to explore new ideas in the field. To these many colleagues I express my thanks. At the publishers I have received considerable editorial support from Dilys Jones, Victoria Yogman and Keith Povey.

I have also been lucky enough to receive the continued support and help of my wife, who fortunately is the same as the one who saw me through the first edition.

Cambridge A. J. W.
August 1989

The author and publishers wish to thank the following who have kindly given permission for the use of copyright material for the second edition.

Longman Group Ltd. for material from *Rural Development* by Robert Chambers, 1983, p.112

New Left Review for material from 'The Global Economy' by D. Gordon, *New Left Review*, March/April 1988

United Nations for material from *World Economic Survey 1987*, Table 11.2

Every effort has been made to trace all the copyright holders but if any have been inadvertently overlooked the publishers will be pleased to make the necessary arrangement at the first opportunity

1

The Sociology of Development

1.1 INTRODUCTION

> The tragedy of famine in Ethiopia will have serious consequences for its neighbour, Sudan, as new refugees flow into the country . . . [in Port Sudan] 45 000 Ethiopians are spontaneously settled in a community of about 350 000 people who have an area of wasteland called Kuria. There is no sanitation in Kuria. There are no taps, and families can spend up to a third of their income buying water brought round in an oildrum on a donkey cart. All the children suffer from malnutrition and there is one small UN clinic with two staff to deal with the entire population.
>
> (*Guardian*, 29 March 1983)

> Sudanese relief workers distributed flour to people displaced by flooding yesterday as the Blue Nile continued rising and overflowed into new areas of Khartoum. But fears receded of epidemics following earlier floods in which 1.5 million people lost their homes in the Sudanese capital.
>
> (*Independent*, 25 August 1988)

Two stories separated by the five years that have elapsed since producing the first edition of this book: a period through which we move from a drought-stricken Ethiopia to a flooded Sudan, whose own refugees search for a safe haven, perhaps in a neighbouring state. Drought and flood can bring famine and both are ecologically linked: desertification and flash flooding are the twin results of farming practices that remove trees and allow top-soil erosion. Yet these human disasters are as much to do with complex social and economic processes as they are with environmental management. The scale of these disasters seems to get worse as time passes: in September 1988, 75 per cent of the entire country of Bangladesh was under water, with 25 million homeless. Future tragedies on a bigger scale are likely, perhaps most particularly in Latin America.

Yet why do these events occur more frequently in the poorer countries of the world? Would they be less likely to happen if they were developed? Why aren't they developed, with better irrigation systems, more effective agriculture, less susceptibility to extremes of weather? How did the rich countries of the world cope with these problems, if indeed they ever had to? The historical and contemporary experiences of the poorer countries of the world appear so different from well-established industrial states, that it appears they exist within another world, the 'Third World'. In order to decide whether there is anything unusual about less developed countries, and so to make sense of inequalities within and between countries, we have to have some idea about the conditions that encourage prosperity and those that work against it. Over the past two decades social scientists have set themselves the task of understanding patterns of 'development' and social change, particularly those that promote prosperity.

This book gives an introductory guide to the range of debate this has generated among social scientists. While many specialists have contributed to this field of research, including geographers, economists, anthropologists, and political scientists, the book is primarily though not exclusively interested in the work of those who have concentrated on the sociological aspects of development, those who, in effect, have created the specialty known as the 'sociology of development'.

In Western Europe and the USA this specialty has grown rapidly since the early 1960s. In England, for example, a number of important academic centres for development studies have been established (such as at the Universities of East Anglia and Sussex) which have promoted important research in the area. Overseas, in Third World countries themselves, academics and political leaders have made and are making increasingly important contributions to the development debate. Official international agencies attached to organisations such as the United Nations (for example the International Labour Office), financial institutions such as the

World Bank and the commercial banks spend many millions of dollars each year encouraging economic growth in the Third World.

Before this, Western research, including sociological research, was more concerned with what was going on in Western societies. After the Second World War the development of research techniques encouraged social surveys that embodied more and more statistical data. These statistics could be more conveniently, cheaply and reliably obtained in one's own country. Besides, Western social science tended to be home-centred as much of it was tied to the demands of governments that sought advice and information in connection with the growth of the 'Welfare State'. Research on overseas countries was typically carried out by anthropologists interested in patterns of preindustrial culture rather than in wider social processes connected with patterns of world development.

If one goes further back however, to the contributions of the great sociologists such as Marx, Weber and Durkheim, there we do see the beginnings of a global perspective inasmuch as all three put forward ideas that they thought were relevant to all societies, both preindustrial and industrial. Their models of society were in fact built on a number of assumptions about the very origins, passage and future of society. In some ways, then, classical sociology was directly concerned with the analysis of social 'development'. However, much of this, as we shall see, relied on nineteenth century theories of evolutionary social progress that bore little resemblance to the processes that were at that very period of history beginning to lay the foundations for the underdevelopment we now see in the Third World.

The growth of detailed research on less developed countries which began during the early 1960s was prompted in part by the political events that accompanied the end of the old Western empires. Third World countries struggled for national independence and did so often under the banner of nationalist socialism. To a large degree, the rapid expansion of work on specific Third World societies can be attributed to the West's concern over its loss of influence in the old colonial areas.

Western politicians and academics courted the leaders of the newly independent states, urging Western backed economic 'development.' The United States, both militarily and economically strong, played a key role as sponsor of these development programmes. Thus, the interest in analysing the details of development was as much a political as it was an academic matter. As we shall see in Chapter 4, the failure of many of these development programmes subsequently led to a full-blown critique of the modernisation programmes then in fashion.

From the 1960s, then, there has developed a large body of literature on development issues, work that has generated a mass of detailed information as well as a range of theoretical perspectives. Thus one should not expect to find today a general consensus among the participants in the sociology of development debate. While there is of course widespread recognition of the basic facts of poverty and hardship in the world, there is considerable disagreement over the causes of this situation and, consequently, over the sort of policies that should be devised to cope with it.

1.2 AIMS OF THE TEXT

The text provides a review of the field and offers a basic introduction to development issues. While this will involve detailed discussion of the Third World the book examines general processes of social change, including industrialisation and urbanisation, that have occurred throughout the world. Processes such as population growth, educational expansion, political change and so on, are examined with reference to developed and less developed countries. A Sociology of Development should not be merely a Sociology of the Third World.

There are some general themes that the newcomer to development studies should recognise. First, the present state of poorer countries in the world can only be understood by examining their place in a global system of social and economic relationships. To some extent, to say that this Earth has 'first' (industrial capitalist), 'second' (industrial socialist), and 'third' (less developed, poor, primarily rural) worlds tends to create the impression that parts of this planet are culturally and economically entirely separate. But this is clearly not the case. Links are apparent in sports competitions, economic trade, super-power confrontation, job vacancies, tourism and many other areas, showing a planet whose peoples have become, for better or for worse, increasingly interconnected.

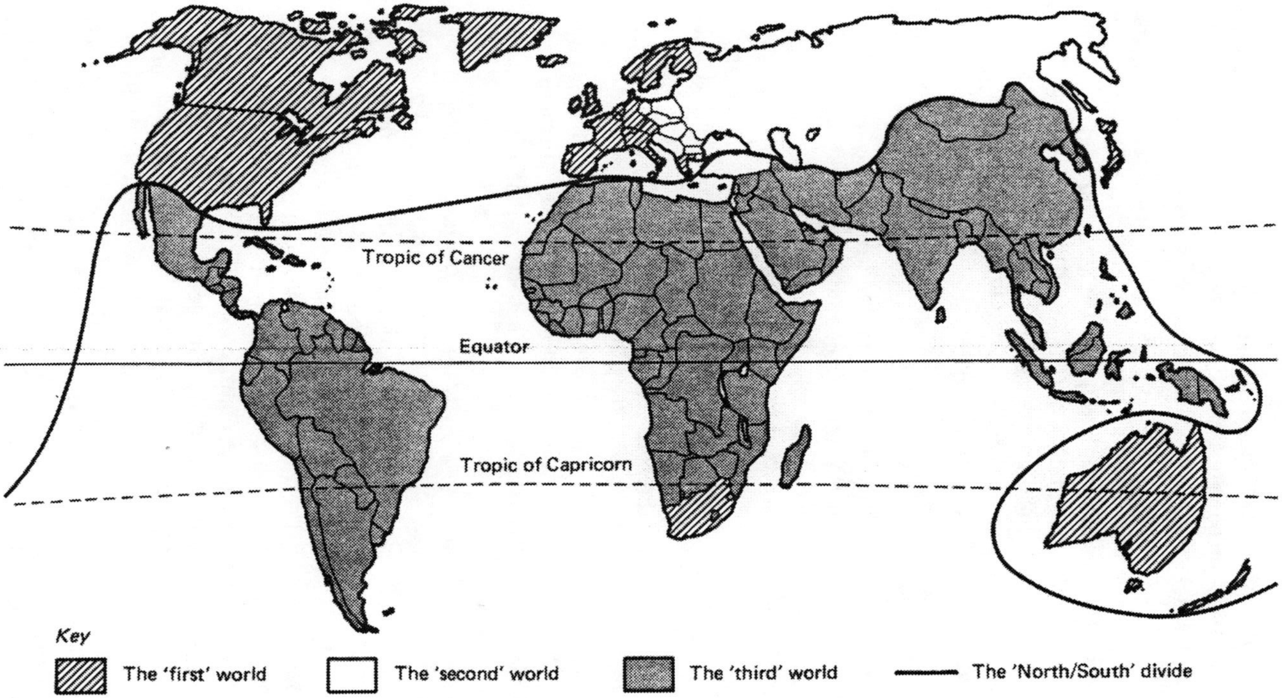

MAP 1.1 *The 'three' worlds and the 'North/South' divide*

While we might want to keep the term 'Third World' to describe a large number of societies that are relatively poor, it would be wrong to see this poverty as being unconnected with the relative wealth of the 'First World'. In short, we need a broad global perspective if we are to make sense of the pattern of affluence and disadvantage in the world. Map 1.1 indicates the location of the three 'worlds', the first two being primarily in the northern hemisphere, the third in the southern.

At the same time, however, it would be wrong to say that the particular cultural and economic features of societies can be ignored. To speak, as above, of a global system does not necessarily imply that the parts of that system are becoming more and more similar. For example, one of the major forces at work today is industrialisation. But its impact on the world has been uneven both culturally and economically. Some societies are more fully industrialised than others and while consumer goods like *Coca Cola* are marketed internationally, it does not mean that the conditions under which they are consumed are identical. The explanations for this state of affairs vary considerably as we shall see, but it is clearly the case that processes at work *within* certain countries have so far limited the development of an industrial base, and that this is particularly true of many Third World countries. The second guiding theme, then, is that it is important to study the particular features of a society that will affect its development.

Thirdly, a crucial aim of the text is to show how the relationship *between* cultural and economic processes influences social development. As we shall see in Chapters 3 and 4, theories of development have too often stressed either one of these to the point of virtually ignoring the other. Such a one-sided view leads to models of development that are less likely to take account of the specific way in which people *respond* to new cultural and economic influences at work in their communities. They may respond by *adapting* (rather than necessarily completely abandoning) the old ways of doing things. New and old may combine in quite unexpected ways. Both cultural and economic dimensions shape the strategies that people devise to sustain or enhance their livelihood, whether in the prosperous North or the less prosperous South.

Fourthly, any investigation of society will be better if it is conducted with a regard for the past. If we want to know 'where

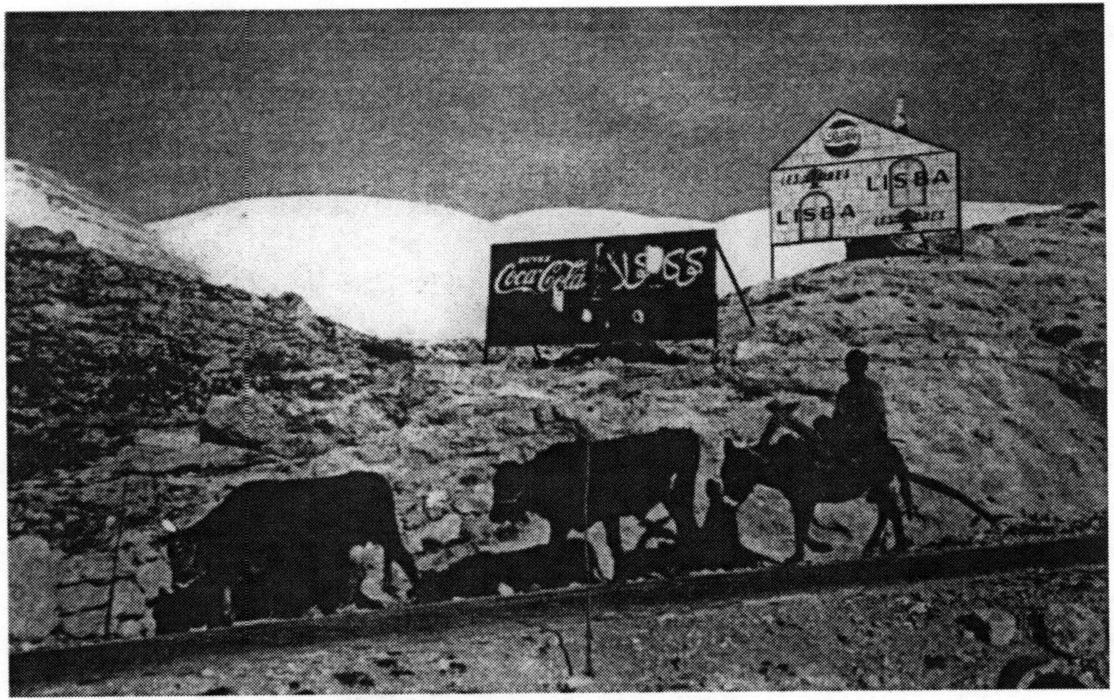

Illustration 1.1 *The global market: the multinationals in Lebanon* (Photo: Marc Riboud)

ILLUSTRATION 1.2 *The modern media as a vehicle for tradition* (© Mark Edwards Picture Library for Publishers)

we are' today we need to know where we have come from, and to know what aspects of our history continue to play a significant role in society. The significance of events or processes from the past is however not self-evident: we will select those historical features which we think are important according to the theory of social change that is thought to be most plausible. So, for example, different theories of change see the impact of colonialism in different ways, from being highly beneficial to being positively harmful. Whatever theory one adopts, history does record that empires have come and gone, dominant countries collapsed and international trading systems been destroyed and established elsewhere. This should tell us to have a dynamic view of social change. This will open us to the possibility that over time and for certain reasons, the pre-eminent countries of today may become weak in the future. Some economists have already remarked on the long-term decline of Britain, no longer the industrial or political power it once was, experiencing high levels of chronic unemployment and an erosion of services provided by the welfare state.

Finally, the text aims to show how the various theories of social change have influenced governments' plans for development, particularly in the Third World. Most Third World societies – whether 'capitalist' or 'socialist' – have tried to implement national plans for improving rural and industrial sectors of the economy. These plans are usually strongly influenced by the international aid and commercial banking agencies that provide capital, technology and know-how for long term development programmes. These programmes have changed as donors have altered their view of the 'problem' of development. The implementation of development plans is no simple matter but involves political decisions about access to material resources, the beneficiaries of the policy, and so on. The administration of any society by government is never simply a technical matter of 'efficient management' or 'good housekeeping'. Whether one is speaking of advanced or less developed countries, governmental institutions operate according to political priorities which hurt some of the people most of the time, and perhaps even most of the people some of the time, though presumably the latter could not persist without a challenge to the government's authority at some stage.

Summary

To summarise the points made so far: we need to have

(i) a broad global perspective focusing on the interconnection between rich and poor countries;
(ii) an awareness of the specific cultural and economic features of the Third World;
(iii) an awareness of the interaction between old and new forces at work in society;
(iv) a dynamic conception of development that recognises the possibility that advanced sectors of the world may decline;
(v) a view of development planning that recognises its inherently political character and impact.

1.3 KEY SOCIOLOGICAL QUESTIONS

Apart from the general themes sketched out above that underlie the text, what more specifically sociological questions will be asked in the book? After all, someone may say, isn't development all about economic growth; so surely then it is an area best dealt with by an economist? But the sociologist might reply, this raises the question as to what is meant by 'development': what, for example, do the 'ordinary' members of society think 'development' is? Their version of an improved world may be very different from that of the economist oriented towards the expansion of industrial production. Sociologically it is important to examine people's own conception of their lifestyle, life-chances and motivations in order to see how they respond to apparent 'development opportunities'. If people themselves do not think that an opportunity exists, whatever prompting the economist may give, they are unlikely to want to make a move.

Moreover, we need to know about the social implications associated with, say, the growth of consumer markets and the introduction of modern technology in a society. Do such things always undermine existing cultures and traditional ways of life? It may be the case that even when people participate in new economic activities they may act in ways that improve their life chances and their standard of living without undermining their traditional culture. This suggests that in some circumstances material prosperity may increase without cultural patterns changing markedly. But it may also be the case that, ultimately, without a *thorough* change in cultural values and norms only a restricted improvement in material prosperity is possible. This and related matters will be discussed in Chapter 3.

The way in which people regard their lives depends very much on the resources they can command especially through their membership of social groups. If people are well off in a society it is likely that they will attempt to sustain their relative advantage over others by acting culturally and economically in ways that will create obstacles for others trying to rise from below. The advantaged will become an interest group, perhaps a social class or status group. So, for example, in the Third World we should be interested in examining the activities of the colonial and ex-colonial elite: what resources did they and do they command to sustain their advantage? Since the world is unevenly developed as we have suggested, it is crucial to ask to what extent this is the result of groups defending their interests at both international and national levels. This question lies at the heart of a number of related approaches to development that are distinct from and highly critical of modernisation theory. These are 'dependency', 'underdevelopment' and 'urban bias' theories. They will be examined in Chapter 4.

In order to offer a convincing account of global inequality any sociological theory needs to show how to identify group, and especially class, interests. Can we happily use the models of class and power advanced many years ago by writers such as Marx and Weber, designed primarily to account for patterns of inequality found in relatively advanced industrial contexts? Does the analysis of Third World inequality require a slightly different model? In advanced industrial societies the lines of conflict between groups that produce the most striking pattern of inequality tend to be most clearly drawn between wage workers and the owners of factories and other enterprises. Each group uses the resources that each possesses, labour or capital, to pursue their interests, which may lead to conflict. This division between labour and capital is also in evidence in all Third World societies, and particularly evident in those that have a relatively large industrial sector, such as Brazil, Mexico and India. However the divisions between social groups and the resources on which they might draw in defence of their interests can be more complex than this. A wide range of cultural resources can be used to enhance one's economic life-chances. In India, for example, as the economy has failed to generate sufficient jobs for the many thousands who arrive in Calcutta (or any other important urban centre), many have begun to use their caste status as a resource to improve their chances of getting a job. Members of different castes who have by tradition been associated with specific occupations make a claim to any such jobs that become vacant in the town. In these circumstances caste divisions become accentuated. However, in times of an expanding labour market, caste divisions may become less significant as there is plenty of demand for workers, as happened in the textile industry in Bombay in the 1920s. Caste, ethnic, family and other status distinctions influence patterns of inequality in an important way in the Third World, and overlay the patterns of stratification more directly determined by class.

Industrialisation in Western Europe and other industrialised countries has been accompanied by educational expansion, population growth, mobility and urbanisation; at the political level it has typically meant the development of sovereign nation states. A key question is, therefore, whether industrial expansion and international commerce has a similar impact on the Third World. Towns have grown, universities have been built, sovereign states recognised, and populations increased. The skyline of most modern Third World cities would be familiar to any Western traveller. Yet we need to know about the real character of the urban centres: does it derive from an expanding industrial base that requires mobility, education and political stability or is it in some ways a pretence – modernisation without industrialisation? How does the development of education and urban centres compare with a similar development in the advanced industrial societies? These questions will be discussed in Chapter 5.

Chapter 6 examines the general relationship between class and political development. Class interests are often regarded as playing a major role in the way political institutions develop. Some have argued, for example, that the particular class relations that characterise capitalist societies are invariably associated with the growth of liberal democratic traditions coupled with mature state bureaucracies, both of which serve the broad interests of the dominant social classes. In contrast, where class structures are less developed – both economically and culturally – the political institutions may be inherently weak. This creates political instability and chronic social unrest. Many social scientists believe that it is the weakness of both social classes and their alliances in the Third World which causes persistent instability, a view which, as we shall see, derives from more general models of power and politics.

Educational expansion is an important priority for many less developed countries seeking to improve literacy rates and the overall level of skill in the population. This expansion is funded by governments who have relatively little capital. Cost are increasingly being met by borrowing from international aid agencies, even though these debts are becoming more and more difficult if not impossible to repay. Chapter 7 looks at the origins and implications of 'aid' and the 'development' plans it accompanies. As we shall see, many radical scholars argue that aid creates more problems than it solves, a view which is also held, but for different reasons, by a minority among the 'modernisation' theorists. The claim that aid is the answer to Third World poverty is then highly debatable.

Finally, in more recent years many people have become interested in pursuing alternative development paths that do not seek industrial expansion that is environmentally damaging and socially disruptive. Instead, many regard the future security and well-being of Third World countries to lie in the hands of those who seek to fashion a technology and a form of work which will provide social needs, create full employment, develop workers' skills and be environmentally sound.

Such ideas have in fact a long history stretching back into the early nineteenth century, when populist writers throughout Europe challenged the onset of industrialism and urban growth as a threat to small scale (family) enterprise and community/village life: the momentum of industrial competition and growth was thought to divide one section of the community from another. These ideas are still with us today, and in many ways have a much wider intellectual base and popular appeal than in the past, although they still have only a small impact on industrial policy and political programmes. Nevertheless, in both industrialised and Third World societies it has become increasingly common to hear that we should move away from producing wasteful, useless, and environmentally harmful products made because they are profitable, towards producing socially worthwhile products through an 'intermediate technology' in the workplace. This critique of industrialism is, therefore, in attacking the profit motive, a critique of capitalism. Political links between ecologists and those on the left have become more explicit in recent political campaigns in Europe. After presenting some key themes of the ecological critique of industrialism, Chapter 8 offers a brief look at one country that was once considered to be a model of self-reliant environmentally sound development, that is Tanzania.

The book concludes with a look towards the future examining the policy implications of different approaches towards the Third World and asks whether industrialisation is likely to occur there through either capitalist or socialist routes.

These then are the specific questions that organise the vast range of material that now goes to make up the 'sociology of development'. Before we examine competing accounts of the development process we shall in the next chapter look at the actual data on patterns of inequality that exist within the world, principally between the developed 'North' and the less developed 'South'.

2

Measures of Inequality and Development

2.1 INTRODUCTION

Over the past two decades less developed countries have experienced an increase in their per capita income. However, the relative gap between the poorest and the richest countries of the world has remained the same, while the absolute gap has even widened. Why, despite some gains, does this inequality remain so persistent?

Comparisons between countries such that some are called 'rich' and others 'poor' are usually based on estimates of the Gross National Product (GNP) that each has. This is an approximate measure of the total value of goods and services produced by an economy for any one year.

While comparisons between countries can be made in this way, it is also necessary to compare sections of society within countries to show that there may be many poor people even in rich societies. Subsequent international comparison creates the paradox that the poor in, say, the United States, may be relatively rich compared with the Third World poor. As Harrington (1969, p. 1) has said,

> There is a familiar America. It is celebrated in speeches and advertised on T.V. and in the magazines. It has the highest mass standard of living the world has ever known. In the 1950s this America worried about itself, yet even its anxieties were products of abundance.... While this discussion was carried on, there existed another America. In it dwelt somewhere between 40,000,000 and 50,000,000 citizens of this land. They were poor. They still are. To be sure, the other America is not impover-

ished in the same sense as those poor nations where millions cling to hunger....

Poverty
Poverty is a relative term, a condition that can only be defined by comparing the circumstances of one group of people or an entire economy with another one. The problem of defining poverty arises since the measures one uses to compare populations will depend on a whole range of assumptions about 'adequate standards of living' which some enjoy and which some do not.

Whatever standards one eventually chooses, if one acknowledges that poverty is primarily a relative concept, what then can 'absolute poverty' be – a condition experienced, says the WDR, by about 750 million people? Absolute poverty describes a situation in which people are barely existing, where the next meal may literally be a matter of life or death as the cumulative effects of malnutrition and starvation enfeeble all, particularly children, whose weakness gives them the tragic distinction of having the highest mortality rate for any group anywhere in the world. Thus in these circumstances poverty takes on an 'absolute' status since there is nothing beyond or 'beneath' it except death. Many in the Third World are in or close to this very vulnerable position, relying on aid, food relief or their own meagre returns from squatter farming, scavenging on refuse tips, prostitution, street hawking, and so on. For such people, statistics about relative GNPs can have no meaning or worth.

Absolute poverty is then fairly easy to define in objective though gruesome terms. Relative poverty is much more difficult to establish as an objective concept. Definitions of poverty can and do vary quite dramatically among those who have a professional interest in it, such as official government agencies and academics. While one might expect there to be considerable variation between countries it is perhaps surprising to find substantial disagreement about the *nature* and thereby the amount of poverty that exists within one country. For example, in 1973 a representative of the national Welfare Rights Organisation in the United States estimated that a family of four needed $7200 per year to satisfy

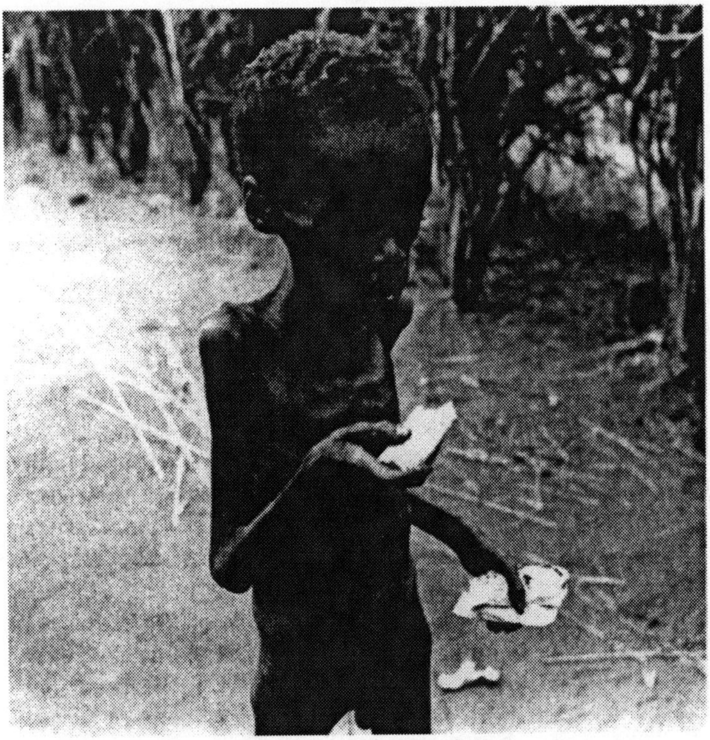

ILLUSTRATION 2.1 *Absolute poverty: so familiar an image of fund-raising campaigns that it has almost become a cliché – even though it is a harsh reality* (Photo: Arild Vollan)

their basic requirements – below this and the organisation considered people to be in poverty. Yet at the same time, the US government estimated the poverty line for a similar household at an income below $4500, while one of the States, Mississippi, established its State poverty line at $600! Such discrepancies indicate that divergent definitions are based on different assumptions of what 'basic needs' are and how family budgets are supposed to meet them. Two of the more important definitions of poverty are based on notions about adequate 'subsistence' and 'relative deprivation.' These are examined in the following section.

2.2 THE CONCEPT OF POVERTY

There are two predominant definitions of poverty: a *subsistence* definition and one based on an analysis of *relative deprivation*. The latter assesses disadvantage in wider terms than the subsistence approach and so usually produces a much wider figure of those said to be in poverty. This means that these differing measures of poverty have very different cut-off points distinguishing those said to be 'poor' from the non-poor.

The subsistence concept of poverty

This concept is based on an estimate of the level of income necessary for buying food sufficient to satisfy the average nutritional needs of each adult and child within a family. The cost of this food is seen as the basic cost of subsistence, which, when added to an allowance for basic clothing, fuel (for heating) and rent, produces an income figure below which families can be said to be in poverty.

This concept of poverty has dominated official policy in Western Europe and the United States since the turn of the century. Its attraction lies in its apparently objective, scientifically derived assessment of the nutritional levels necessary to keep the body physically healthy. For example, the food equivalent of approximately 3000 calories per day is considered necessary for the average adult. In 1989, the British government estimated that a man with a wife and two children could satisfy their basic requirements on £61.93, based on their entitlement to unemployment and child benefit. Had this amount kept pace with inflation over the past decade, their entitlement should have been £111.95, so the British poor are worse off now than in 1979.

At first sight this method for calculating the poverty line seems reliable and sufficiently scientific to warrant its continued use. Indeed most governments seem firmly committed to an approach of this sort. However on closer inspection a number of problems emerge:

(i) the estimates of nutritional needs are typically only averages and do not take into account the composition of households, the age of family members, their jobs and non-work activities;

(ii) poor people have to meet the increasing price of foodstuffs whose extra cost does not necessarily mean an increase in nutritional value, indeed in many cases much of the food in advanced societies is losing its food value;
(iii) estimates of what clothing is needed can be challenged since they are often based on what the *poorest* family spends on clothing;
(iv) the family budget and pattern of expenditure deemed to be adequate relies on a degree of rigorous accounting and disciplined personal behaviour which in its virtue and self-discipline borders on saintliness;
and finally,
(v) the estimates are rarely revised to reflect changing customs and needs that develop in the wider society, and, as we saw in the British example, usually fail to keep pace with inflation.

These five criticisms of the subsistence approach challenge its simplistic assumption that the basic needs of an individual or family can be determined merely through an assessment of the biological and physiological demands of the human body for food, warmth and shelter. Hence one might argue that the definition of 'needs' must be more broadly defined in terms of what things are socially expected. Thus instead of being defined in terms of a shortfall in some notional subsistence, poverty might be defined in terms of the degree to which people do not enjoy the basic standards of diet, living conditions, leisure activities and amenities which are socially perceived as 'customary'. Compared with these standards, poor people could be said to be 'deprived' to a greater or lesser extent. This brings us to the second major concept of poverty, that of 'relative deprivation'.

Poverty as relative deprivation

An important exponent of this approach is the British sociologist Peter Townsend (1979) who has produced the most recent survey on the poor. Townsend shows how the concept of need is very much a matter of *social* definition. For example, families will have to meet the cost of those 'needs' which the law may specify for them such as the cost of supporting a child at home for an extra year when the school leaving age was raised. Or again, parents may believe that their young infant 'needs' a bed of its own to encourage its development. Yet this need can only properly be satisfied by having the room (and the beds) necessary to do this. In societies where this practice is considered needful, deprivation occurs as soon as two or more children are without choice consigned to the same bed. In a similar fashion, the basic needs of health care will in part be determined by the availability of a health service.

In order to make sense of relative deprivation therefore, Townsend urges us to examine the social perceptions of approved needs, customary values and lifestyles and how they vary over time. From this analysis one can construct an index or list of those things and activities (such as, in western society, eating meat once a week, sending Christmas cards, etc.) which are considered 'normal' in a society. When people find that they have to exclude any of these features through lack of income, they can be said to have begun to experience 'relative deprivation,' and the *start* of poverty. As Townsend (1979, p. 31) says,

> Individuals, families and groups in the population can be said to be in poverty when they lack the resources to obtain the types of diet, participate in the activities and have the living conditions and amenities which are customary, or at least widely encouraged or approved, in the societies to which they belong. Their resources are so seriously below those commanded by the average individual or family that they are in effect, excluded from ordinary living patterns, customs and activities.

The great strength of Townsend's approach is that poverty is seen as a *process* of encroaching deprivation by which people gradually slip out of the mainstream of social life, almost unnoticeably, without being the stereotype paupers in rags and tatters. In addition, Townsend lays great stress on the need for *participation* in the customs, leisure pursuits, and political culture of everyday life: if people's circumstances militate against this participation then they are relatively deprived. Thus deprivation has to be measured both materially and socially.

Critics of Townsend's approach challenge his view that one can construct an objective list of deprivation indicators especially as he explicitly requires that 'needs' should be derived from their social convention. Thus opponents have said that he fails to distinguish between personal taste and true basic needs in referring to 'a customary style of living' as his yardstick. One could argue, for example, that one might decide not to eat meat or send Christmas cards as a matter of personal taste. Is one thereby suffering deprivation? No, say the critics. Townsend would probably reply that this decision not to eat meat has been made by someone who has a *choice* in these matters: there are many low-income families who do not have the resources to make this a viable choice. While both prosperous vegetarians and the poor in the towns and country may forgo meat-eating they will do so for very different reasons. Choice is a resource itself which is not equally distributed throughout society.

We have seen then two very different conceptions of poverty, that of subsistence and of deprivation. These could be applied to *any* society in the world to describe poverty though they would of course come up with different stories and draw different conclusions about its extent. In addition, since each defines poverty differently, the policy implications of how to cope with it would also be fundamentally different.

A subsistence approach would suffer from all those inadequacies noted earlier. Nevertheless, assuming a Third World government could afford it, it would clearly make some provision with regard to satisfying people's needs for food, warmth and shelter. This would certainly be an advance in the context of the desperate malnourishment experienced in many Third World countries. But such a strategy would serve primarily to relieve some *symptoms* of poverty rather than its cause. Much of the hardship suffered by people in the Third World is due to a steady reduction in available land. As it becomes increasingly difficult to hold on to what land one has to feed the family, a *small*, reduction in land holding leads to a sharp *increase* in the level of deprivation for all in the household. The increasing difficulties the poor face are captured in Chambers' ideas of the 'poverty ratchet' (see Fig 2.1). Acknowledging this situation, a policy based on the relative deprivation approach would confront the primary cause of poverty and propose a major redistribution of land (and probably income) in favour of the rural farmers and pastoralists.

Without such a policy it is likely that the number of people in serious difficulty will increase dramatically: the number of people

FIGURE 2.1 *The deprivation trap: Chambers' poverty ratchet*

Townsend's approach to deprivation in industrialised countries is similar to Chambers' analysis of rural poverty in the Third World. Like Townsend, Chambers argues that people experience worsening deprivation rapidly after the initial onset of poverty: as the poverty ratchet twists it creates increasing vulnerability which in turn produces powerlessness and so on, thus creating a cross-linked cluster of deprivation.

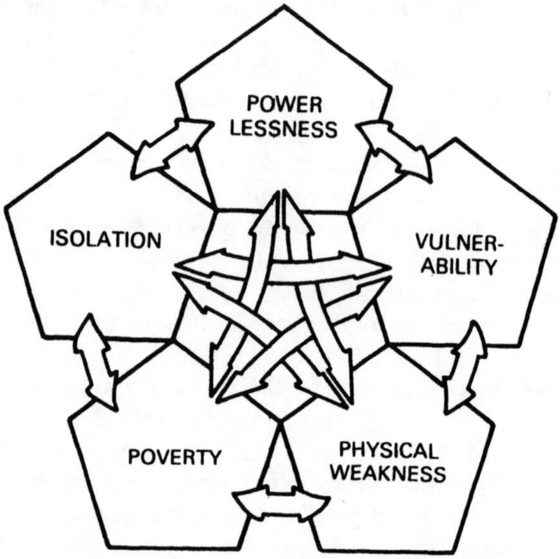

Source: R. Chambers, *Rural Development* (London: Longman, 1983)

dependent on agriculture in the Third World is growing all the time, and in the last twenty years has almost doubled, reaching a figure of about 1250 million.

If we look at the policies that have been advanced to cope with serious poverty and inequality in the Third World we can see a gradual shift, at least in principle, away from a subsistence approach to a strategy based on a broader social evaluation of basic needs that is more akin to the relative deprivation approach: this is suggested by the World Bank's attempt to develop a 'Physical Quality of Life Index'.

We shall now examine in more detail the character of the Third World, its poverty and the shift in development strategy based on the welfare policy of tackling relative deprivation.

2.3 THE THIRD WORLD AND ITS POVERTY

Variation in the Third World

Before we can examine Third World poverty we must look closely at what we actually mean by 'the Third World'. The phrase is a familiar one but this does not necessarily imply that there is universal agreement over its meaning. This can cause some confusion for those new to the area. For example, it is a phrase used to describe many evidently impoverished countries such as Ethiopia, yet is also a label applied to describe many evidently prosperous countries, such as the oil-producing states of the Middle East, for example, Iran and Kuwait. Or again, some texts include China in the Third World while others do not. Clearly this suggests that notions about the Third World can vary dramatically; yet despite this we still seem to have a rough idea of what we are talking about. A number of scholars have, perhaps, taken the search for a precise definition a little too far, producing various lists of countries that (they claim) can be said to be reliable. For example, Abdalla (1978) counts 108 (out of the world's total of 185) countries in this category though he excludes China whereas other researchers claiming a similar degree of precision would include it. Since such lists vary, it is an indication that one can only claim to be precise on the basis of a set of initial *assumptions* about 'development' or the lack of it. Change one's assumptions and the list of Third World countries changes. In addition, the search for a precise list tends to lose sight of the *dynamic* character of world processes that gradually change the economic and political character of countries, including that of advanced states, some of which may suffer a serious decline in the future.

The poor countries of the world do, however, have some similarities that allow us to decide on the approximate boundaries of the 'Third World,' as suggested by Map 1.1. Third World countries

(i) tend to have a larger agricultural than industrial workforce;

(ii) tend to rely on a limited number of raw material products for export;
(iii) have relatively poor diets and high levels of illiteracy;
(iv) have often experienced a colonial past.

However such indicators of 'Third World' status are always provisional since there are a number of countries traditionally placed in the Third World which do not share all such characteristics, or have only one or two of them: this is particularly true of the newly industrialising countries.

We must in fact recognise that Third World countries are considerably different from one another. This means that, as argued in Chapter 1, the Third World should not be treated as a homogeneous or uniform bloc. While their relatively poor condition might be the most important feature of the vast majority of Third World societies, it is experienced in varying ways and to a greater or lesser extent. Mabogunje (1988) has suggested that this variety can be demonstrated by looking at three aspects of the societies: their populations, natural resources and current 'levels of development'.

Population

Mabogunje shows how population size and density vary between Third World countries quite dramatically. For example, many countries have only about 5 million inhabitants while a few, such as India with over 620 million, are very large. He then draws attention to an important population factor influencing subsequent growth. This is the degree to which a country has been subject to population migration from the 'central industrial countries' (of Europe in particular). In Asia and Africa, despite colonial expansionism, there were relatively few *settler* groups from overseas (apart from settlement in South Africa), but in Central and Latin America the immigrant settlers became the dominant population group so that the native population struggled to preserve its cultural identity. Mabogunje stresses that the important socio-economic implication of this is that the countries of Central and Latin America have been much more easily penetrated by US and European capital, which has been used in such a way as to encourage considerable industrial growth, even though this has been shackled by rampant inflation (of 200–300 per cent) and an increasing debt-burden.

Resources

A second distinction between Third World countries can be made in terms of their 'natural resource endowments'. Countries can be grouped into three types according to the sort of raw materials they produce. First, there are the temperate agricultural economies of Latin America where the rich farmlands have been extensively commercialised by European business over the past century specialising in arable and meat products. Secondly, there are the tropical countries that, since the colonial days of the mid-1880s, have been pushed into producing agricultural crops, such as sugar, coffee, and rubber for the central industrial countries. Despite these products being of some importance to manufacturing industry in Europe in the nineteenth century, they were cultivated by traditional farming techniques with little intervention from the 'North' in controlling production directly. Since the Second World War, however, the rise of the multinational corporation with extensive international interests in agriculture – the so called 'agribusiness' companies – has brought a much greater interest in owning and controlling farmlands in the Third World. Finally, the third group of countries are those which have been of long-term importance to the industrial economies of Europe and elsewhere because of their *mineral* resources. Countries such as Mexico, Chile, and Bolivia in Latin America, Iran and Malaysia in Asia, and Zambia, Zaire and Libya in Africa are just a few in this group. The need to exploit the mineral wealth of such regions for the development of European industry led to a much greater direct control by overseas concerns in mining. Foreign companies not only introduced their own technology but also rigorous and often harsh measures for controlling workers and the whole system of production.

Whatever natural resources they produce, it seems clear that many Third World countries are the cultivators or extractors of raw materials rather than being the refiners or processors of them by manufacture. One might then be tempted to regard the world economy as being divided into two, with farmers and miners in the 'South' and factory workers, engineers and scientists in the

'North'. However, while much of the Third World is predominantly reliant on agricultural produce for export, there are significant exceptions to this pattern such as Brazil, Mexico, India and other Asian countries. South Korea, for example, the host country for the 1988 Olympics, has experienced a rapid growth in its urban-based industrial workforce. By 1986 two-thirds of the labour force worked outside agriculture. As Harris (1986) says, 'a nation of peasants had become one of urban workers' (p. 33), and much of this change had occurred through strong government control over the economy. Nevertheless, many Third World countries still rely heavily on selling raw material commodities as their principal source of income.

Levels of Development

As the preceding section suggests some countries may have a greater productive capacity than others. This may be the result of state policy – especially an effective land reform – as well as higher investment from banks and commercial companies from the North. Thus a third way to compare Third World countries is in terms of the value of their productive output, or GNP. In 1987, the poorest African and Asian countries had an average income of \$400 or less per person, the newly industrialising countries such as Brazil and Mexico about \$2500, while the rich OPEC states of the Middle East averaged over \$5000 of which Qatar, with a population of only 1.3 million, enjoyed an average of almost \$25 000 per head, making it in these terms the richest country in the world (the US figure was \$15 500). Yet even these OPEC states still suffer serious problems with regard to health, literacy, the development of both their agricultural and their industrial bases, and display a massively unequal distribution of income and wealth. Moreover, the Middle East's capacity for development based on oil can be seriously disrupted by long-standing regional hostilities such as the recent eight-year long war between Iraq and Iran. The economic difficulties this has created indicate the way in which these OPEC states are still, like many other Third World countries, heavily dependent on a single primary commodity, in this case oil.

This brief look at population, resources and levels of GNP gives some idea how Third World countries differ from one another. We can begin, therefore, to see that their opportunities for overcoming poverty are consequently unequal. Countries likely to experience the most serious hardship ahead are the low-income, non-oil agricultural societies, especially those of Africa, such as Tanzania, that face the prospect of increasing costs for imports, declining export values and limited opportunity for commercial borrowing. Poor farmers have little incentive to grow crops for export if they get declining returns: on average, prices for primary commodities declined by 25 per cent between 1980 and 1987. In these circumstances it would be more sensible for farmers to grow crops solely for their own household consumption.

Problems with using GNP to indicate 'development'

Information about GNP and other economic data can be obtained from a number of sources including two annual publications, the World Development Report and the World Bank Atlas. These are official World Bank texts that provide statistical data on the performance of the majority of countries gathered through its agencies around the globe. The Bank recognises that these data indicate rather than properly represent the true extent of relative inequality between countries. Despite their limitations which we shall examine shortly, they do give a stark indication of the unequal distribution of income in the world economy, as Table 2.1 shows. Not only does this table indicate the great differences between rich and poor countries in terms of GNP per person, it also shows the negligible 'growth' in GNP for the low-income countries which, although higher on paper, has not improved in real terms since 1960.

TABLE 2.1

GNP per person (in 1980 dollars)

	1950	1960	1980	1987
Industrial countries	4130	5580	10660	12500
Middle-income countries	640	820	1520	2000
Low-income countries	170	180	250	300

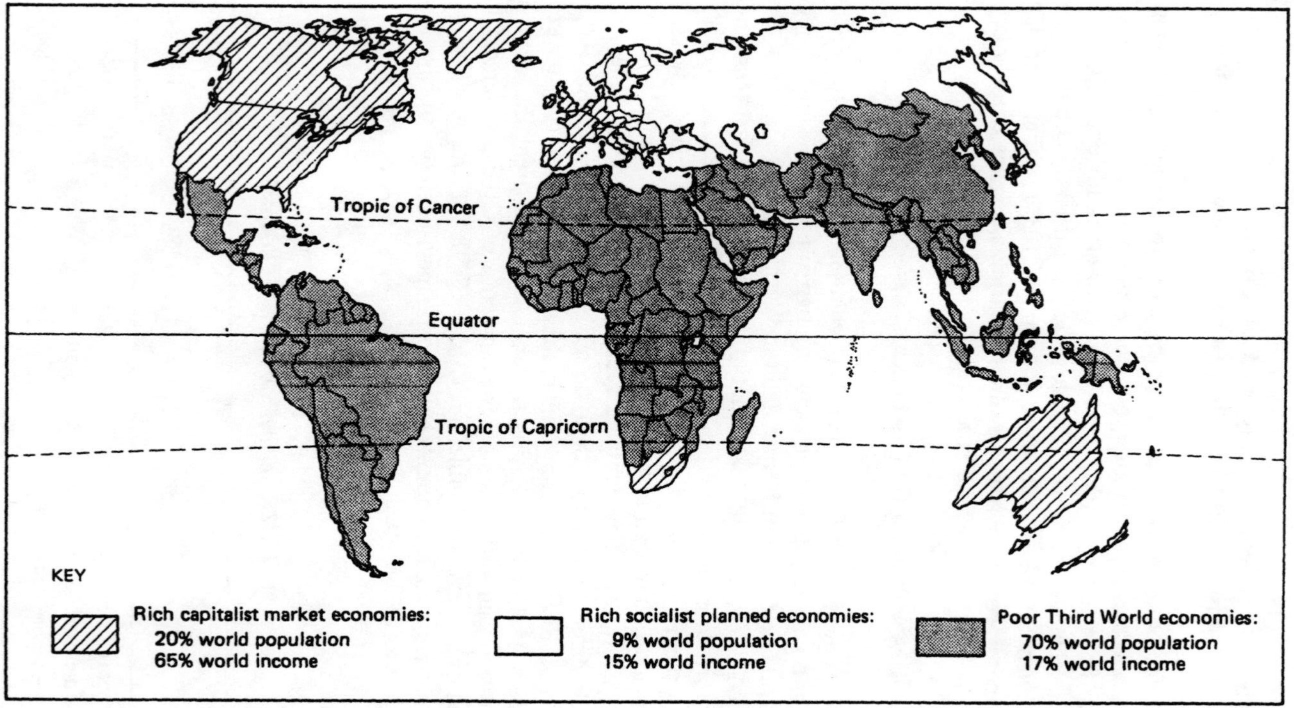

MAP 2.1 *Share of global income by population*

These figures are a valuable source of information about the relative levels of development in different parts of the world economy. Yet it must be recognised that the data are partial in three ways:

(i) they are usually national *averages* which in themselves say nothing about the distribution of resources among the population;
(ii) they omit certain activities that have an economic value;
(iii) they imply that development can be measured in straightforward quantitative money terms.

Let us examine these three criticisms more closely.

(i) GNP refers to the total money value of goods and services that are exchanged within a nation and GNP per person describes the average of this value for each member of the population. However, averages are notoriously unreliable. They typically hide much greater deviations from the norm than say the figure for the average physical height of a population does. That is, detailed investigation of the actual income received by members of a population shows great inequalities within all nations, but particularly so within the Third World. For example, although the GNP per person is notionally \$2000 or so in Brazil, in reality the top 5 per cent enjoy thirty times as much income as the bottom 20 per cent. These very wealthy people have the effect of raising the overall income per person, although in reality the great mass of Brazilians have very low incomes and in many thousands of cases absolute poverty is the norm.

(ii) At the same time, however, since GNP is a measure of the value of 'products' (goods and services) which are *exchanged* through markets in the economy, it excludes other activities which have an economic value but which are hidden, either because they are illegal or because they do not enter into exchange. There are three main activities that fall into this category, all of which occur to a greater or lesser degree in all societies:

(a) the work of domestic labourers (usually women) who receive no payment for running and caring for the household, an activity that takes many hours of unsocial labour time;

(b) the work of families in producing food for their own consumption through cultivation or animal husbandry: this so-called 'subsistence production' is important in sustaining the livelihood of many peasant homes in the Third World that still have access to land;
(c) the illegal and 'informal' activity of the economy that occurs in every country in the form of corruption, cash payment for casual labour that is not recorded by the authorities, and so on.

It is the last two activities which are of particular importance for poor urban and rural households in generating, albeit on a precarious basis, some extra food or income for livelihood, the value of which is not included in their country's GNP estimates, estimates that depend on surveys of those in full-time employment, a much easier activity for officials to count.

(iii) Finally, as we have seen, GNP figures are used to compare countries' levels of 'development', measured in terms of the growth in the value of products in their economies. Yet societies may 'develop' in this sense while many people within them become progressively poorer in absolute and relative terms, as has happened for example in Brazil. To understand development in bald GNP terms is to ignore the way in which the value it represents is *distributed* among members of society, including access to employment, the provision of welfare, education services and so on. Nevertheless, the notion of GNP dominated development thinking for many years, especially during the decade after 1960.

This period is known as the first 'development decade', a time during which development policies were formulated by international aid agencies in tandem with Third World governments. They assumed that rising GNP levels meant real growth whereby poverty would be eventually eradicated.

These policies were in part based on assumptions about the causes of rural and urban poverty and low growth. It was thought that poverty was in many ways the result of limited ambition on the part of families: farmers were merely content to produce sufficient for their immediate needs, and workers were said to have a poor work ethic and low ambition, working only to satisfy their limited desires. Lack of development was seen as a fault of the people themselves whose malnutrition, ill health and poor living conditions reflected insufficient production by them, indolence, the distractions of their lifestyle with its archaic social institutions, and their backward looking attitudes and beliefs. To help the people to overcome these self-inflicted ills, a range of development programmes was established.

For the rural population programmes were developed that encouraged families to produce crops for *commercial* markets both abroad and in their expanding urban regions. In order to encourage this change as quickly as possible, foreign experts, accompanied by sophisticated technology, were introduced. External assistance was considered crucial since it was thought that the poor were unable to change things adequately by their own efforts, and that growth would occur only through *diffusion*, or a spreading of ideas and technology from the advanced countries to the Third World. It was assumed that modernisation was best brought about by the exchange of goods and ideas on the national and international markets. One gave the peasants the opportunity to produce for these markets. Thus for example, the Kenyan government Development Plan of 1966–70 placed great emphasis on agricultural development, whereby increasing agricultural productivity would encourage growth in the industrial sector as rising rural incomes would lead to a rising demand for consumer goods.

However, it would be of little use to the Third World country if these consumer goods were to be all *imported* from countries with a more developed manufacturing sector. This would merely lead to a drain of capital overseas and increasing 'balance of payments' problems. Thus, accompanying the programmes to raise agricultural prosperity were programmes designed to limit imports of consumer goods, to encourage instead the growth in urban regions of new domestic industries that could satisfy the demand for consumer products. This policy of 'import-substitution' sought to provide capital and business opportunities for those in the urban regions, and was pursued with great vigour, though not exclusively, in Latin America and Asia.

As an approach to overcoming poverty these agricultural and industrial policies attempted to give the poor a kick up their collective backside, to demonstrate what could be were they to grasp the opportunity, to give them a nudge forward so that they might eventually progress under their own steam.

These policies have the hallmarks of the subsistence approach to poverty outlined earlier in section 2 of this Chapter. That is, this growth oriented development strategy sought to expand the agricultural and industrial sectors in such a way as to give the rural and urban poor the chance to pull themselves up: helping the poor to help themselves. As we shall see in Chapter 3, a number of sociologists and social psychologists made important contributions in the 1960s to this economic strategy and so were instrumental in sustaining its credibility in international development circles.

For a decade this philosophy dominated development thinking. Yet by the early 1970s it was clear that all was not well. While a number of countries' per capita income had grown over the period, and health and education had improved, the standard of living in many countries which had experienced a rise in their GNP did *not* improve for the vast majority of the population. Indeed, over the period in question, many tens of millions joined the hundreds of millions already suffering from absolute poverty.

Critics of the growth oriented approach argued that this was because it had failed to give sufficient attention to real human welfare through prioritising industrial growth and agricultural commercialisation. Rural deprivation was falsely regarded as a problem that any sufficiently motivated peasant could overcome in an expanding economy. Critics, such as Streeten (1978), argued that the economic priorities of the growth model had been *both* economic and social failures inasmuch as they had done little to strengthen the economic structure of the Third World, and had done a great deal to harm the material and social well-being of the rural producers. Lipton (1977) claimed that most of the advantages that came from these development policies were creamed off by the more articulate, organised and powerful urban classes: 'The urban classes have been able to "win" most of the rounds of the struggle with the countryside; but in so doing they have made the development process needlessly slow and unfair' (p. 13).

Streeten and others such as Seers (1977), as well as bodies like the International Labour Office (ILO), argued for a complete change of approach to Third World poverty and development. They argued that proper growth can only be encouraged by a programme that has as an essential ingredient a *redistribution* of income and resources downwards (for example through taxation) towards poorer rural households.

Famine comes from income insecurity

Who are the victims of famines? Rarely, it would appear from a study done for the International Labour Organisation, does famine result simply from a reduction in food production and affect all people in the area uniformly. In 1943 in Bengal, in 1974 in Bangladesh, in 1973 in Ethiopia those who suffered most from famine were the landless – casual laborers employed in agriculture or providing unskilled or semi-skilled services – and pastoralists, who had to trade their emaciated beasts for expensive food grain. In short, the vulnerable were those whose "exchange entitlements" were removed or massively devalued by the events preceding the famine.

It was not a decline in food availability itself that caused the famines. In Bengal in 1943 the food supply was lower than in many years but higher than in 1942 and well within a normal range of fluctuations. In Bangladesh per capita food availability was, if anything, higher in 1974 than in earlier years. In Ethiopia, on the other hand, a drought sharply decreased food supplies in a localized but by no means inaccessible area.

The mechanisms that caused marginal groups to suffer varied. In Bengal a wartime inflation debased the real value of their already low wages, which bought much less food than before. In Ethiopia, low yields caused farmers to dismiss farm servants, not hire laborers, and reduce their demand for other services. Food prices did not rise, but the poor, losing their employment, lost their source of earnings (entitlement) to buy food. Similar problems plagued the Sahel region in the early 1970s. Pastoralists saw their herds diminish while animal prices fell, and more had to be marketed in exchange for food grains. In Bangladesh a long period of flooding similarly reduced employment opportunities. Simultaneously, food prices rose and thousands starved.

Famines are therefore compatible with adequate food supplies within a country or within large regions. In Ethiopia the national supply of food did not decrease. But major groups of the poor, especially the landless, were extremely vulnerable to a sudden reduction in their earnings. In such cases, and particularly if prices rise suddenly, these are the people who starve.

Source: *World Development Report*

Such direct intervention in the distribution of resources is completely contrary to the philosophy behind the market-oriented growth models of the 1960–70 period. It also involves a change in the view of poverty: no longer a condition to be overcome by the individual, it came to be seen as the product of the deteriorating social and environmental circumstances of the poor. Great stress was laid on the failure of the market model to create enough jobs, particularly in the context of an increasing population. As in advanced industrial societies, poverty is very much a problem associated with either underemployment or unemployment.

A valuable illustration of how unemployment, poverty and famine are linked through socio-economic processes is provided by the boxed extract taken from the 1982 edition of the *World Development Report*.

The recognition that the nature of poverty had to be reconsidered led academics, development agencies (such as the World Bank), and some aid donors in the North to propose a radically different approach to Third World development. This became known as the 'basic needs strategy.'

2.4 THE BASIC NEEDS STRATEGY

Rather than giving priority to gradual economic growth measured in terms of increasing GNP which, as we have seen, leaves many millions of social casualties in its wake, the basic needs strategy seeks to do two things:

(a) to relieve as quickly as is possible absolute poverty through intensive direct assistance to those in desperate circumstances:

(b) to meet the 'basic needs' of all in terms of material wants such as food, clothing, shelter and fuel, and also, as some argue, social needs such as education, human rights and what is called 'participation' in social life through employment and political involvement.

At the heart of this approach lies a desire for social justice and welfare based on a concern that the material resources of a society should be distributed more evenly throughout the population. This includes all the assets or resources of the society, including 'public goods' (government funded services such as hospitals and schools) and capital for investment in agricultural or industrial enterprise.

For rural regions this new approach stresses the need for *land reform* to make land available for poorer farmers, opening up new farmland and making cheap loans or grants available to the rural households.

In urban regions, the ILO has argued that the government should assist all those who have had to rely on their wit, chances and kin assistance to make some work for themselves in the towns. Many people attracted to towns in search of work find that there are very few full-time jobs available on the 'formal' job market. In response, an 'informal' job sector has developed: people engage in a mixture of legitimate and illegal activities such as distilling drink, trading in goods at stalls, roadside booths or just by hawking, laundering, removing night-soil, and a range of other trading and service activities (see Hart [1973]). The ILO argues that any government should encourage rather than check this informal sector. Commenting on the development of this informal sector in Kenya, the ILO (1972, p. 504) noted that:

> On the basis of any reasonable calculation, the urban informal sector in 1985 will include a larger proportion of the urban labour force than it does today. We do not view this inevitable development with dismay, for we see in the informal sector not only growth and vitality, but also the source of a new strategy of development for Kenya.

It seems reasonable to suggest that these rural and urban strategies for relieving deprivation and satisfying basic needs have much in common with the view of poverty as 'relative deprivation' discussed earlier in this chapter. This is indicated in a number of ways, perhaps most clearly in its combining material with social needs to encourage great *participation* in the economy and culture of a society. This echoes Townsend's concept of 'participation' and is premised on the assumption that the provision of the human 'rights' of employment and political involvement in decision-making are basic needs of every individual in any society.

However, despite the move away from the earlier growth model of the first 'development decade', there has been little real attempt to implement the basic needs policy properly. There are relatively few cases, for example, of rural development programmes directly benefiting the rural poor, while there are many examples of richer farmers receiving most of the gains. The World Bank still extends most of its credit to countries or groups within countries that are seen as a good commercial bet. The increasing debt-burden of many Third World countries during the 1980s has meant that the Bank has been more interested in policies designed to promote stabilisation, restructuring and growth. As Hoeven (1988) has shown, this has meant that the little genuine attention that was given to basic needs has all but faded away.

One might not be too surprised, therefore, to find that in these circumstances poor farmers and residents in urban centres become somewhat cynical about so-called 'development' programmes. The response that such people make to development policies is a crucial factor influencing the outcome of planned social change. A weakness of many of the policies of recent years is their failure to examine the perceptions of 'development' held by the ordinary men and women who are the subject of all this expert attention.

It is these perceptions that are of particular interest to a number of sociologists and anthropologists who have examined the aspirations and the values of people subject to the development process. If people do not like what they see, or interpret development programmes in ways that are significantly divergent from developers' intentions then no matter how *economically* viable they are on paper, they may be completely impractical *socially*. It is, then, important to consider perceptions of 'development from below', from the ordinary folk who live and work in the factories, streets, rice fields, sugar plantations, mountain villages and so on.

2.5 THE PERCEPTION OF DEVELOPMENT FROM BELOW

In the earlier sections of this chapter we looked closely at the concept of poverty. It is clear that poverty implies a lack or loss of something and that development for most theorists means making good this loss (however defined). In Chapters 3 and 4 we will look at the work of the more important of these theorists. They all make differing assumptions about what development 'really is': but, before we let the more abstract issues of this development debate take over, it is wise to pause for a moment to consider what people themselves regard as their priorities for development.

Wallman (1977, p. 2) points out that there are two good reasons why people in both the Third World and in industrialised countries may be disillusioned with 'progress and development':

1) However successful a particular region's development effort, the economic gap between it and its industrialised technological superiors continually widens. 'Progress', far from being the explicit arrival point of the development process, tends to recede as one advances. Even the poor are beginning to realise that they cannot catch up with the rich. In many cases they are no longer trying.
2) High GNP and/or rates of industrial growth are precisely *not*

> progress for the developed regions any longer – apparently bringing more ills than we yet know how to cure.

There are two crucial points to note in Wallman's remarks. First, the lack of 'ambition' among the poor, so frequently noted by some social scientists, may be a perfectly reasonable response to a set of circumstances in which 'they cannot catch up with the rich'. We shall return to consider this point in more detail in the next chapter. Secondly, while most people regard the acquisition of material goods as worthwhile, many might not welcome such gains if it meant they came at the expense of their personal independence and privacy. People's perceptions of development or progress are a complex mixture of these two objectives which do not necessarily lie easily with one another. Wallman (1977, p. 14) gives us some idea of the tensions that arise:

> Most of us want to live better *and* to live the way we have always done; to participate *and* to remain separate; to keep up with the Joneses *and* to distinguish ourselves from them; to give our children more options than we have had *and* to see them choose as we would have chosen.

While the growth oriented economist may regard such a confusion of ideas as an absence of economic rationality, these are some of the thoughts people have which will influence, for example, the sort of response they will make to economic 'opportunity'.

Development experts may decide that communities need to grow in order to remain viable. But the people within them may believe that all is well and may resist any disruption. Many studies have shown this. One of these, by Ralph Matthews (1977), looks at the attempt by the Canadian government to encourage resettlement of the inhabitants of small fishing villages in Newfoundland, in order to relocate the population in larger 'growth' areas, on the assumption that the villages were no longer economically viable.

Matthews shows how this limited economic view of the villages by the Canadian authorities ignored the way in which, for the people, the villages *were* socially and culturally viable. The people thought that even economically things were not as bad as the experts believed, since they had access to a number of material resources, such as food grown on household plots, which were ignored by the experts in their calculations. The majority of the villagers resisted the move not because they were opposed to the potential material gains to be had elsewhere, but because they sought to meet development 'in their own terms', without having to abandon their community. They wanted 'a style of development related to their own goals and values.' As Matthews (1977, p. 130) reports:

> Most emphasised that it was cheaper to live on the island than anywhere else, for they owned their own house and had few expenses. Others felt that they were more 'self-sufficient' there. Some also felt that the people just seemed 'more contented' than elsewhere. There can be no doubt that those who remained have a high level of commitment to the community and its way of life.

Development v. indigenous community

Today tribal peoples are still seen as barriers to the spread of 'civilization' and 'progress'. Indigenous lands are under enormous pressure from an ever-expanding industrial economy which is probing every corner of the earth for new resources. Lands once considered worthless desert or inhospitable jungle (suitable only for 'reserves') are now resource frontiers. In the US alone an estimated 80 per cent of all uranium reserves and a third of all strippable coal reserves are on native land. So highly prized are these resources that Navajo land around Big Mountain, Arizona was declared a 'National Sacrifice Area' by the US government in 1974. No points for guessing who gets sacrificed.

In Third World countries, too, indigenous lands are under pressure. And the stakes are high – tribal peoples are intimidated, beaten and sometimes killed for opposing modern-day land grabs. In countries like Brazil and Malaysia governments want to open up new territory to mining and lumber companies. In Sarawak, Malaysia, the Orang Ulu have protested about unchecked logging by blocking roads into their territory. And in Madhya Pradesh, India, more than 60,000 tribal people are fighting a huge dam project that would flood their traditional homeland.

Source: *New Internationalist*, August 1988.

Conclusion

The studies by Wallman, Matthews and others show how people's development goals may be very different from those of the planners. Choices for 'development' are not self-evident. What counts as being 'poor', 'in need' and 'development' depends on the value judgements that people make when they perceive social inequality. Debates over inequality and development are then ultimately ideological disputes that involve political as well as economic choices. Some are at the receiving end of this debate and will find that, whatever their perceptions of how things should be, the choices will be made for them. There may be those who try to resist this with the inevitable breakdown in social order as a result. Development is not, then, always a peaceful and effective process. Commenting on recent experience in India, Singh (1987) writes:

> As the size of youth in our society has grown, as the magnitude of unemployment both rural and urban has increased, and as the disenchantment of the poorer and weaker sections of society with the national ideology of development has also grown significantly, it has resulted in large scale delegitimation of the civic structure of authority and power. The incidence of violence and lawlessness, the growth in protest movements and movements based on violent separatist or alienative ideologies in many parts of the country is indicative of the writing on the wall (p. 65).

However, it is not merely the poor who may resist development: in prosperous countries the more affluent social classes are just as likely to oppose the growth of towns, industry and transport systems when they disturb their countryside retreats. As Newby (1987) has shown, the 'escape' of the urban middle classes in Britain to commutable country homes has had to contend with a highly intensive, uncountrylike, agriculture as well as a massive growth in countryside leisure activities that suck in large numbers of urbanites and their cars. The affluent rural residents will try to limit how much of the countryside is 'consumed' by these other social groups. As Newby says:

> The countryside has become a 'positional good' – that is, something which is fixed in supply and whose consumption is dependent on one's position in society. . . . Concern for the rural environment thus became a public issue partly because there

> was now residing in the countryside an affluent and articulate population, no longer dependent upon local farmers and landowners for housing and employment, and which was capable of mobilising itself politically (p. 227).

In the Third World, of course, for the vast majority of rural residents, it is the urban centre that has become the equivalent 'positional good' as large numbers migrate to towns in search of greater economic security.

Summary

A number of points may be made to summarise this chapter.

1. In the first two sections of the chapter the problem of defining poverty, and, by implication, material and social needs was discussed. The measurement of poverty is often based on the concepts of 'subsistence' or 'relative deprivation'. Different *conceptions* of poverty give rise to different *policies* to alleviate it.
2. The poor countries that make up the Third World share some important features but they are not a uniform bloc. A number of variations were seen in terms of population size, natural resource endowment, and current levels of development.
3. Gross National Product (GNP) is conventionally used to indicate economic development, and was the measure that dominated policy in 'the first development decade' (1960–70). It ignores the real distribution of income and resources, fails to register activities that have a real material value to people, and distracts attention from social welfare.
4. There has been a shift, at least in principle if not in practice, away from a growth orientated development philosophy to one based on 'basic needs', a broader socio-economic philosophy that in its breadth and approach is more attuned to the social justice approach of writers such as Townsend.
5. People's perception of progress or development may be very different from that of the planners: people are likely to combine a desire for greater material prosperity with the hope that the pattern of social life is not radically altered. Their conception of development is an important factor influencing planned social change.

3

Modernisation Theory

3.1 INTRODUCTION

We have seen in Chapter 2 that there is considerable inequality and poverty in the world today. However, we have also seen that the nature of this disadvantage depends on the perceptions one has of social and material 'needs' and thereby how a society should 'develop' to make good these 'deficiencies'. The various policies of planned social change which are implemented today to alleviate such problems are rooted in general conceptions of socio-economic change and development that can be traced back to the nineteenth century.

The widespread interest in socio-economic change among European scholars in the nineteenth century was in part a direct reflection of the circumstances of their time. Among other processes, the period saw the rapid expansion of industrial manufacturing, a growth in population and urban centres, and the increasing national importance of the political and bureaucratic activity of the State. These processes were not, of course, initiated during the nineteenth century but much earlier, in the British case, for example, as early as the 1600s. Moreover, all European countries did not experience such developments to the same extent. Indeed many, for example Spain, Portugal and the Scandanavian countries, remained relatively untouched by the dynamics of industrialisation. But within certain countries, particularly Britain, France and Germany, the pace and extent of change were comparatively massive. Polanyi (1944, p. 73) speaks of this period as the 'great transformation' and writes of the 'acute social dislocation' created by the 'ravages of [the] satanic mill'. The demands of businesses for cheap materials and low labour costs have always existed, but in the nineteenth century such demands were given new meaning principally because of the development of new systems of production entailing large scale factory manufacturing. In addition, labour productivity and new sources of power (for example the replacement of water by steam-power), along with the growth of national markets, made nineteenth century capitalists much more effective and ambitious than any of their forebears: hence the so-called 'Industrial Revolution'.

The changes this brought about were, according to Dobb (1963, p. 256), 'entirely abnormal, judged by the standards of previous centuries'. He suggests that the period saw a major change from 'the more or less static conception of a world . . . where departure from tradition was contrary to nature, into a conception of progress as a law of life and of continued improvement as the normal state of a healthy society'. As Dobb remarks, given such a change in consciousness, 'it is evident . . . that interpretation of the nineteenth century economy would most essentially be an interpretation of its change and movement'. And indeed there were many in the universities, academies, philosophical societies and political clubs who regarded an analysis of such changes as their most important task.

The interpretation of these processes of social change varied considerably among those whose work is now regarded as constituting 'classical sociology', in particular that of Marx (1818–83), Durkheim (1858–1917) and Weber (1864–1920). They produced very different theories about the origins, character and future path of industrial society. They also had divergent views about the positive and negative effects of this transition. While their specific ideas on deviance, religion, education, politics etc. have been a source of much interest, it is their general theories of social change that have commanded most attention and which inspired in the twentieth century the emergence of the 'sociology of development'. As we shall see later on, however, the more information that is obtained about past and present day societies of the Third World the more evidently limited are these classical, European-centred analyses.

Despite their considerable differences, Marx, Durkheim and Weber shared the intellectual concern of their time in trying to identify the basic features of societies that promote or inhibit their development. They all, more or less, shared in the spirit of

Darwinian thought that came to dominate the philosophical, scientific, economic and political spheres of debate. Darwin's theory of the evolution of nature challenged the established notion of an unchanging, predetermined, God-given order to the world. The idea that one could not only identify but also explain the origin of things and how they develop gripped the imagination of the early social scientists. They were especially interested in Darwin's use of the *comparative* method. He compared different animal forms and organisms in distinct kinds of environments suggesting which were, as biological structures, more functionally adapted for survival.

Darwin's ideas raised the possibility that social change could similarly be charted according to some principle of social evolution: do societies develop through certain 'stages', what have these been in the past and what will they be? Could such questions be answered by comparing aspects of different societies, such as their economic patterns, kinship systems, religions and so on, in order to find out how far they had 'developed'? These were the issues in which the classical sociologists, especially Marx and Durkheim, immersed themselves. Weber was not so obviously tied to the evolutionist approach though he too has elements of it within his work.

The twentieth century has seen the critique, refinement and even attempted synthesis of the ideas of these men. Two main schools of thought now dominate the literature on development and change. The first, which came to prominence in the 1950s and 1960s, is called '*modernisation*' theory. This offers an account of the common features of the process of development drawing on the analyses of Durkheim and Weber. The second, which came to occupy a central place in the development debate in the 1970s, is called '*underdevelopment*' theory and draws its ideas from the analysis of the economic system of capitalism developed by Marx. We shall look at this second school of thought in Chapter 4. In this chapter we shall examine the origins and development of the first approach to social change, that being modernisation theory.

3.2 THE THEORETICAL ORIGINS OF MODERNISATION THEORY

As noted above, modernisation theory has its roots in the ideas of Durkheim and Weber which we can now examine more closely.

Emile Durkheim

To appreciate Durkheim's theory of the development of complex modern society from a simple 'primitive' past we must understand his theory of social order and stability. For Durkheim, the crucial question was how do people combine in stable groups to form cohesive societies and what is the nature of their relationship to one another as society grows and becomes more complex?

Durkheim tried to answer this question in his doctoral thesis, which subsequently became his first major book, *The Division of Labour in Society*, published in 1893. In this he proposes that there are two basic types of society, the 'traditional' and the 'modern' which have very different forms of social cohesion between their members. The people of a traditional society perform the limited tasks of a simple agrarian community based on groups of families or clans in village settlements. One village is like any other in what people do, think and believe. In these circumstances, social cohesion is based on the simple common lifestyle and beliefs that prevail within and between settlements. Durkheim calls this form of cohesion 'mechanical solidarity', 'mechanical' in the sense that the separate groups are very similar to one another, conforming to a rigid pattern of traditional norms and beliefs.

The similarity of groups within traditional society does *not* mean that they are heavily dependent on each other: quite the contrary. Each group, though similar to all others, is relatively self-contained, its members performing all the required roles of farming, childrearing, social control, defence, and so on. In other words, the 'division of labour' is restricted and within the capabilities of all in the group. Each group is then a sort of 'segment' – a discrete unit – in a larger society: hence Durkheim also called this a 'segmental society'.

The traditional or segmental society is contrasted with the modern society. How does the latter develop? The basic mechanism that undermines the traditional way of life is the ever increasing number and density of the population. This leads to more people competing for relatively scarce resources. Adopting his evolutionist position, Durkheim believed that in these circumstances, when competition was most fierce, a social resolution to this problem had to emerge: society had in some way to adapt to the circumstances or go under. The problem was resolved by a gradual increase in the social division of labour. New resources could be generated by people taking on the role of producers (as cultivators, livestock farmers, etc.) on a full-time basis while others became similarly specialised in other areas of life outside of material production. Thus, the division of labour became more complex and created an increasing *interdependency* among people. Just as the cells in a growing body differentiate to form specialised organs for particular functions, so social differentiation occurred as specialised institutions were formed by people to deal with particular needs of society (religious, economic, political, educational, and so on). And so, in this way modern society is created. It is more complex and integrated and has a cohesion Durkheim called 'organic solidarity': each part, like a natural organism, is specialised in function and reliant on others.

The modern system creates a new pattern of morality and a system of norms; these social rules are much less rigid than those of a traditional society since they have to act as guides for much more complex and diverse social activities. This means that the 'modern' individual has a much greater freedom of action within a general set of moral constraints. Durkheim believed, however, that this carries potential dangers to society if the individual's desires and ambitions get out of step with the general moral code. When individual desires go beyond the moral order then people become dissatisfied with life and social cohesion begins to break down. Thus, Durkheim believed, being the conservative moralist he was, that the individual must be encouraged to conform to the collective morals of society and to do so for his or her own good.

Some key features of Durkheim's argument can be isolated. First, one should note the stress on the system of morality and norms as the foundation stone of social integration, whether 'mechanical' or 'organic' in form. Secondly, although Durkheim regarded the coming of modernity as progress inasmuch as modern society was more cultured, less rigid, and allowed more scope for individual expression, it is also clear that this flexibility could potentially be a source of individual frustration and unhappiness. At a more theoretical level two comments are worth making. Primarily, it is clear that Durkheim give us little *explanation* for the passage to modernity other than population growth and density. His arguments about increasing social differentiation are not explanations but *descriptions* of the modernising process. His theory is then, relatively limited in its explanatory power. Secondly, we ought to be cautious about his claims for the good reason that they are speculative with little regard for historical evidence.

We shall see shortly how Durkheim's ideas have influenced the development of modernisation theory. The other major sociologist whose work has had at least as great an impact was Weber whose theory of the development of capitalism we can now consider.

Max Weber

Like Durkheim, Weber sought to explain the emergence of industrialisation, though he focused his attention on answering why capitalist manufacturing became dominant only in the economies of Western Europe. In his work, most of which appeared in the first decade of this century, he argued that the basic explanation for this occurence was the existence of a cultural process peculiar to Western society, namely, 'rationalisation'. Weber proposed that a crucial element in the expansion of capitalist manufacturing was the rational organisation of business enterprise to establish steady profitability and the accumulation of capital. This involved a number of tasks, including an assessment of the most efficient use of capital, expansion through cost reduction and diligent investment, a continual effort to better one's competitors, and an attempt to meet consumers' demands. Weber (1971, p. 7) characterised the transition from the 'traditional', 'leisurely' pre-capitalist culture to the diligent hard working ethos of 'modern' capitalism in the following manner:

> What happened was often no more than this: some young man from one of the putting-out families went out into the country, carefully chose weavers for his employ, greatly increased the rigour of his supervision of their work, and thus turned them from peasants into labourers. On the other hand, he would begin to change his marketing methods by so far as possible going directly to the final consumer ... and above all would adapt the quality of the product directly to their needs and wishes. At the same time he began to introduce the principle of low prices and large turnover. There was repeated what everywhere and always is the result of such a process of rationalisation: those who would not follow suit had to go out of business

> . . . [T]he new spirit, the spirit of modern capitalism, had set to work.

While this rational economic activity would no doubt bring good profits, making money was not, argued Weber, the principal factor behind it. Such a motive had always existed throughout the world in business transactions. The particularly significant additional force at work which brought about the transition from just money-making to large-scale capitalist enterprise was that to which he alludes at the end of the above quote: the rational ethos of the 'spirit of capitalism'. Unlike other societies, especially in the East, when the profits of business were 'wasted' on the purchase of exotic or luxurious items for immediate consumption, Western Europeans were typically committed to hard work and the steady accumulation of capital through careful investment. Weber suggested this was not an easy nor natural form of behaviour. One of the important factors that promoted this work ethic was, according to Weber, not economic but *religious*.

In his now famous text, *The Protestant Ethic and the Spirit of Capitalism*, Weber argued that the distinctive care, calculation and hard work of Western business was encouraged by the development of the protestant ethic which came to pre-eminence in the sixteenth century and which was promoted most forcefully by the doctrines of Calvinism. John Calvin (1509–64) was a major Christian reformer. His central doctrine was that of *predestination*. This is the belief that God has already decided on the saved and the damned. The 'sting in the tail' is that according to an additional doctrine no one can know whether he or she is one of this chosen few. Moreover, salvation cannot be earned through good works or declarations of faith. These beliefs must have aroused considerable anxiety among followers of Calvin: Weber suggested that believers must have experienced 'salvation panic', The only way to bring about a degree of calm, claimed Weber, would be to think that, like the good tree that cannot bear evil fruit, people could not be successful in this world without God's blessing. Thus, the doctrine of unknowable predestination was made less awesome by believing that success was a *sign* (though never a proof) of election.

For this reasoning to work, however, believers had to ensure that they glorified God through all that they did: any weakness, self-indulgence or failure would be an immediate sign of damnation. This would be true in whatever one did, including work. Diligence, discipline, moderation and success was as crucial in business as anywhere else. Thus, according to Weber, these *religious* concerns shared by Protestants throughout Western Europe helped fashion a work ethic which was in tune with the spirit of capitalism, a combination that led to the development of modern capitalist society throughout the west.

Unlike Durkheim's primarily speculative analysis, Weber actually supported his propositions with historical evidence. As suggested earlier, supporting evidence is always a matter of selection and thus there have been those who have challenged Weber's particular selection of data and interpretation of the history of capitalism. We shall not go into the details of this debate which have been carefuly discussed by Marshall (1982). Perhaps the central theme in Weber's entire body of work is his belief that as Western society has developed, more and more of its members act in ways that are guided by the *principles of rationality* and less by the *customs of tradition*. Like Durkheim, Weber thus draws a distinction between traditional and modern society and again like Durkheim sees much of this distinction in terms of a fundamental contrast of ideas and values. Both see the coming of the 'modern' era as the social birth of the 'individual' as a relatively free agent not bound by rigid and unquestioning conformity to past tradition.

In their different ways Durkheim and Weber have provided many of the basic themes of present day modernisation theory in particular their contrast between traditional and modern societies. Each conceives of this contrast in different terms yet this has not discouraged today's social scientists from attempting to combine Durkheim's and Weber's notions into a grand theory of development that incorporates an analysis of changing normative systems, differentiation, rationalisation, business motivation and individual ambition. Such a synthesis on occasions does an injustice to some of the original ideas on which it relies. (As we shall see, this is particularly true of the use of some of Weber's ideas.) Nevertheless, drawing on these ideas, modernisation theorists identified the basic features of 'development' and believed that they could construct a useful model which could be used as a yardstick to measure the stage of development of *any* society today: much of the deprivation of the world could then be seen in terms of the continued stranglehold of backward looking traditionalism. We can now consider these ideas more closely.

3.3 MODERNISATION THEORY

In the 1950s and early 1960s modernisation theory was developed by a number of social scientists, particularly a group of American scholars the most prominent of whom was Talcott Parsons. As noted in chapter 1, much of this interest in modernisation was prompted by the decline of the old colonial empires. The Third World became a focus of attention by politicians who were keen to show countries pushing for independence that sustained development was possible under the western wing (rather than that of the Soviet Union). Academics reflected this interest by examining the socio-economic conditions conducive to modernisation.

Tradition versus Modernity

In constructing their accounts of development, theorists drew on the tradition-modernity distinction of classical sociologists. Like Durkheim and Weber, these theorists placed most emphasis on the values and norms that operate in these two types of society and their economic systems. Like Durkheim, most argued that the transition from the limited economic relationships of traditional society to the innovative, complex economic associations of modernity depended on a prior change in the values, attitudes and norms of people. Bauer (1976, p. 41), for example, argues that:

> Economic achievement and progress depend largely on human aptitudes and attitudes, on social and political institutions and arrangements which derive from these, on historical experience, and to a lesser extent on external contacts, market opportunities and on natural resources.

Development then depends on 'traditional', 'primitive' values being displaced by modern ones.

In a 'traditional' society, three crucial features are noted:

(a) The value of traditionalism itself is dominant: that is, people are oriented to the past and they lack the cultural ability to adjust to new circumstances;

(b) The kinship system is the decisive reference point for all social practices, being the primary means through which economic, political and legal relationships are controlled. One's position in the kinship system and hence in the society is ascribed, not achieved – that is, is a reflection of the status or standing of the family, clan or tribe into which one is born; one's position only changes as one moves up the family hierarchy. Status is then, not earned or achieved, but conferred by virtue of kin relationships;

(c) Members of the traditional society have an emotional, superstitious and fatalistic approach to the world: 'what will be will be; 'things have always been this way'.

In contrast, 'modern' society is made up of completely opposite characteristics:

(a) People may still have traditions but they are not slaves to them and will challenge any that seem unnecessary or get in the way of continued cultural progress (that is they do not suffer from 'traditionalism');

(b) Kinship has a very much less important role in all areas of society (even within the family) because of the need for geographical and social mobility which weakens family ties; moreover, one's position in the economy, polity etc., is earned through hard work and high achievement – motivation and not determined by kinship;

(c) Members of the modern society are not fatalistic but forward-looking and innovative, ready to overcome the obstacles they find in their way, particularly in business affairs, reflecting a strong entrepreneurial spirit and rational, scientific approach to the world.

It is evident that various ideas from classical sociology are incorporated in these profiles of the two types of society. For example, the description of the modern society includes reference to the splitting off or 'differentiation' of kinship from the economy, stresses individual freedom from constraint especially in business and points to the rational, calculating character of innovative entrepreneurs. Parsons (1951) develops this model in considerable detail elaborating on the choice of actions or behavioural orientations that tend to typify the two types of society. For example, he argues that in modern society an achievement orientation is the likely choice of action for people particularly within the economic sphere since it is a much more rational criterion for deciding who should be given what sort of jobs with what level of reward, than are ascriptive criteria. In the achievement oriented society jobs are allocated and rewarded on the basis of achieved skills and hard work: it is what one can do, not who one is that gets rewarded.

The necessity of developing an 'achievement' orientation in the values system has not merely been regarded as part of a wider process of development. For some theorists of social change the desire to achieve has been seen as the crucial or determinant factor of development. For example, McClelland (1961) and Hagen (1962) claim that the level of achievement in a society is expressed in terms of the level of innovation and entrepreneurship. In traditional cultures both are at an exceptionally low level. Economic constraints or limitations can be overcome given a sufficiently high motivation to do well by the individual entrepreneur. As McClelland (1961, p. 105) argues,

> Men with high achievement will find a way to economic achievement given fairly wide variations in opportunity and social structure... These results serve to direct our attention as social scientists away from an exclusive concern with the external events in history to the internal psychological concerns that in the long run determine what happen in history.

The stress on ideas and psychological factors in shaping history and the rate of development is clearly evident.

Lerner (1964) adopts a similarly socio-psychological approach to explain the transition from traditional to modern society. There is in fact, he believes, a 'transitional' society, a society which has, through the process of cultural diffusion from more advanced sectors of the world, been exposed to modernity. For Lerner, the 'transitional society' is the 'empathetic society'. The society is defined by what it *wants* to become: the transitional man 'wants really to see the things he has hitherto "seen" only in his mind's eye, really to live in the world he has "lived" only vicariously'. (p. 72). Empathy involves the ability to 'rearrange the self-esteem on short notice', the capacity to 'incorporate new roles', and to have a publicly minded orientation that encourages participation. Lerner's description of traditional society is similar to that offered by Durkheim's notion of mechanical solidarity: Lerner (1964, p. 50) says that,

> Traditional society is non-participant – it deploys people by kinship into communities isolated from each other and from a center ... [it lacks] the bands of interdependence, people's horizons are limited by locale.

In general, then, for Lerner, the more a society exhibits empathy the more it will be engaged in the process of modernisation and the more likely is it to be modern. Like McClelland's measurement of achievement orientation in society, Lerner's empathetic criterion of modernity has quantifiable dimensions:

> The latent statistical assertion involved here is this: In modern society *more* individuals exhibit *higher* empathetic capacity than in any previous society (1964, p. 51).

Lerner's account of modernisation is somewhat different from the simple model of two societies, traditional and modern, seen so far, since he tries to identify an *intervening* stage, the 'transitional society'. A more elaborate 'stage' model has been provided by the development economist W. W. Rostow. In his *Stages of Economic Growth: A Non-Communist Manifesto* (1960, p. 4) he claims that,

> It is possible to identify all societies, in their economic dimensions, as lying within one of five categories; the traditional society, the preconditions for take-off, take off, the drive to maturity, and the age of high mass-consumption.

These five stages are derived from an analysis of the British industrial revolution, and take-off he defined as the 'great watershed in the life of modern societies' when obstacles to economic growth are removed, particularly by the onset of an adequate rate of capital investment so that growth becomes a normal condition.

It seems clear that entrepreneurial ambition combined with sustained capital accumulation and investment are seen by most modernisation theorists as two of the principal forces of development. As Roxborough (1979, p. 16) says,

> This emphasis on entrepreneurship and capital accumulation is the single most pervasive theme in the literature on economic growth. It always appears as *the* lesson to be learnt from Western experience and to be mechanically applied to the rest of the world so that they can repeat the transition.

Let us briefly summarise some of the basic themes of modernisation theory and draw out their implications particularly for development policy in the Third World.

3.4 SUMMARY OF MODERNISATION THEORY AND ITS IMPLICATIONS

By way of summary the following points seem most important:

(a) there is a clear mixture of sociological, psychological and economic features to modernisation theory including, for example, reference to value systems, individual motivations, and capital accumulation;
(b) most accounts give greatest priority to the role played by the values, norms and beliefs of people in determining the sort of society – traditional or modern – that they create, and thus value changes are the most important conditions for social change;
(c) the history of the development of industrialisation in the West is no longer regarded as something unique as Weber thought, but as the blueprint for development throughout the world. As one of the contributors to modernisation theory, Eisenstadt (1966, p. 1) claimed: 'Historically, modernisation is the process of change towards those types of social, economic and political systems that have developed in Western Europe and North America from the seventeenth to the nineteenth centuries.'
(d) the evolution of societies occurs as traditional behaviour

patterns give way under the pressures of modernisation. While these pressures built up gradually *within* Western societies, the 'developing' countries of the Third World can be *exposed* to them from outside. That is, they can be helped along the road to modernity with the assistance of the developed countries whose ideas and technologies can be introduced and diffused throughout these poorer countries;

(e) this process of 'modernisation by diffusion' should encourage the development of a number of features in the Third World, including urbanisation based on nuclear family households, educational growth for literacy and training, the development of mass media to disseminate ideas and encourage increased awareness about society, heightened political awareness and participation in a democratic system, increased business opportunities through providing capital for investment, the replacement of patterns of authority based on traditional loyalties (for example monarchies, local chiefdoms) with a rational system of law coupled with representative national government;

(f) different societies are at different stages of development because they have been more or less successful in introducing the features of modernity highlighted above in (e).

These, then, are the major tenets of modernisation theory. What theoretical implications do they have for an understanding of development?

1) Lack of development is seen as a condition prior to development: that is, that present day Third World societies are underdeveloped countries gradually moving towards modernity. This may seem self-evident: however, as we shall see, this lack of development may *not* reflect obstacles apparent from the internal history of these countries but be instead a result of the relationship they have had over the past few centuries with outside countries.
2) Lack of development is the 'fault' of Third World countries' socio-economic systems that create obstacles to modernisation and encourage little ambition or incentive among individuals, particularly in their work: they tend to have little

interest in commercial production and rationally planned long-term enterprise being content to work only as long as they need to satisfy their immediate (limited) demands.

3) Development is presented as a relatively straightforward process of efficient social adaptation to periods of strain (for example one brought about by increasing population); there is little debate about the possibility of fundamental *conflict* between social groups.
4) Development occurs not only along Western lines for Third World societies but also for those countries which are now socialist states (for example the Soviet Union, China), whose future paths will, because of the forces of industrialisation, converge with the road beaten out by the pioneering West.
5) The Western economies will continue to grow and develop so that, in Rostow's (1960) terms, they enjoy the prosperity of the period of 'high mass consumption'. There is no sign given of the possible collapse or steady decline in the fortunes of these economies.

The social scientists who developed these arguments in their professional capacity as academics were co-opted to work with the development agencies, particularly of the United States and the UN. Given that their diffusionist thesis explicitly argued that the developed countries could have nothing other than a benign influence in the 'developing' countries their ideas were a great source of justification for the activities of the development agencies. A whole range of policies were fostered by modernisation theory. These will be discussed in detail in Chapter 9. They have included the injection of capital to aid both industrial 'take-off' and the commercialisation of agriculture, the training of an entrepreneurial elite in the values and motivations most likely to promote free enterprise, the expansion of educational programmes, and only assisting 'democratic' (or notionally democratic) countries.

This policy role for modernisation theory and its evident support of the economic strategies of the development agencies gave it a virtually impregnable position in academic circles, particularly in the United States. Parsons' work came to be regarded as having a significance of classical proportions and his fellow contributors provided further credibility for the whole theoretical edifice. It remained intact for almost twenty years, but, by the late 1960s and early 1970s a number of criticisms began to appear that developed into an out and out attack on its central assumptions and propositions. The main and most devastating attack came from those working within radical, Marxian sociology, till then very much on the margins of academic social science. Their specific criticisms we consider in Chapter 4. Here we can examine a range of general criticisms made by sociologists, anthropologists and economists that initiated the attack on the foundations of modernisation theory.

3.5 THE CRITIQUE OF MODERNISATION THEORY

Modernisation theory claims to identify those factors crucial for economic development such as achievement motivation and a decline in the significance of extended family relationships. While it may be the case that substantial economic growth cannot occur without changes in, say, technology, the level of capital investment and market demand, it need *not* be the case that such growth requires major alterations to value systems and social institutions as modernisation theory claims. Indeed, there is a good deal of evidence to the contrary. The following section illustrates this through presenting a number of important empirical and theoretical criticisms that have appeared in the literature since the late 1960s.

First, many critics have pointed out that the principal terms of the theory – the 'traditional' and the 'modern' – are much too vague to be of much use as classifications of distinct societies. The two terms do not give any indication of the great variety of societies that have and do exist; instead, the 'traditional' label is offered as a blanket term to cover a range of pre-industrial societies that have exceedingly different socio-economic and political structures such as feudal, tribal and bureaucratic empires. A much more careful historical analysis is required of these distinct pre-industrial forms in order to have any hope of understanding the subsequent processes of social change they undergo. Eisenstadt, one of the more historically sensitive of the modernisation school, recognised the force of this criticism, and in a later contribution (1970, p. 25) wrote:

> The process of modernisation may take off from tribal groups, from caste societies, from different types of peasant societies, and from societies with different degrees and types of prior orientation. These groups may vary greatly in the extent to which they have the resources, and abilities, necessary for modernisation.

Secondly, although the theory is supposed to be about the way society develops there is little explanation offered for this process. This is a serious weakness. Apart from reference to the need for forward looking attitudes and healthy economic motivation we have no idea which mechanism it is that brings about the process of social differentiation of which so much is made.

Thirdly, even if, for the sake of the discussion, one were to accept the use of the terms 'traditional' and 'modern' societies is it the case that they are so mutually exclusive as the theory states? Remember, the claim is that, as societies develop, the 'traditional' world gets squeezed out by the force of modern values and attitudes. Yet there is a wealth of evidence to indicate that economic growth and the advent of modernity does *not* necessarily mean the abandonment of so-called 'traditional' patterns of action, values or beliefs. For example, Gusfield (1973) points out that the 'traditional' religion of Islam has been *reinforced* by the diffusion of modern technology, particularly transport, that makes the visit to the shrine of Mecca a much more practicable proposition for many more people than had been true in the past. At the same time, as Mair (1984) argues, the trip to Mecca may be very expensive for Muslims living a great distance from the shrine, so much so that in order to meet the costs of the journey great care had to be taken with household revenues: 'In Java the organisation of retail trade on a capitalist basis was the work of a reformist Muslim movement which not only valued austerity but insisted on the duty of making the pilgrimage to Mecca. It was that duty, a costly one, that drove the members of this sect to practise thrift' (p. 25). In this case then, *in order to sustain traditional religious practices*, the Muslims had to engage in activities typically associated with capitalist investment and economic growth, similar in character to those identified by Weber in his study of Protestantism.

There is also evidence to show that in 'modern' industrial society 'traditional' values not only persist but actually play an important role in keeping it going. Frank (1969, p. 26) shows how the norm of ascription (judging people according to their family background, age or sex for example) plays an important role in allocating reward in Japanese industry, a paragon of 'modernity' if ever there was one. Frank shows that, although recruitment to Japanese companies is based on achievement criteria – the skills and qualifications applicants have – once they are employed their level of pay and promotion prospects depend very much on the age, background and family responsibilities of the workers, highly ascriptive considerations. Frank in fact offers considerable evidence of the persistence of so-called 'traditional' values in many modern industrial societies, including Japan, Britain and the United States. At the same time, we can find evidence that modern industrial society does not necessarily encourage achievement by motivation among all its members, but in fact the very opposite, a lack of ambition: thus, gender relations in modern capitalist society whether expressed in the family, schools, the mass media or in employment discourage equal levels of achievement between the sexes resulting typically in male dominance and female subordination; or again, there have been many sociological studies of the educational system in advanced economies and some suggest that for many working class youths the experience of schooling is to dampen down their ambitions, being socialised into *low* achievement motivation (for example, Willis, 1977), rather than high, as McClelland would assume.

Fourthly, one should question the proposition that as industrialisation and its attendant urbanisation develop the wider kinship system is weakened as people become primarily concerned with their own nuclear family. As Long (1977, p. 37) says,

> Several studies have concluded that certain extended family systems not only survive in a modern economic context but that they often function positively to enable individuals to mobilise capital and other resources essential for modern capitalist enterprises.

Moreover, for urban poor as well as the middle class, and for those who move to towns in search of work, extended family kin are an important source of support as British studies by Anderson (1971), Penn (1986) and Willmott and Young (1971) have shown. While it would be foolish to suggest that urbanisation does not change kinship relationships it would be wrong to claim that it completely undermines the value of extended family ties; rather, these are modified or sustained in a manner different from that which prevailed prior to urbanisation. Yet again, the essential weakness of the tradition-modernity thesis is revealed here, namely, its persistent recourse to generalisations that such and such will happen without inspection of the historical or current evidence.

Fifthly, much use is made of Weber's ideas by McClelland in his analysis of 'achievement motivation' which he believes lies at the heart of economic growth. But Weber's thesis is distorted by McClelland's theoretical handiwork. As we saw at the beginning of this chapter, Weber saw the activity that derived from the concern for salvation among Protestants as an important contributory factor in the rise of rational capitalism. McClelland effectively ignores the importance Weber gives to this religious anxiety by reducing it to a latent psychological drive for success which can be found not ony in post sixteenth-century Western Europe but also in a wide range of societies that experienced economic growth later. This does an injustice to Weber not only in terms of an abuse of his particular thesis about Protestantism but also in term of its failure to respect Weber's general approach which was much more sensitive to the sociologically distinct patterns of change that have occurred in history.

Sixthly, as already hinted at above in our fourth criticism, it seems that people may be able to use their 'traditional' roles and expectations (such as those associated with kinship) as *resources* that can be drawn on to serve their social and material needs. A good example of this is provided by Ortiz (1970) who examined the impact of a Mexican government development scheme on a northern community, Tzintzuntzan, whose villagers produced pottery. The government wanted the potters to develop higher quality items for sale on a wider market but, after the failure of initial attempts to do this through the installation of more sophisticated kilns, the project was abandoned. Subsequently, however, pottery production and sales increased dramatically. Ortiz argues that this was due to the growth of the local urban market for domestic cooking pots and the construction of a much better road for the potters to take their wares to town. What is of interest here is that this expanded business enterprise relied on the *traditional personal ties* of friends, kinship and immediate family, so, rather than being an obstacle to commercial growth, these ties were harnessed in such a way as to promote entrepreneurial productivity and success. Commenting on this survey, Long (1977, p. 50), in an excellent summary of many similar case studies, writes:

> It is difficult in the light of this example to accept the view that peasant culture is a major brake on change. On the contrary, once a viable set of opportunities presented themselves the peasants showed every willingness to increase production and become more involved in the market economy.

The notion, therefore, that 'traditional' peasant culture is necessarily contrary to the development of economic growth must be subject to serious question. But surely, one *does* find evidence for peasant conservatism and fatalism? After all, studies of rural development programmes in Africa have suggested that many problems were associated with the lack of peasant motivation: as DeWilde (1967, pp. 176–7) argued, 'the conservatism of the peasants, unless closely supervised, is a major problem'. However, while such conservatism may exist it is more likely that it reflects the *insecurity* of the rural producer, who is more vulnerable than the higher social classes to disease, death, adverse weather, fluctuating income from produce, and last but not least, exploitation by the political and social system that ultimately makes the peasants' land holding so uncertain. In many ways, then, peasants are *more* likely to be exposed to socio-economic change than other social groups. Conservatism may represent the attempt to establish some continuity and order in these precarious circumstances. When opportunities are more favourable, however, many case studies show that the peasantry will respond in an innovative and commercial manner. As Moore (1969, p. 387) says,

> They will not change simply because someone has told them to do so. That has been going on for some time. It is necessary to change the situation confronting the people on the land if they are going to alter their behaviour. And if this has not yet happened, as by and large it has not, there are likely to be good political reasons.

Religious fatalism?
While many sociologists have shown that peasant conservatism is a rational response to insecure circumstances, what of those societies where religious dogma appears to demand that its adherents adopt a fatalistic attitude towards life? Many modernisation theorists would claim here strong evidence for the inhibiting effect of traditional beliefs on development. But matters are perhaps sometimes more complex, as Mair (1984, p. 25) suggests:

> In some religions, the idea of an individual fate that one cannot escape may lead people to take little interest in plans to improve their fortunes. Hinduism and Islam both include such an idea, but it is very important to be aware how much or how little in a given case people's attitudes towards the practical problems of their own lives are affected by it. It is too easy to ascribe resistance or indifference to development projects to 'fatalism'. The belief may be temporarily forgotten; or there may be a way of getting round it, as there is with the Yoruba in Nigeria. They believe that everyone is endowed with a destiny at the moment of birth; it may be good or bad. But there are ways of getting the better of a 'bad destiny', and even a good one may come to nothing if its holder does not bestir himself to make the most of it. Certainly the Yoruba have not been behindhand in economic activity. We need to learn more about the real effect of such beliefs on the everyday decisions of those who hold them.

The final and in many ways most forceful criticism of modernisation theory, is that it entirely ignores the impact of colonialism and imperialism on Third World countries. This is a staggering omission. It is also a failure to acknowledge that economic growth is as much if not more about the *power* to control resources as it is about the 'ambition' to do so. With this in mind, Hoogvelt's (1976, p. 18) sarcasm is deadly:

> In Parson's approach one gets the impression that the history of mankind has been one happy, relaxed and peaceful exchange of ideas, stimulating progress here, there and everywhere where contact between societies was made. Cultural diffusion appears as a friendly merchant traveller, a timeless Marco Polo, innocently roaming the world, gently picking up a few ideas in one place and harmlessly depositing them in another. Incredulously,

the 'domination', 'exploitation', 'imperialism', and 'colonialism' are *not* discussed in any of Parsons' works on evolution.

This is perhaps not as surprising as it might first appear, since, in basing much of his analysis of Durkheimian evolutionary theory Parsons was merely repeating the omissions of Durkheim's original work. The latter too had little to offer by way of an analysis of power in general and nothing about the specific impact of the imperialism at work in the Third World at the very time Durkheim published his first text on the division of labour. His thesis on the division of labour itself lacks an adequate conception of power. It implies that the differentiation of roles and institutions occurs as a process of harmonious adaptation in which people choose roles appropriate to the needs of modernisation. Clearly the division of labour in the economy *has* occurred but it might be the case that certain groups in society, elites or upper classes, have the power to *impose* this division on subordinates, determining the reward for and control over the work task. As we said in the previous chapter, choice relies on an exercise of power that is unlikely to be equally shared by all people.

The next chapter discusses an alternative way of conceptualising development and the lack of it that relies very heavily on an analysis of conflict and inequalities of economic power: this is 'underdevelopment' theory.

3.6 CONCLUSION

In conclusion, two general remarks can be made. First, modernisation theory is clearly an oversimplified model of development that lacks two essential ingredients: an adequate historical input and a structural perspective. Historically, it ignores a wealth of evidence, some of which has been presented above, which indicates that the process of economic growth cannot be encapsulated in simplistic notions about the displacement of 'traditional' values systems and institutions by 'modern' ones. Structurally, the theory is insensitive to the specific ways in which factors for economic growth such as the introduction of new technology or markets may be interpreted, or modified or accommodated within *existing* social relationships. In addition, the inequalities of power and social class that structure these relationships are virtually ignored.

'Modernisation' in practice: the case of a French colony

Niger is one of the poorer countries of West Africa and until the exploitation of uranium reserves in the late 1960s was one of the poorest countries in the world. It has relied on groundnut oil as its primary source of export revenue for decades. It was once a French colony (1922–60). When the French first established control over the territory there appeared little prospect, at least in their eyes, of development – which meant the extraction of raw materials and the sale of French goods: the land was poor, the population small so that, as Roberts (1981) says, 'French colonial officers found little justification for their presence, either military or economic.' The indigenous Hausa people were accused of being idle and lacking any real commercial spirit: what is particularly interesting is why the French thought this the case. Any observer would have noted that the Hausa were in fact exceptionally successful farmers producing considerable quantities of grain from poor, rain-fed fields. For example, using only one hectolitre of seed, on marginal land Hausa farmers could with fairly limited effort produce 300–400 hectolitres of grain, whereas farmers in France could produce only 30–40 hectolitres 'after *incessant* labour *and* the use of manure and fertilisers'. Rather than applauding the Hausa's efficiency, the French declared them idle for not developing their productive capacities further in the service of the colony. Such 'natural improvidence' could only be overcome through 'civilising' the Hausa.

But as Roberts writes, '"Civilisation" had not much chance to prove itself since the improved methods of cultivation, including ploughs brought over from France, had produced disastrous results. By the end of the 1920s, government promotion of agricultural development in Niger was limited, consisting mainly of crop trials and model sheep and ostrich farms. Any peasant resistance to these marvels of Gallic civilisation simply confirmed the French in their view that the Hausa were backward, rather than an understandable reaction to inappropriate 'development'. For example, the authorities required the Hausa to stock cereal in case of drought; the Hausa resisted doing this because their custom was to trade surplus cereal for livestock from local pastoralists. In times of shortage the cattle were traded for grain from cereal farmers based in the more fertile regions to the south. Roberts comments, this north–south trade was not to the advantage of the French colonialists whose subsequent imposition of 'compulsory grain reserves hindered the development of regional trade and certainly contributed, like forced labour and conscription, to driving some of the population into Nigeria' (p. 199).

Secondly, despite the weakness of its thesis, modernisation theory is right to focus our attention on the role of values and attitudes in affecting people's behaviour and thereby their response to and fashioning of social change. It may be the case that economic opportunities existed for many entrepreneurs in Western European modernisation who could thereby give full rein to their innovative, calculative spirit. Yet it may well be the case that such opportunities do not exist in the Third World (nor for that matter in some of today's advanced states) for reasons we shall see in the next chapter. Thus, the values and attitudes that people in the Third World draw on do not necessarily express the ambitions of an 'achievement' drive since this would be unrealistic where economic opportunities are typically very limited.

The problem faced by the Third World peasantry is its increasing insecurity: agricultural production in the world economy is now dominated by rich industrial countries, such as the United States. This vulnerability is nothing new: as Worsley (1984) says, 'The world has never been a place where the peasants have held power, even when they constituted nine out of ten of the population. They will have even less political influence in the future' (p. 166). Perhaps in order to maintain the little influence they have, peasants may draw on 'traditional' values as respositories of some security, and be prepared to support political parties that champion nationalism, popular socialism and 'self-reliance'.

The relationship between values and the economic context is, therefore, a complex and dynamic process inadequately conceived by the traditional values/traditional economy – modern values/modern economy dualism of modernisation theory.

4

Theories of Underdevelopment

4.1 INTRODUCTION

In the preceding chapter we considered the theory that global modernisation could be explained primarily in terms of the development of certain values, norms and motivations – such as the drive for high achievement. Among those who cultivate such modernising attitudes, it is claimed, are the entrepreneurs of the business world who use the monetary surplus accumulated through wise and steady investment to expand industry and so generate more investable surplus for further expansion. Thus, countries which have yet to develop, lack the necessary values-system and entrepreneurial skills to invest any surplus remaining after people's immediate consumption needs have been met. We saw that this theory has serious weaknesses in terms of lacking supporting evidence and analytical strength. In particular, we concluded that it does not have any conception of the inequalities of power and class conflict that for many social scientists are an important and for some *the* most important factor influencing the pattern of social change and development. While modernisation theory has its origins in the Durkheimian and Weberian explanations of industrialisation, those who regard class conflict as a central dynamic of historical change trace their ideas back to the nineteenth century work of Karl Marx.

Marx's work offers a very different explanation for the inequalities within and between societies. Those who belong to the 'underdevelopment' school of thought find Marx's work to be of great value in accounting for the inequalities in the world economy and the lack of development in the Third World. As we shall see, however, there is some disagreement over the possibilities for future industrialisation in the Third World. For example, Frank (1981) believes that Third World development is unlikely, while others such as Warren (1980) and Williams (1978) argue that large-scale industrial capitalist development is very probable. Let us first examine some of the basic propositions that Marx made about the source of economic inequality and social division before going on to see how these have been incorporated into underdevelopment theory.

4.2 MARX'S THEORY OF CAPITALISM AND CLASS CONFLICT

While the modernisation theorist might ask 'Are there any entrepreneurs who can invest surplus capital?', Marx would ask 'Who produces this surplus in the first place?' For Marx any material surplus that is produced in excess of what people use for their own needs only has a value because of the fact that it is a product of their labour: without people working on the land or in the factories there would be no surplus. Any value that a product has is a reflection of the value invested in it by the workers' 'labour-power' expended on it.

In capitalist society the capitalist exploits this labour by employing it to produce items for sale – commodities – in return for a wage. This wage is used to support workers in order that they can continue to exert labour-power week in week out. But this wage is *less* than the *value of the production* which their effort has *created*. Capitalist profits are made by the employer taking or 'appropriating' this newly created value. This Marx calls 'surplus value'.

In capitalist societies most people cannot make a living without selling their labour: in these circumstances labour-power is itself a commodity – an 'item' available on the labour market to be purchased by employers, the capitalist class. Marx says that this class originates from the affluent Western European families of the seventeenth century. Before this, wealth came mainly through the ownership of land concentrated in the hands of the feudal lords on whose estates worked the serfs. These were not paid labourers but peasants who, in return for farming a few acres of the estate were allowed to keep a proportion of the produce for their own consumption, the remainder going to the lord. Thus, the feudal economy did not exploit serf labour through wages.

It was only when the concentration of private wealth was put to productive use in the employment of 'free' wage labour on a large scale to accumulate capital that the capitalist economy appeared. Those playing the crucial role in establishing capitalism were the rich, those with 'monetary wealth, merchant's capital and usurer's capital'. The first term refers to those whose riches derived from land ownership – the large estates; the second refers to wealth gained through merchant trading and plunder on national and overseas markets; and the third refers to that capital generated by the lending of money at high interest. During the eighteenth century in particular the money that these groups held began to be put to use employing wage labour on a considerable scale in the new manufacturing industries.

The existence of the moneyed few, the landed, merchants and usurers, had to be accompanied by the existence of 'free' wage labour in order for capitalism to emerge. The availability of 'free' wage labourers resulted from the historical process through which the agricultural population was driven from the land during the sixteenth and seventeenth centuries by nobles seeking to enclose their lands (particularly for sheep-farming) and by the dissolution of the Church estates after the Reformation. This meant that peasants were 'suddenly and forcibly torn from their means of subsistence, and hurled onto the labour market as free, unprotected and rightless proletarians' (Marx, 1976, p. 876).

Eventually the 'free' workers were organised by capitalist manufacturing in one of two ways:

(a) assembled in one workshop or factory where a variety of trades or crafts are used to produce one product – for example a carriage (or car today on the assembly line);
(b) assembled in one workshop or factory where each worker uses the same skills to produce an identical product from start to finish, although in order to meet that increasing demand for the product the task is likely to be divided among the workers.

In these ways, argues Marx, capitalist manufacturing exploits workers' labour-power and craft skills. A crucial aspect of the productive process is the division of labour into restricted tasks. We have seen a similar argument made before by Durkheim (see Chapter 3). Durkheim saw the division of labour as a necessary feature of industrialisation that encourages efficiency of task, interdependence between people and so an integrated, harmonious economy. Marx argues that *in its capitalist form*, while it may be more productive, it is at the same time harmful to the workforce: they lose two things, control over the only 'means of production' they possess (their own labour) and control over the actual product they make.

The division of labour not only makes capitalist investment more profitable it also involves the continual undermining of workers' skills. Skilled trades are broken down into operations requiring little thought or craft, or are eventually completely taken over by machines. Thus according to this view, the division of labour does not enhance workers' skills but quite the opposite: most workers are being deskilled all the time.

Deskilling is symptomatic of the way in which a worker's labour

Child labour in early capitalism

Marx argued that the power of the employers was evident not only in the way tasks were divided but also in the way workers were actually brought into factory work in the first place. For example, he writes at some length about the forced recruitment of labour in England – especially child labour – to the large mills of Derbyshire, Nottinghamshire and Lancashire. These first factories relied on power from the river driven water-wheel and were often situated in the countryside. This meant that local labour was in short supply and so, to remedy this situation, young children (aged between 7 and 14) were often taken from the London or Birmingham 'workhouses' by employers or their agents to work in the mills. As Marx (1976, p. 922) saw it, 'the birth of large-scale industry is celebrated by a vast, Herod-like slaughter of the innocents. Like the Royal Navy the factories were recruited by means of the press-gang.' Marx (p. 923) cites a contemporary commentary on the plight of these young workers by Fielden (1836) who noted that

> having tired out one set of hands, by working them throughout the day, [the employers] had another set ready to go on working throughtout the night; the day-set getting into the beds that the night-set had just quitted. . . . It is a common tradition in Lancashire, that the beds *never get cold*.

is taken possession of by the capitalist. Unlike Weber, Marx is little concerned with the attitudes of capitalists: he argues that they seek profit to accumulate capital in order to remain viable in the capitalist system to which they themselves are enslaved; capital is needed to generate profit to generate more capital and so on in a never ending circle of production – the capitalist treadmill.

This is the basis of class conflict in capitalist society. The dominant class, the capitalists, own and control the means of production and thereby exploit the subordinate working class. Thus, a person's material security is crucially dependent on his or her class membership, or to put it in more abstract terms, on his or her relationship to the means of production. Within and outside work people find their lives shaped by this relationship which creates much of the inequality in society. This state of affairs cannot be changed without removing the class structure itself. This clearly means challenging the position of the dominant capitalist class. Class conflict is inevitable. When workers become conscious of their exploitation and strive to stop it a revolutionary situation develops which, according to Marx, leads to the end of capitalism: capitalism sows the seeds of its own destruction.

Marx describes how the exploitation of workers' labour is not limited by national boundaries. Capitalists will seek to take possession of labour-power abroad as well. Marx refers to that time from about the sixteenth to the late eighteenth centuries when wealthy merchants built up their fortunes in western Europe by plundering the raw materials and labour of other nations. For example, Marx (1976, p. 915) writes that,

> The discovery of gold and silver in America, the extirpation, enslavement and entombment in mines of the indigenous population of that continent, the beginnings of the conquest and plunder of India, and the conversion of Africa into a preserve for the commercial hunting of blackskins, are all things which characterise the dawn of the era of capitalist production.

The 'treasures' yielded by these activities, 'flowed back to the mother-country and were turned into capital there'.

Clearly, this account of exploitation by European capitalists raises the possibility that the current socio-economic problems of Third World societies originated during this period of 'primitive accumulation', as the productive power of their peoples was geared to serve the interests of the industrialising west. The development of western capitalism seems, therefore, to have been dependent to some extent on this source of capital accumulation from abroad, and thus, it developed at the expense of Africa, Asia and Latin America. It is this basic proposition that underlies much of recent Marxian writings on underdevelopment. Shortly, we shall examine the theoretical debates within this school. At this point we can try to construct an account, with which most underdevelopment theorists might agree, of how the growth of western capitalism relied on the exploitation of countries elsewhere.

4.3 THE EXPLOITATION OF THE THIRD WORLD: AN ACCOUNT OF MERCHANT CAPITALISM, COLONIALISM, AND NEO-COLONIALISM

The account is divided into three parts: the analysis of merchant capitalism, colonialism, and neo-colonialism. These are seen as distinct stages of Third World exploitation associated with the growth of industrial capitalism in the west. We shall consider each in turn.

1 Merchant Capitalism

Merchant capitalism which, as we have already noted, refers to the accumulation of capital through trade and plunder, predominated during the first period of capitalist expansion that began around the sixteenth century and continued to the late eighteenth century. Kay (1975) and Amin (1976) have discussed the role played by the merchant class over this period whose transactions profited European business. The merchants themselves were not necessarily directly involved in organising the labour force in the African, Asian or American countries where they conducted their trade, though many of them did begin to use their profits to organise production in Europe. One of the most profitable forms of merchant capitalism was the slave trade – 'the commercial hunting of blackskins' as Marx called it.

The slave trade involved a three-cornered system of exchange.

First, European (mainly British) merchants exchanged goods – often inferior quality weapons and clothes – at a profit for African slaves supplied by local chiefs mainly from the countries around the Gulf of Guinea in West Africa. Secondly, they were then carried as cargo by ship across the Atlantic to be traded at a profit as slaves for the plantations of the Caribbean Islands and the American mainland. Finally, the merchants filled their ships with agricultural produce – especially sugar and cotton – which had been produced by the slaves on the plantations and sold this at a profit on their return to Europe. Map 4.1 illustrates this three-cornered or 'triangular' trade. It is important to note that profits were made at every stage of the triangular trade, since this allowed a steady accumulation of wealth which was funnelled back into Europe, and particularly to England. Moreover, the agricultural commodities that were taken to Europe for refinement and processing encouraged industrial development around the ports and cities (for example London, Bristol and Liverpool).

The merchants took advantage of the system of local slavery that was long established in Africa. They did not create it themselves. The empires of the African states of Dahomey and Mali in the west had used slave labour for many years for crop production. The merchants struck up deals with the local African elites to supply slaves in return for guns, clothes, etc., although many slaves were not traded but simply taken through warfare, trickery, banditry or kidnapping. Over a two hundred year period (1650–1850) it is estimated that about 9 million Africans aged between 15 and 35 were shipped across the Atlantic and almost 2 million of these died as a result of the harsh conditions of the voyage.

The trans-Atlantic slave trade had at least two damaging consequences for the African countries affected. First, as Rodney (1972) argues, it is likely that the trade had a serious impact on the growth of the African population, that is, had it not occurred the population would have grown much more quickly than it seems to have done. This implies that population growth is an important factor encouraging social and economic development. Secondly, the European traders had a particularly harmful affect on the existing political and economic patterns of African society. The French traders, for example, drove a wedge between the traditional dominant elites in West Africa and the subordinate groups,

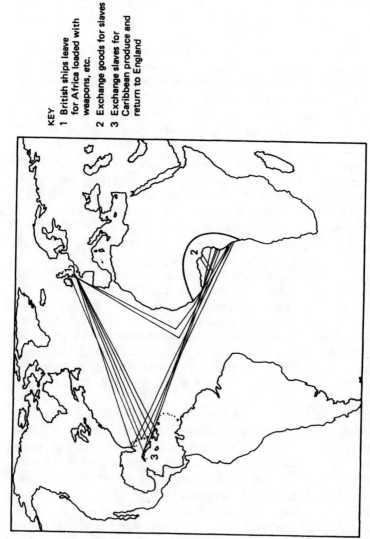

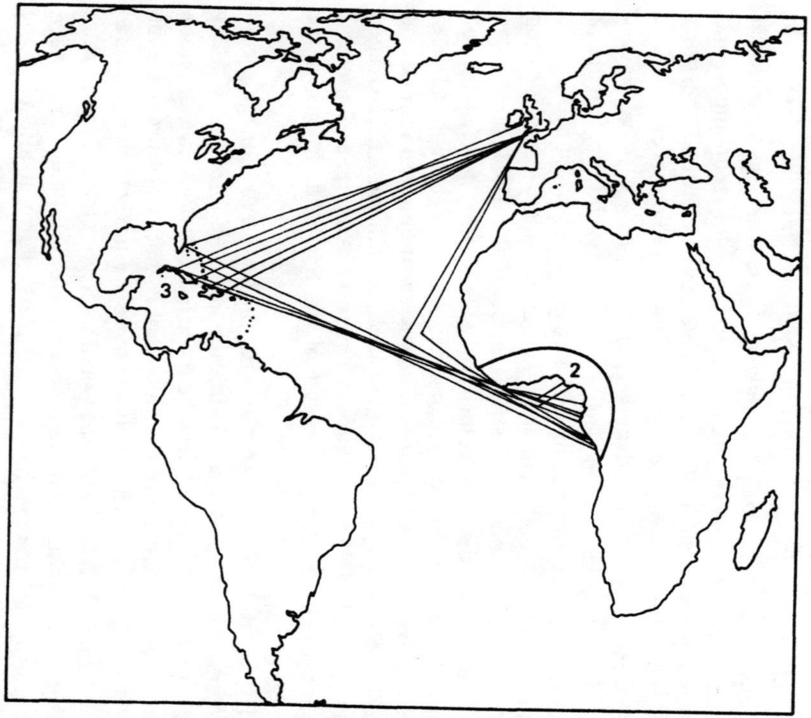
1
2
3
KEY
1 British ships leave for Africa loaded with weapons, etc.
2 Exchange goods for slaves
3 Exchange slaves for Caribbean produce and return to England

MAP 4.1 *The 'Triangular Trade': the slave route*

supporting the latter in order to weaken the negotiating strength of the former. Over the years, this undermined the political structure of the empires and fragmented the authority and trade patterns which had been built up over the centuries. What suffered most appears to have been the traditional trans-Sahara trading between African Kingdoms. The trans-Atlantic slave trade meant a re-orientation towards the exterior: African eyes looked to the sea either in anticipation of gain or in fear.

Although the European dominance around the African coastline was not always achieved easily, its superiority was usually assured by virtue of its technological and military power compared with that of African society. Worsley (1984) draws attention to the brutality that often accompanied this superior fire power, noting that in the Belgian Congo, '10 million were killed in thirteen years and those who failed to bring in their ivory or rubber quota had their hands chopped off. It was enough to demoralise even the bravest' (p. 4).

On a long-term basis, merchant capitalism sowed the seeds of economic weakness and dependency on European states in a number of ways. For example, it introduced western currency systems into African and Asian economies undermining confidence in the local money forms which, during the subsequent colonial period, were virtually completely displaced (see Ake [1981, pp. 32–5]). Moreover, it encouraged the emergence of a relatively small, prosperous elite in societies that had a close association with European business. It made African, Caribbean and other countries highly dependent on the export of their resources (for example crops and labour) in exchange for the import of manufactured goods from capitalist societies. Finally, it ushered in a period of an increasing interlocking of economies on a world scale dominated by a capitalist centre. These processes were inaugurated by merchant capitalism and were to become more developed during the subsequent period of colonialism and neo-colonialism. We can now see how they figured in the second stage of this historical account, colonialism.

2 Colonialism

Most neo-Marxist writers argue that merchant capitalism, while hugely profitable to Western Europe, was nevertheless an obstacle to the more efficient organisation of production and control over raw materials that the new manufacturing capitalist class sought as their businesses expanded and competed with one another. Merchant capitalism had been primarily a period in which growth occurred through profitable trading: colonialism potentially allowed much greater profits because it meant the introduction of more efficient systems of farming and mining, as well as greater control over the labour force. What merchant capitalism had done, however, was to establish the basic pattern of production in the Third World countries: that is their economies were geared towards the provision of a narrow range of raw materials for export to the developing industries of Europe.

The main period of colonial expansion was between 1850 and 1900. There had been formal colonies established as early as the sixteenth century by the Spanish and Portuguese in Latin America but these were basically run as overseas feudal estates for the Spanish settlers, and most were granted independence by 1830. Nineteenth century colonialism was seen as a valuable political instrument controlling overseas territories for the further development of industrial capitalism in the West. An important stimulus to what turned out to be a veritable race for the colonies was France's protectionist policies of the 1850s, which sought to defend its markets and access to overseas resources. This sparked off a European scramble for control over lands, people and raw materials, a process encouraged by the technological innovations in transport and communications, such as the steamship, the new Suez Canal and the telegraph. This dash for colonial territories was not always as profitable as the colonial authorities might have wished. On some occasions lands were taken by colonial officials without the blessing of their authorities. For example, a number of British governor-generals in the colonies claimed additional territory without consulting their London superiors – Lower Burma was established overnight as a British crown colony by a governor who was annoyed by the Burmese government's refusal to pay a debt of £1000. Such precipitate action meant considerable expense for the colonial power which was obliged to make arrangements for the administration of the new region. Indeed, as Fieldhouse (1967) shows, many colonial conquests were neither economically needed nor profitable for the capitalist centre.

The 'scramble for Africa' represented colonial expansion at its most rampant. Although British colonialism was extensive in Africa by the end of the nineteenth century, France had by far the largest territorial control in the continent – an area of approximately four million square miles holding a population of about sixty-four million. It controlled the greater part of the north, north-west, west and equatorial Africa. Britain's interests lay to the east and south, Germany, Belgium, Portugal, Italy and Spain controlling (in declining order) much smaller regions. Map 4.2 illustrates the extent of colonialism throughout the world at the turn of the nineteenth century.

What were the social and economic consequences of the imposition of colonial rule? There was some variation in this regard as different colonial powers pursued different expansionist policies. Nevertheless, we can identify a number of features of colonialism which apply in general.

(A) As suggested above, the colonies were a source of cheap raw materials (crops and minerals) as well as an expanded outlet for manufactured goods from Europe. The rivalry between the European powers meant that it was important that each established a strong presence in its claimed overseas territory. Apart from the introduction of a colonial political, legal and administrative structure to establish 'authority', the economic resources of the colony were often secured through the activities of the large capitalist companies from Europe with the backing of their governments. The capitalist penetration of the colony was typically led by one main company to which the authorities granted monopoly rights over what was produced as well as legal powers over land use, taxation and labour regulations in the territory. In West Africa, for example, the Royal Niger Company was granted a charter by the British government in 1886 which gave it power to collect taxes and maintain and administer the law. Moreover, the Company was free to use arms to sustain and expand its presence in the Niger region, which it did do against local sultans and colonial competitors from France and Germany. The great economic and political power of these companies was enhanced when they received concessions from the authorities in the form of sole land rights over vast areas to prospect for and mine minerals and gemstones as well as clearing land for plantation crops. Not surprisingly, the presence, power and activities of these capitalist

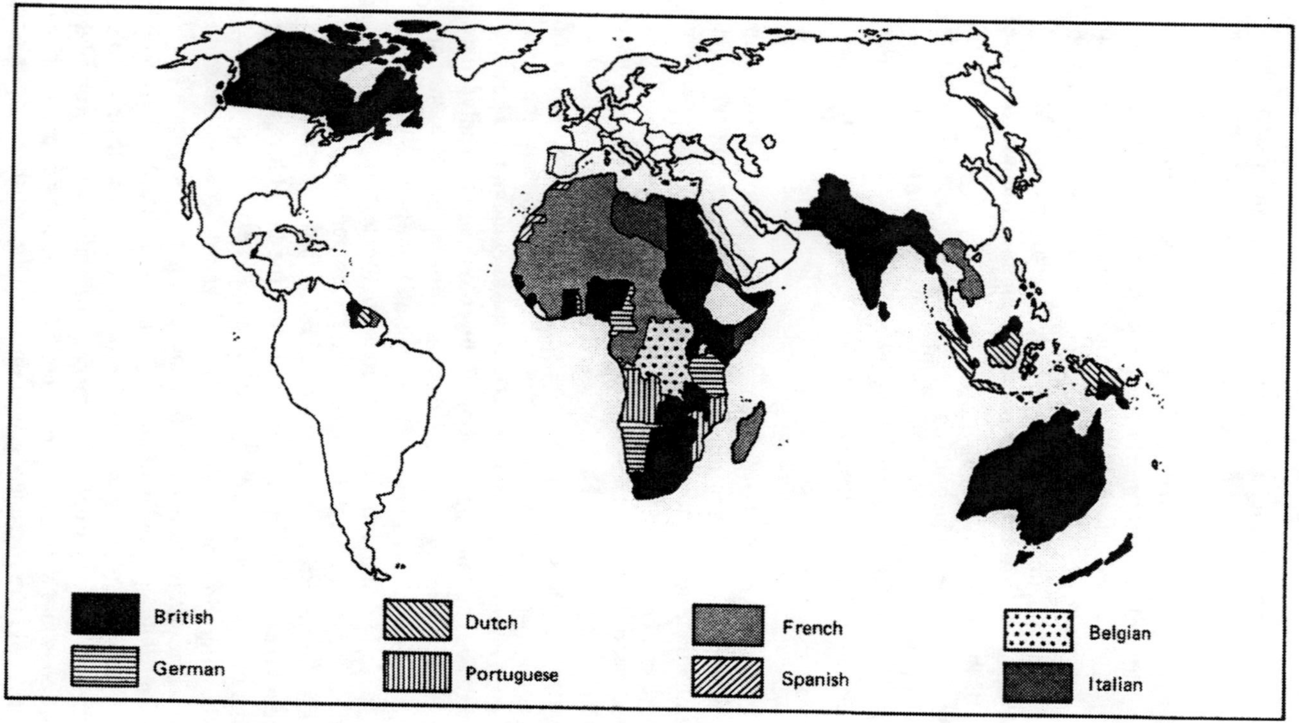

MAP 4.2 *The colonial empires, 1914*

firms had a considerable impact on the lives of the local people, particularly with regard to their access to land. Land tenure patterns that had existed for centuries were displaced. Moreover, the monopolistic companies developed only those forms of agriculture and mineral extraction that would have a commercial market or a productive use in Europe. Over time, the traditional crops which fed the local population were squeezed out as rural farmers lost land to the companies interested only in the new crops – like coffee, cocoa and tea – for export, the so-called 'cash crops'. As land, crops and the labour that was employed became subject to the cash economy the local inhabitants found that their ability to sustain their families through their own farming efforts was threatened. Many lost land and had to sell their labour for a wage on the company plantation or in the mine.

(B) The capitalist enterprises needed wage-labour to work the mines and plantations. Apart from there being little alternative because of landlessness, many local people were additionally compelled to seek a cash paying job in order to pay the money taxes imposed by the colonial authorities. So much labour was needed in a relatively short period of time that compulsion also came in the form of forced labour, indentured labour, and intimidation. Many workers were brought great distances to work, even from other countries (for example, the Tamils of India to work on the tea estates of Sri Lanka); thus, colonialism inaugurated the first real pattern of large scale labour migration and displacement in the world. Wage labour became established in both rural and urban regions in the colonies in the productive and service sectors.

(C) Finally, colonialism meant the imposition of a system of law and order that suited the colonial administration. This system prevailed over a colony whose territorial boundaries were not determined by the pre-colonial boundaries recognised by the indigenous populations. Geographically and politically, the colony was the creation of the competition between European powers, and its shape was determined as much by the seizure of land as by negotiation. The legal system that operated was usually a mixture of local customary law and European law. Thus, the colonial system did not necessarily mean the complete destruction of local political and legal institutions; indeed, not only would this have been socially impossible but it would also have been regarded as foolish by many colonialists. They saw their task as being the introduction of the new capitalist rigours of production as quickly as possible without, however, encouraging the local population to become competitors to the colonial power by establishing their own enterprise. While clearly, the companies' own behaviour did much to restrict this, it was also felt that the maintenance of local authority structures would help to check any threat from local ambition. A few indigenous structures were allowed to prevail so long as the capitalist interests in the colony (and Europe) were served. The British were most adept at this system of indirect rule, ruling the colony through the local elites and chiefs. It was often the case that colonialism gave *more* power to the indigenous authorities. This was true, for example, in Africa and India: in India the Permanent Settlement Act imposed by Britain made the Zamindary notables landowners thereby giving them private property rights which they had not enjoyed previously.

These three general features of the colonial period indicate the scale of the impact colonialism had on existing forms of production, land ownership, labour patterns and political structures. The unifying theme is, of course, that this transformation was geared to serve the interests of the development of European capitalism, thus disrupting the social and economic character of the colonies. As we shall see in section 4.4, those who subscribe to underdevelopment theory frequently write about the 'distorted', 'incoherent' or 'imbalanced' character of the Third World economies because of their association with western capitalism. With the society geared towards and dominated by European interests there has been little opportunity for the development of an independent, locally controlled system of production serving the needs of the local market. As Stavenhagen (1973, p. 87) has said,

> Nowhere in the underdeveloped world has a generalised system of rational and well-balanced mixed-farming orientated towards supplying the internal market developed. This is one of the characteristics of agriculture in underdeveloped areas; perhaps it is one of the causes of underdevelopment itself.

Arguments of this type imply that the Third World has been subject to a socio-economic experience that is unlike anything that the advanced industrial societies underwent in their period of industrialisation. While most neo-Marxist theorists would want to support this claim and thereby challenge the Eurocentric models of modernisation theory, there is considerable disagreement among them as to the implications of the specific historical route taken by the Third World. To recall, for some, the penetration by capitalism of the Third World will lead to chronic underdevelopment; for others, this penetration, while certainly unique in its historical form, could promote the evolution of industrial capitalism in the future.

There are many more detailed aspects of colonialism that we could have discussed such as its impact on language, religion and gender relations; shortage of space prevents this here although the last will be examined in Chapter 5. Let us now turn our attention to the final and still prevailing process that is said to sustain the exploitation and poverty of the Third World; namely, 'neo-colonialism'.

3 Neo-colonialism

Neo-colonialism was first examined at length by Nkrumah, the Ghanaian President of the early 1960s. He argued as follows (Nkrumah, 1965, p. ix):

> The essence of neo-colonialism is that the state which is subject to it is, in theory, independent and has all the trappings of international sovereignty. In reality its economic system and thus its internal policy is directed from the outside.

Nkrumah himself experienced the full force of this outside direction when his socialist policies were undermined by capitalist groups in Ghana supported by foreign agencies, causing him to be deposed by military coup in 1966. Neo-colonialism literally means a new form of colonialism, a form of socio-economic domination from outside that does not rely on direct political control.

It appeared that, about a decade after the end of the Second World War, the old colonial dominance had finally collapsed: the weakness of the European powers, the emergence of the United States and nationalist movements in the Third World combined to bring about a fairly swift end to the empires. By the mid 1960s most colonies had won their independence and by the mid 1970s the world was virtually free of colonies. Many of the new sovereign states took their places in the United Nations. However to argue that a chair in the UN meant the end of the economic dominance of the Third World would be to misconceive the processes whereby such domination is sustained.

As a political weapon, colonialism was used in most (but not all) cases to effectively transform and control the colonies in the interests of the capitalist expansion occurring in Europe. This process involved the establishment of international laws and regulations covering prices, currency dealings and banking systems. Once established, these arrangements and the capitalist penetration they facilitated were strong enough to withstand the granting of formal political independence to the colony. Little would be changed economically by such a move. At the same time, the political demise of Europe and the strength of the United States (US) meant that capitalist enterprises, particularly from the US had much greater freedom to invest in the world economy. The principal source of growth in the world economy after the Second World War were the US multi-national corporations (MNCs). Untrammelled by the old imperial systems of influence, the MNCs established subsidiaries outside the US in many nations, particularly in those offering cheap labour.

According to this view, therefore, the growth of the MNCs is the principal feature of neo-colonialism, as corporations increase their economic grip on the raw materials and labour power of Third World, nominally independent, countries. MNCs use their worldwide business structure to control production from the raw material, through the processing, to the final retail stages. The MNC represents, therefore, the increasing *concentration* of capital and the *integration* of production on a world scale. Their strength should not be underestimated: as Girvan (1976) notes a large and growing share of world production is under the control of a few hundred MNCs and by the end of the century about 400 MNCs will own about two thirds of the fixed assets of the entire globe. Institutional changes of a political and legal nature reflect this internationalisation of capital. The European Economic Community (EEC) helps to channel capital and sustain the health of European based MNCs as well as to maintain trade, production and political links with the ex-colonies of Africa, the Caribbean and the Pacific.

Merchant capitalism, colonialism, and neo-colonialism – these are the three stages which historically mark out the increasing penetration of Third World countries by capitalism from the advanced industrial centres of the world economy. Most neo-Marxist theorists would refer to part or all of the historical account sketched out above as support for their various analyses of underdevelopment. Yet there are a number of important differences with regard to the theoretical lines of argument taken by members of the underdevelopment school, to which we now turn.

4.4 EXPLANATIONS FOR UNDERDEVELOPMENT

We saw above in section 4.2 that Marx argued that the dynamics of capitalist production and capital accumulation were not restricted to the national boundaries of Europe. Marx wrote comparatively little about this process of the international expansion of capitalism being more concerned with a general analysis of the economic character of the capitalist system. Lenin was one of the first theorists who examined the international growth of capitalism from a Marxist perspective. We should note though, that he was not directly concerned with analysing its detailed *impact* on the rest of the world, but instead tried to explain the *reasons* why capitalism needed to expand globally. This he attempted in his theory of imperialism (Lenin, 1966).

The Leninist Theory of Imperialism

Non-Marxist theories of imperialism describe it as a relationship between one dominant power and subordinate states that fall under its political sway: in these terms could one speak of the Roman, Moghul, or Chinese empires. This essentially *political* definition of imperialism is not shared by Lenin. He argues that imperialism is basically an economic phenomenon restricted to a particular phase of capitalism, a stage at which crisis appears in capitalist profitability. Imperialism is primarily a result of the capitalist system attempting to resolve its crisis of profitability. Drawing on Marx's ideas, Lenin argued as follows:

Marx had said that as capitalism grew through industrialisation and mechanisation it became more and more difficult for it to maintain its levels of profit as capital investment in plant and equipment increased. The rate of profit therefore always tended to decline. But this tendency could be offset in a number of ways. For example, the cost of machinery could be reduced or the rate of exploitation of labour could be increased through increasing labour productivity, cutting wages or demanding longer hours. Lenin claimed that one of the most important ways in which the rate of profit could be sustained was through advanced capitalism expanding overseas. Such imperialism would allow (a) control over a global market, (b) access to cheap foreign labour and (c) a cheap supply of raw materials.

Lenin saw the relationship between imperialism and capitalism in terms of four related propositions:

(i) to maintain profitability capitalist enterprises in advanced countries exported capital to the colonies assisted by the political and military strength of European governments;
(ii) this made it possible to obtain on very favourable terms raw materials in the colonies;
(iii) this also meant that capital was needed in the colonies to build railways, roads and ports to service the capitalist penetration; and
(iv) these developments led to a concentration and centralisation of capital by large transnational monopolistic firms.

Critique

There are many criticisms that have been made of Lenin's thesis. Roxborough (1979, pp. 55–7) raises a number of questions two of which seem particularly important:

(a) Lenin portrays colonialism as the inevitable result of the appearance of monopoly capitalism: however (as we saw earlier), colonial empires have all but gone yet international monopolistic corporations thrive. This either means that Lenin's basic explanation for the emergence of colonialism is wrong or, (and this is more likely) the sort of monopoly corporations we now have are radically distinct from those of Lenin's time at the beginning of this century.

(b) Roxborough argues that empirically Lenin's theory has a

number of weaknesses, especially, for example, the fact that a large amount of capital did not go to the new colonies of Africa and Asia in the latter part of the nineteenth century, but to areas where white settlers had established themselves in New Zealand, Australia and South Africa.

On theoretical and empirical grounds, then, Lenin's theory is open to question. What is of crucial importance, however, is Lenin's general attitude towards the effect of capitalist expansion for this has bearing on the question of Third World underdevelopment. Lenin adopted Marx's view that capitalist expansion would have a 'progressive' affect on those non-capitalist societies it penetrated. Both believed that although it was true that capitalism would disrupt, plunder and exploit these societies this very exploitation would lead to the development of the more productive industrial capitalism in these 'backward' regions. As Marx (1976, p. 91) said,

> The country that is more developed industrially only shows, to the less developed, the image of its own future.

Thus, the classical Marxist–Leninist view is to see the global spread of capitalism as destructive of the old (pre-capitalist) order yet constructive of a new, more productive society, although we must not forget that for Marx and Lenin the antagonisms of class conflict and social inequality would be as much a part of this process as they have been in Western Europe.

According to this view, therefore, a lack of development is a reflection of the uneven impact of capitalist penetration in the world. Although the exact route taken by the first capitalist states will not be repeated since societies can, as Marx said, 'shorten and lessen the birth-pangs' of economic growth, they cannot avoid experiencing more or less directly the logic of capitalist accumulation and the class antagonisms this creates. The primacy of the development of European capitalism means that the working class will be most progressive there and will, in their eventual revolution in the centre, bring about the liberation of the immature working class still developing in the less capitalist regions of the world. This is a thesis based on an analysis of economic forces which in its evolutionary character is not unlike that of modernisation theory though clearly its substance and its projections for the future concerning the eventual appearance of socialism make it radically different. For both however, but for different reasons, a lack of 'development' is likely to be overcome.

What therefore appears as something of a surprise in the Marxian literature after Lenin's death (in 1924) is the growth of a thesis about capitalist imperialism completely contrary to that advanced by Marx and Lenin. This is the view that imperialism must be considered as an obstacle to industrialisation and the development of the productive power of capitalism. Warren (1980) who does not subscribe to this view, suggests a number of reasons for this dramatic shift of opinion. One that seems to be of particular importance was the alliance between the nationalist organisations that developed in India and China during the 1920s and a number of prominent Soviet Marxists who disagreed with Lenin that the Western working class are to be the source of world revolutionary struggle. Instead, they sought strength for their socialist cause through allying the Soviet regime with the anti-imperialist struggles of Asia. In supporting the Asian socialists the Soviet theorists denied the 'progressive' role of capitalist imperialism and championed the cause of peasant-based socialist struggles in agrarian societies.

This basically strategic revision was subsequently given analytical support through the theoretical work of more recent members of the neo-Marxist school. The central tenet quickly established itself that imperialism is a block to Third World development draining the resources or *economic surplus* from these societies which stagnate as they become *more* underdeveloped. This notion that the surplus is being transferred from the poor countries to the rich capitalist states is one which lies at the heart of the second major theory of underdevelopment that claims a Marxist pedigree, namely, dependency theory.

Frank's Theory of Third World Dependency

Dependency theory originated in the 1960s through the work of a number of academics and development economists who were particularly concerned over the continuing economic failure of Latin American countries. They dismissed the notions of modernisation theory that a lack of development could be attributed to a deficiency in appropriate modernising values and that exposure to advanced industrial countries could only be of positive benefit to the Third World. Instead they argued that the massive and persistent poverty in countries like Argentina, Peru, Chile and Brazil was *caused* by exposure to the economic and political influences of the advanced countries. The view that the impact of advanced society is progressive, whether in the form of the diffusionism thesis of modernisation theory or in the form of the imperialism thesis of classical Marxism, was completely rejected. The growth of the advanced industrial centres in the world today meant the *simultaneous* underdevelopment of those countries whose economic surplus the West exploited. Poor societies should not therefore be regarded as in some way 'immature' or 'underdeveloped' in their economic development; given time, their growth will occur. So long as they are subject to the dominance of the economic imperialism of the West their poverty will persist.

One of the major representatives of this position is Andre Gunder Frank who is most closely associated with the view that the persistent poverty of the Third World is a reflection of its 'dependency'. Frank argues that the periods of merchant capitalism and colonialism forced a specialisation of production on Third World countries that was primarily export oriented, of limited range and geared to the raw material needs of the imperial powers. The Third World elites were incorporated into this system and could do little to establish a more diverse, independent form of economic activity. They became the mere intermediaries between the rich purchasers and the poor (peasant) producers. Frank dubs them the *comprador* (literally 'interpreter') elites whose wealth and lifestyles were more and more tied to and so heavily dependent on the activities of the economic elite in the centre, or in what Frank calls the 'metropolitan' country. While the Third World elite enjoy a high standard of living from this relationship, the masses experience chronic deprivation as their surplus production is taken from them in the local rural region and transferred to the rich farmers and merchants in their own country and then on abroad. Frank argues that there is a 'chain of dependency' running down from the highly advanced centres of the world, a hierarchy of 'metropolises' with their subordinate 'satellites' through which the economic surplus is passed upwards within a nation and then internationally; there is he says (Frank, 1967, p. 34):

> a whole chain of metropolises and satellites, which runs from the world metropolis down to the hacienda or rural merchant who are satellites of the local commercial metropolitan centre but who in their turn have peasants as their satellites,

While countries of the advanced centre can develop through self-growth, others since they are dependent, can only possibly expand if the dominant metropole expands. But such an expansion is always under the control of the metropole since any expanded surplus will be automatically passed upwards out of the satellite.

For Frank, and other dependency theorists, the only way of stopping the exploitation of this surplus is by breaking the chain of dependency by which it is transferred. The only people who can do this, it is argued, is the Third World working class and the only weapon strong enough is socialist revolution which removes the *comprador* elite, the weak link in the chain.

Critique

Frank's thesis received much support from Latin American neo-Marxists and nationalist economists such as Dos Santos (1973) and it was quickly incorporated into the broad school of radical underdevelopment theory where it remains today. There have been a number of attempts to subject Frank's theory to empirical investigation, and a useful discussion of these is provided by Long (1977, pp. 77–84). These seem to have had some success in identifying different levels of exploitation from local through to higher regional levels much as Frank's metropolis/satellite thesis claims. Nevertheless, there are a number of serious theoretical weaknesses that can be identified in Frank's account of dependency which we can now consider.

(1) The concept of 'dependency' is much too vague to be of use, failing to clarify sufficiently the sense in which Third World countries are dependent on metropolitan centres. As O'Brien (1975, p. 24) says, Frank gives us 'a circular argument: dependent countries are those which lack the capacity for autonomous growth

and they lack this because their structures are dependent ones'. By itself, this tells us very little other than that economies are not autonomous but depend on each other for growth. There is clearly nothing in this that is peculiar to Third World countries: for example, Canada is very much dependent on US capital yet it is a developed economy and the US can be said to be 'dependent' on Third world reserves as the oil crisis of 1973 demonstrated and as Caldwell (1977) shows in his examination of the use of world resources. Moreover, as Therborn (1979) argues, the proposition that the world economy is a *system* means that all parts are in one way or another 'dependent' on each other.

As Kitching (1982) has argued, the only real *measure* of dependency that gives it meaning is the assessment of the amount of money that is invested in a Third World country and the amount over and above this that is taken out by the metropolitan centre: this is the exploited 'surplus'. But simple measures of the net transfer of money say nothing about the possible benefits that may have arisen from the initial investment – the spin-off perhaps from the construction of a railway. As Kitching (1982, p. 167) says:

> Certainly a simple comparison of money capital inflows into developing countries with money capital outflows is . . . a totally inadequate basis on which to build a theory of exploitation.

(2) In describing the character of Third World underdevelopment, Frank's earlier work appears to argue that Third World countries are static. As the surplus is sucked out of such countries, no indigenous development is possible. However, given the relatively recent (post 1970) economic growth that has occurred – especially in Brazil, Mexico, Argentina and some East Asian countries, a number of radical Latin American scholars have had to rethink their theoretical position with regard to dependency. Cardoso (1979) for example believes that capital investment *does* promote the development of some locally controlled manufacturing, he now speaks not of 'dependency' but 'dependent development'.

Petras (1969) acknowledges that some 'development' has occurred but rejects the view that this can lead to autonomous industrial growth. Instead, he suggests that a distorted 'enclave' development is happening: this means that pockets of technologically advanced manufacturing are established geared to export but which cannot transfer their 'dynamism and high productivity to the rest of the economy'.

In his more recent work Frank (1984) accepts the need to account for this growth in industrial production and his analysis no longer supports a stagnationist position, but is similar to that of Petras. He argues that the new industrial sectors are socially and economically inherently defective and vulnerable because they depend on the continued support of foreign MNCs, a strong handed government to curb unions, and demand from high-income consumers who are in a minority in Latin America. It has not he claims, led to an increase in the national wage rates nor to an expansion in the internal market but instead requires a repression of wages to make 'profitable production and competitive exports possible.' The growth in the money sector in the urban centres of Latin America has not been matched by a general increase in employment:

> The whole development is limited to between 5 and perhaps 20% of the population while the other 80% (perhaps up to 95%) of the people are excluded by economic, political and military force from all benefit and often from any participation. 56% of Brazilians are 'absolutely marginalised' and limited to basic food consumption, 75% of the population is relatively marginalised and limited to primary necessities only. (Frank, 1981, p. 10).

If Frank's view on the *inherent limits* of the industrialisation of Third World economies is accurate then we cannot expect these figures to change much in the future; presumably they will only change if the comprador elite is challenged from below. If, however, a broader distribution of economic growth does occur then his view of the impact of capitalist penetration must be open to serious question. Moreover, a number of South-East Asian countries, such as South Korea and Taiwan, have demonstrated a remarkable capacity for sustained real growth via a strongly directive central government that has marshalled indigenous labour and capital very effectively. The organisational strength of such state capitalist societies questions Frank's claims about an inherently weak comprador elite prevailing throughout Third World states.

(3) We have seen above in our first criticism that Frank spends too much time measuring underdevelopment in terms of the *exchange* and *transfer* of the surplus from satellites to metroplises. This has led a number of critics to argue that the basic flaw in his work is his failure to examine the *way* in which surplus is extracted through the system of *production* that prevails in Third World societies. Critics such as Laclau (1971) point out that the exploitation of a surplus through a more powerful country enjoying a trade advantage over another is not a defining feature of the capitalist economic system. Such trade advantages can be found among feudal economies. As Laclau argues, the crucial problem is to know *how* the surplus that is transferred is produced and whether there are any specific features of the productive system that limit its 'development'. He therefore suggests that capitalist development has taken place in (parts of) the Third World but in an uneven, and unfinished manner: for example, capitalist enterprises may have been located in the Third World and wage labourers employed yet these workers may rely on additional non-capitalist sources of material support available in their productive system (such as crops from plots they cultivate on communal land). This allows the employers to pay low wages and to maintain profitability but it also *limits* the extent to which wholesale capitalist development based on the full exploitation of a wage labourer's surplus value is possible.

In other words, capitalism is said to *articulate* with rather than completely incorporate the local social and economic system of production. Laclau and a whole host of 'articulationist' theorists criticise Frank's simplistic assumption that capitalism permeates and subsequently completely displaces pre-existing, non-capitalist systems. Hence, rather than examining how much capital is taken out of Third World countries, as Frank does, the neo-Marxist articulationists prefer to explore the relationship between different systems of production and the implications this has for general economic growth.

(4) One important neo-Marxist, Bill Warren, like the critics mentioned in the preceding remarks, challenges Frank for failing to analyse production relations properly. However unlike them, he does not believe that the underdevelopment of the Third World will persist even if it is true that at the moment its productive

system is a complex mix of capitalist and non-capitalist activities. Warren argues that what are thought of as aspects of underdevelopment are in fact the features typical of any society going through the socio-economic transition to capitalism. In other words for Warren, Third World societies are not doomed to stagnation or enclave development and while their historical experience is distinctive, it is not unique. Warren accepts that they do rely heavily on advanced industrial societies for economic growth, especially for advanced technology. Yet he argues (Warren, 1980, p. 170):

> The distribution of world economic power is becoming less concentrated and more dispersed, and the countries of Asia, Africa, and Latin America are playing ever more independent roles, both economically and politically.

Warren claims then, that the Third World contains the newly industrialising countries of the world economy and as capitalist penetration becomes deeper and more successful in the Third World it generates its own capacity for growth. One must recall here the classical Marxist view of the progressive role of capitalism, for Warren explicitly allies himself with this position.

Attempts to resolve this question of the potential for industrial growth in the Third World have shifted away from exploring as Warren did, the evidence for specific individual countries. Instead, the *global economy* is the primary focus of attention. Research conducted at this level suggests a rather different picture of development than that produced by Warren.

Many of Warren's neo-Marxist critics acknowledge that there has been a steady flow of capital investment to the South from northern-based MNCs. But they argue that this fact does not herald the arrival of a new period of industrial development in the Third World: rather the capitalist world economy is said to be 'restructuring' itself to take advantage of the very cheap labour force found there, and so is establishing a 'new international division of labour'. Extending this argument, others (such as Ernst, 1981; Lipietz, 1986) argue that in addition to this process, the large transnational corporations have developed much greater corporate flexibility in the way they use and control their workforce and resources. They will spread productive activities across a network of global locations to take most advantage of local conditions, encouraged to do so by compliant Third World states.

The flexible approach to production is said to signal the end of global 'Fordism', a term coined to describe the once-common mass production systems of large scale assembly-line manufacture that was located in First World states, most classically represented – hence the name – by the Ford Motor Company. International recession, oil price rises and increasing unemployment accompanied by relatively high production costs in First World states have led many large companies to restructure their activities, to spread component production across a wider range of countries including many in the Third World. Ford itself did this during the early 1980s, opening, for example, large component plants in Mexico.

However, many Marxists believe that northern-based investment does not serve the long term needs of poor countries, either in the sense of redistributing resources towards them or in terms of enhancing their capacity for self-determined development (Lipietz, 1982). Rather the Third World is primarily a source of cheap labour, making up the manufactured items designed in the North: this simply means that yesterday's 'banana republics' are today's 'pyjama republics' (Adam, 1975).

However, though there is some evidence to support this thesis, it has been challenged by fellow Marxists, such as Gordon (1988). Gordon provides considerable evidence that suggests that a planned global 'restructuring' may have been overstated. He points out, for example, that recent data show that transnationals get a *lower* return on their Third World investments than on their equivalent in the North. Gordon believes that rather than an efficient 'restructuring', the global economy has in fact become increasingly unstable, symptomatic of which have been the rapid fluctuations in commodity prices and exchange rates over the past decade. Thus, large corporations have sought to cope with uncertainty by investing in locations they perceive to be relatively secure which *may* include some Third World states: '[corporations] search among potential investment sites for institutional harbours promising the safest havens against an increasingly turbulent world economy' (p. 56).

There remains, therefore, within underdevelopment theory some doubt over the correct interpretation of the global activities of capitalist corporations and their particular impact on Third

World development. Frank's dependency theory tended towards a stagnationist position, while Warren's view, dismissing underdevelopment altogether, has perhaps exaggerated the expansionary impact of investment in the Third World. The 'global restructuring' theorists are convinced that underdevelopment will remain but that some sectors, or enclaves, might experience a distorted, Northern oriented capitalist growth. Gordon's analysis calls for a longer term perspective and points to the inherent instability of world capitalism today.

Lipton's Theory of 'Urban Bias'

Following in the broad tradition of underdevelopment theory, Michael Lipton's theory of 'urban bias' as an explanation for distorted, uneven development in the Third World, has generated considerable debate among writers on the left. In placing a particular emphasis on the advantages that the urban centres in the Third World enjoy – by cashing in on most of the development aid and exploiting the surrounding rural regions – Lipton's thesis differs from that of many other underdevelopment writers. While not denying that there is a political and economic 'global rift' between the rich North and poor South, brought about through a history of imperialism and neo-colonialism, Lipton believes that the main reason why development is held back in the Third World, and 'why poor people stay poor', is because of the existence of parasitical and corrupt urban elites.

In defending his thesis, Lipton presents a mass of evidence that shows how little of the real investment capital that is available goes to the agricultural sectors, and what does tends to go to the more prosperous farmers: while poor farmers are very efficient it is the richer ones that receive the cheap loans and subsidised fertiliser. When development for the rural sector is advocated by the urban elites, their objective is not necessarily to improve the lot of the rural poor, but to increase the revenue from cash crops, most of which will go to support the urban centres.

Many Third World countries have declared their ambition to develop through profit-oriented industrial growth orchestrated by modernising urban classes to be spread subsequently throughout the rest of society. This is supposed to emulate the historical experience of already industrialised countries. But Lipton claims that such a path is unavailable to the Third World. First, there is no large, 'organisable' urban-based, literate working class as there was in Europe whose labour was not only very productive but also received increasing real wages. Secondly, the organisational and political strength of national governments in the Third World is much less than that of nineteenth-century states, particularly with regard to control over finance capital and the circulation of money and credit. Thirdly, capitalist investors in the Third World have never sought to undermine indigenous feudal or other non-capitalist interests: 'feudal' power is often enhanced, not removed, by capitalism and is located in urban-based elite groups.

Finally, and most important of all, because of these circumstances there is a massive imbalance between the city and the country in the Third World which did not happen in, for example, nineteenth-century British development (see Chapter 5, p. 109). This urban bias is found in both 'socialist' and 'capitalist' states in the Third World. As such, it is not, says Lipton simply a result of capitalist class exploitation, as others might want to claim. It is rather the result of the power of an 'urban class' over a 'rural class', where 'class' is defined in terms of shared group interests and the actual or potential power to defend them. Though weak internationally, the urban class is more effective in mobilising itself to take most advantage of the situation.

Urban bias

Poverty persists alongside development largely because poor countries are developed from, by and for people in cities: people who, acting under normal human pressures, deny the fruits of development to the pressure-less village poor. Few of these can escape the trap by joining the exploitative city elite, because high urban wages (and subsidised capital imports) deter employers from using extra labour. Many villagers, once migration has failed to secure entry to the urban labour aristocracy, return to an increasingly land-scarce village: a village that is by policy starved of public investment allocations, and hence by policy prevented from sharing in development and thus from curing its own poverty.

Source: Lipton (1977) p. 69.

Lipton believes that the only way in which genuine mass development can occur is through a dramatic change in policy favouring a shift of resources to the rural poor: this is the 'overriding development task'. Lipton acknowledges that this could mean that some poor countries would in the future sustain themselves through an efficient, low cost, self-reliant agriculture, with no need to strive for large-scale industrialisation.

Lipton's thesis has been seen as both provocative and inspirational, especially to development workers on the liberal left. But it has also been subject to strong criticism, on both empirical and theoretical grounds, at some length by Byers (1979) and more concisely by Kitching (1982). One of the principal criticisms is that Lipton fails to provide a convincing picture of a unified urban class separate from a similarly homogenous rural class. Socio-economic relations are more complex and overlapping than Lipton's model implies. Moreover, despite Lipton's claim that his thesis is not necessarily *anti-industrial* in its implications, the critics believe that ultimately he advocates a future that is based on development that favours a mass of small peasant farmers, cooperating in an egalitarian rural society. Hence, Lipton has been accused of a utopian rural 'populism' (see Chapter 8, p. 174).

Recent Trends in Development Theory: Towards a New Convergence?

We have seen so far in this chapter that there are a number of differing accounts of Third World disadvantage that can be grouped together as types of 'underdevelopment' theory. Typically, all are highly critical of the assumptions made by modernisation theorists explored in Chapter 3. However, there is increasingly a sense in which neo-Marxists and neo-modernisation theorists are coming together in their respective accounts of the Third World, though this is *not* to say that a new development consensus has been established. But what one can see in recent writings is a recognition by modernisation theorists that they have underplayed the importance of a history of economic and political inequalities – the 'global rift' – between North and South, while underdevelopment theorists have with increasing enthusiasm begun to take seriously the importance of local political and cultural institutions in the Third World as obstacles to further development. Rather than trying to summarise this growing literature, we can consider the views of Apter (1988) and Mouzelis (1988) who represent the neo-modernisation and neo-Marxist schools respectively.

Apter argues that although the two perspectives seem irreconcilable at first sight, 'each can be applied to the same process to show different systemic tendencies simultaneously at work' (p. 28). Modernisation theory, he says, emphasises the growth of a complex, urban-based middle class, which in turn encourages increasing social integration; underdevelopment theory draws attention instead to a process of 'polarisation', or division and conflict between social classes and groups within the Third World. Apter argues that both perspectives can be correct inasmuch as he believes it is possible to demonstrate that there are tendencies towards both integration and polarisation occurring simultaneously as societies develop: 'integrative tendencies and a moving equilibrium can go together with polarisation, and each as a function of growth' (p. 32). As development occurs, the technological innovation it brings tends to create unemployment and marginalise less advantaged sectors of society, who are increasingly likely to resort to violence. But Apter sees such violence as functional to development, as a way of resolving the problems of development rather than being pathological to societal growth. These difficulties resulting from innovation are, he says, apparent in industrialised societies too, though the way conflict is displayed and managed is likely to be very different from that expressed in the Third World.

Apter's attempt to synthesise the cultural, value-oriented focus of modernisation with the more economically oriented underdevelopment theory is still at a provisional stage, and needs much more work. Nevertheless, it reflects a growing interest by theorists of both right and left to go beyond the impasse of modernisation versus underdevelopment.

Writing from within a broad neo-Marxian tradition, Mouzelis (1988) is prepared to criticise previous Marxist analysis for ignoring the role of cultural processes within specific countries in order to stress the role of global economic factors: he believes instead that the economic factors that create underdevelopment are influenced and shaped by local cultures and in particular local political structures, i.e. the state and public sector bureaucracies that manage the development effort (see also Booth, 1985).

Mouzelis compares the way in which different states have related to the global economy. He contrasts the anti-communist military elites of South-East Asia where a sense of 'the public interest' and a 'citizenry' with constitutional rights are both lacking, with Latin American countries which have a stronger sense of 'civil society'. While classic modernisation theory might regard the weakness of the citizenry in South-East Asia as a problem for development, Mouzelis shows that, on the contrary, this has allowed the South-East Asian states to take a much more direct role in determining their economic development, including enjoying greater control over foreign (transnational) capital. 'In the Latin American case, on the other hand, one sees a relatively stronger civil society and a state whose controlling elites are less willing or capable of directing the activities of foreign and indigenous capital towards a more self-reliant and less marginalising type of capitalist accumulation' (p. 31).

Like an increasing number of neo-Marxists, Mouzelis demands that underdevelopment theory takes seriously the proposition that Third World political structures cannot simply be treated as secondary to the global processes of the world capitalist system. They have to be seen, in fact, as being of *at least equal* importance to such processes: 'What has not been given any serious thought is the extent to which at least the internal obstacles to [growth] in the third world are more *political* than economic' (emphasis in original, p. 38).

There is, therefore, a healthy new debate within the sociology of development, in part a reflection of the growing interest in conducting detailed historical examinations of societies and their patterns of development. This has led to a greater recognition of the complexity of development. The focus on understanding how political resources can empower elites, classes or interest groups to shape social change is also growing in sociological theory, perhaps best illustrated in the recent work of Mann (1986) and Giddens (1987).

CONCLUSION

'Underdevelopment theory' embodies a number of linked but distinct perspectives including classical imperialist, dependency, urban bias, articulationist and post-Marxist accounts. The general trend has been towards a more historically informed analysis of economic, political and cultural dimensions of social change which, while still recognising the importance of capitalist economic interests as *globally* determinant, acknowledges that at national and local levels such interests are shaped by and have effect through the indigenous political and cultural institutions (see Cammack, 1988).

Hence, most of the theorists considered in this chapter have argued that the Third World is economically 'distorted' or that an 'unevenness' prevails. At the same time they argue that this distortion is reflected in cultural institutions and patterns, which have the veneer of 'modernity' but lack its structural foundations: in this regard we shall look at population growth, urbanisation and educational expansion in Chapter 5.

5

Population, Urbanisation and Education

5.1 INTRODUCTION

The majority of models of development regard population growth, urbanisation and educational expansion as crucial features of industrial modernisation. They are seen as important preconditions for industrialisation as well as developing more fully as a consequence of it. Yet the simple presence of all three does not necessarily indicate that industrialisation has occurred as is evident when we look at the underdeveloped Third World. One hears of 'over population', 'over urbanisation', and inappropriate educational expansion: are these distortions and the difficulties they imply derived from something specific about social policies in the Third World or are they symptons of more deep-seated problems? This chapter looks at some of the basic issues raised in this debate.

5.2 POPULATION

Population growth is a matter of great concern today, particularly in the Third World. Yet a growing population is also considered to be an important factor encouraging economic growth. Clearly this implies that there is an optimum set of conditions which must balance population growth with sustained economic development. The growth of a population results from the excess of births over deaths as well as the movement of people between regions or countries. The 'natural increase' in a population, that is, the surplus of births over deaths, occurs for two reasons: first, an improvement in the control of disease through widespread improvements in health care, especially public sanitation, and secondly, an improvement in the standard of nutrition throughout the population. Migration into and out of areas clearly is a major social factor influencing population levels in a country, and can be a particularly acute problem for countries in receipt of many hundreds of thousands of refugees at times of warfare, or immigrants seeking to enhance their life chances by leaving their impoverished homeland. Since both warfare and poverty are grim but routine features of the Third World today, it is not surprising to find a substantial volume of migration within it.

From a theoretical perspective population growth is seen as a major stimulant to industrial development. As was noted in Chapter 2, Durkheim and other exponents of the 'tradition-modernity' thesis see the pressure of population as part of social development since the problems it creates can only be resolved by a more productive use of land and an increase in the division of labour. The subsequent increase in economic productivity and social differentiation promote industrial growth in the long term. Indeed, in areas of the Third World that are relatively *under*-populated (primarily African countries) some authors such as Boserup (1965), argue that population increase should be encouraged as the additional demands would stimulate rural cultivators into developing more innovative, productive agriculture so that, as she says, 'genuine economic development' can occur. One implication of Boserup's remarks is that the population 'problem' may in some circumstances refer to a *shortage* rather than an 'over supply' of people. However, Boserup acknowledges that there may be conditions in which a rapidly growing population is not conducive to development. She accepts, for example, that some regions are ecologically less capable of supporting a very sharp increase in population levels over a short period of time. In such cases, inappropriate farming to produce sufficient crops is likely to lead to land degradation fairly quickly, making long term agricultural development much more difficult.

Those adopting a broadly Marxist perspective can be found to place a similar emphasis on an adequate level of population for development, but as Marxists they typically argue that this is to service capitalist expansion rather than simply 'industrial' growth. Population growth is needed for capitalist development inasmuch as a shortage of labour is likely to increase its cost, or it may be so inadequate as to prevent the establishment of factories or large plantations that are labour-intensive (particularly in the early stages of capitalist enterprise); for example we saw in the previous chapter that Marx noted that the lack of available labour for the new cotton mills of Lancashire led to the forced recruitment of child labour from other parts of England. One Marxist, Amin (1977, p. 154), in describing the necessary conditions for the development of 'agrarian capitalism', writes:

> The second condition is an average population density of the order of ten to 30 inhabitants per square kilometre. Any lesser density makes the private appropriation of lands ineffective and the potential supply of paid labour insufficient.

However while it is reasonable to argue that population growth is a feature of economic development this presupposes that the two are in some way mutually beneficial; that the population serves the economy and vice versa. One of the chronic features of Third World societies has been the way in which, from the days of merchant capitalism through to the colonial and neo-colonial days, their export oriented economies, as Gregory and Piche (1978) note, 'have borne little relation to the needs of the population, to precolonial demographic and economic patterns or to current population distribution'. This should immediately alert us to the possibility that the problems of population in the Third World are associated with the historical and current processes of under-development discussed in the preceding chapter.

While we have seen (in Chapter 2) that the Third World population is not uniform there is increasing concern over its global growth rates. Compared with developed countries whose population is estimated to grow by about 300 million over the next thirty years, the underdeveloped countries will expand by over 2500 million people. By the year 2000 the total world population will be about 6200 million of which over 5000 million will be located in the Third World. The major cause of this rapid natural increase in population is the significant improvement in health care throughout the world which has raised life expectancy considerably, while birth-rates have not appreciably declined. Unless the world economy is growing and its produce available to people, this expansion will mean increasing undernourishment, deprivation and 'absolute poverty'. But evidence indicates that many of the poor Third World countries that have experienced rapid population growth are *not* growing economically quickly enough to allow genuine development to occur (see Table 5.1).

TABLE 5.1 *Number of countries with real GDP growth rate at or below population growth rate*

	1970	1980	1982	1984	1985	1986	Population (millions)
World total	21	38	66	45	49	47	850
Developing countries	20	20	54	44	47	44	826
Developed countries	1	6	10	1	1	2	13
Eastern European countries	0	2	2	0	1	1	10

Source: *World Economic Survey*, 1987.

In these circumstances, one wonders why many (but not all) societies in the Third World continue to have high birth-rates, since this can only be irrational given improved health and the potential for real gains in productivity and standards of living. There was according to demographic analysis, a period in the history of Western Europe when high birth-rates prevailed and a natural increase in the population occurred. However this situation found in the latter part of the eighteenth century, was associated with major socio-economic change, that being rapid industrial growth in and around the towns and great advances in rural productivity so that output rose faster than the natural increase in the population. New members of the population could find work to support themselves in conjunction with their families without state support. One might therefore argue, since the Third World lacks comparable industrial and rural growth, population increases can only make matters worse, especially for the young, who comprise an ever larger dependent section of society. Indeed much of the population growth in the Third World is accounted for by young children; in Kenya, for example, 21 per cent of the population was under 5 in 1986.

Consequently, a situation of 'over population' is developing, where communities cannot sustain at an adequate level all those living in them. Increasing density leads to increasing fragmentation of land holdings as farmers divide their land up between their sons and daughters. In response peasants cultivate bulkier but less nutritious crops, such as cassava. Surely then, until Third World populations decline through national programmes of family planning, population pressure will *cause* hunger and shortages.

At first sight this argument seems to be unexceptionable. But a number of questions must be raised before we rush to accept it. First, is it the case that hunger and food shortages are the result of population pressure? There may of course be circumstances in which the food that is available cannot feed people properly. One could suggest that this is not a result of too many hungry mouths but problems with access to food. As we saw in the extract from the *World Development Report* in Chapter 2, famine is often a problem that results from job insecurity, that being from *social* deprivation rather than a lack of agricultural productivity. Taking this argument a little further, one could suggest that it is not so much population pressure that causes hunger but the *distribution* of food and the social (job) and material (land) resources needed to obtain it. If this thesis has any merit it should be possible to find circumstances in which food production is higher than local population growth yet where many in the vicinity still go hungry. There are, in fact, many examples of this process happening, some discussed by George (1976) and Lappé and Collins (1977). Where does the food go? It goes either to local elites or for export to more affluent societies. Lappé and Collins (1977) note that Mexico provides the US with over 50 per cent of its winter and spring vegetables while Mexican infants die from malnutrition. One need not restrict oneself to the Third World for illustration; the same pattern can be found in advanced societies (Lappé and Collins, 1977, p. 17):

> Stanislaus Country, California, in the heart of some of America's most productive farmland was nevertheless designated an official Hunger Disaster Area in 1969. Thousands of jobless and underpaid residents went hungry because they did not have the money to buy the food they could actually see growing in the fields.

Many times then the problem is not one of production but of social access to produce. When food production is connected with a widespread inequality of land ownership and there are inadequate sources of livelihood – jobs – whereby people can earn enough to buy food, hunger will be more than likely to follow.

Adequate land holding or access to common land may therefore be a necessary condition for sustaining one's livelihood in predominantly agrarian societies. Colonial and post-colonial Third World societies have often experienced an increasing concentration of land ownership among richer farmers or foreign companies interested in large-scale farming, the so-called 'agribusiness' multinationals such as *Nestlé* and *Unilever*. Access to land for the peasantry has become more difficult. Substantial land reforms inaugurated by national government and a redistribution of income downwards to the rural poor are much more likely to relieve world hunger than policies of population control. This has been forcibly argued in a detailed study by Repetto (1978) of 68 'developed' and 'less developed' countries and by Gibbons (1980) in a study of Malaysia and Indonesia.

The second question of the earlier argument is this: it seems to imply that population growth in the Third World is a result of completely uncontrolled fertility among its people – is this true? While it is true that the birth-rate is high there are indigenous forms of social regulation of birth practised routinely, in other words, social forms of contraception. For example, despite heavy advertising campaigns for artificial babymilk for bottle-feeding by companies such as Nestlé (and the annual sales market is estimated to be two billion dollars in the Third World), many women prefer to breast feed their babies and continue to suckle their child for a much longer period than in the west which inhibits fertility. Similarly, in some Indian communities widows are prohibited from remarrying according to social custom thus limiting their reproductive potential. Medical contraception has had some affect in reducing fertility levels in India and China but changes in fertility rates are more likely to be brought about by fostering *social* contraception as above, although not in these particular forms since they clearly place a much greater burden on female than male members of society.

Why does population growth continue? One of the reasons most frequently suggested for this is the insecurity that families experience. Until socio-economic conditions change for the better, children will typically be seen as a valuable asset by poor parents in the Third World. They are an extra pair of hands to work on the farm or, if the parents are landless, an extra source of earned income in urban centres. In old age children provide the only security that exists in countries with no state pension or social security. Moreover, the high number of births in a family is offset by the high incidence of infant mortality. As Lappé and Collins (1977, p. 64) report,

> According to a computer simulation an Indian couple would have to bear an average of 6.3 children to be confident (at a 95% level of probability) of the survival of one son. When more children are likely to survive, couples will feel less need for children. Two doctors with extensive experience in Africa, conclude, therefore, that 'the best birth control program is, simply, to feed the children.'

In conditions of insecurity and poverty large families are a rational rather than irrational choice. But this does put an exceedingly onerous burden on women who are required to bear, rear and look after the offspring. Indeed women's position in general seems to be one of increasing hardship as one moves from the pre-colonial to neo-colonial period. Even in some progressive socialist countries (for example Tanzania) women are expected to combine their farming duties with the domestic tasks of looking after children, cooking, cleaning, and so on. In the pre-colonial era, while it would be wrong to say that gender relations were egalitarian, there is evidence that women had greater independence and control over resources by working their own farms, engaging in commercial business or establishing political and military bodies (Hafkin and Bay, 1975). European colonials in Africa sought to impose a more 'suitable', 'feminine' role on women and so for example removed many women from cash crop farming or full-time wage labour.

Today, many women are restricted to cultivating the household plots, often owned by overseas companies, as basic subsistence for all the family. Their husbands are perhaps employed by the companies for very low wages. Many feminist writers, for example Deere (1976) and Van Allen (1974), argue that the companies can

'Civilising' gender relations

That equality of men and women is a sign of backwardness and that it is part of the 'civilising mission' of the British colonialists to destroy the independence of colonized women, and to teach the colonised men the 'virtues' of sexism and militarism are also clearly spelt out by one Mr Fielding Hall . . ., Political Officer in the British colonial administration in Burma between 1887–91. He gives a vivid account of the independence of Burmese women, of the equality between the sexes, and of the peace-loving nature of the Burmese people which he ascribes to Buddhism. But, instead of trying to preserve such a happy society, Mr Hall comes to the conclusion that Burma has to be brought by force on the road to progress. . . . Considering equality of the sexes a sign of backwardness, this colonial administrator warned: 'It must never be forgotten that their civilisation is relatively a thousand years behind ours.' To overcome this backwardness, the Burmese men should kill, to make war and to oppress their women. In the words of Mr Hall:

> . . . the gospel of progress, of knowledge, of happiness . . . is taught not by book and sermon but by spear and sword . . . to declare, as Buddhism does, that bravery is of no account: to say to them, as the women did, you are no better and no more than we are, and should have the same code of life; could anything be worse?

Source: Maria Mies, *Patriarchy and Accumulation on a World Scale* (1986), p. 93.

keep male workers' wages low because of the (unpaid) work their wives do on the plots. As Van Allen (1974, p. 6) remarks, much of the capital surplus drained from Africa by companies

> . . . would not be possible except for the unpaid labour of the wives of their African workers, who feed, clothe and care for themselves and their children at no cost whatsoever to the companies. Far from being a drag on the modern sector, then, as it is sometimes claimed, the modern sector is dependent for its profits on the free labour done by women.

Thus women suffer doubly from the insecurity of Third World life: on the one hand, they (and their husbands) respond to their familial insecurity by having large families; on the other hand, the domestic labour this generates is aggravated and exploited by companies who pay their husbands low wages which simply adds to their insecurity. The problems of population growth and the position of women in the Third World so affected will only really begin to be resolved when the processes of underdevelopment are checked. A few societies have already made some progress in relieving poverty, improving women's position and reducing population growth: this is true for example of Mozambique and Taiwan. However there is still a long way to go to overcome women's subjugation, perhaps most acutely and appallingly represented by the practice of the genital mutilation of young girls in many African countries (Hosken, 1979): it is estimated that 74 million women are now suffering the psychological and physiological damages of clitoridectomy and infibulation (the removal of the clitoris, labia minora and part of the labia majora of the vulva, the two sides of which are then pinned together by catgut or thorns apart from a very small opening for the discharge of urine or menstrual blood). Why do mothers require their daughters to undergo such horrific and harmful operations, usually performed by the old women of the village, with knife, razor blade or glass?

It is not an activity that has been forced on women by colonialism although colonial authorities and missionaries only made half-hearted attempts to check it. In one form or another it has existed for many hundreds of years. Reasons given include the belief that the woman is oversexed and thus her clitoris is removed in order to ensure her chastity – virginity is often considered an absolute necessity for marriage. In these circumstances, the mutilation becomes 'evidence' for virginity so that even when a girl is a virgin but has not been subject to the operation it is likely that she will be ostracised and have to leave her village. There also appears to be some quasi-religious motives for the operation, particularly among Moslem communities in Africa (the Sudan) even though in the 'cradle of Islam', the Arab countries of the middle east, the custom has virtually disappeared. Catholics, Protestants and Animists also practise excision in certain African countries. As in Islam, there are no religious doctrines nor church authorities that require believers to do so. Yet many believe that without excision women will be 'impure', as though they carry some additional 'original sin'. Finally, it is tragic that this practice has been used politically as a symbol of the restoration of Africa's cultural identity by some nationalist leaders, such as ex-President Kenyatta of Kenya, who rallied his supporters by denouncing the attempt to stop the mutilation as yet another example of western imperialism.

This practice clearly has serious implications for women who become pregnant, a likely occurrence where a large number of children are considered a family asset. Population growth has 'problems' which statistics on birth-rates do not even begin to reveal.

One of the features of population growth that is of particular interest to sociologists is its tendency to promote geographical mobility between regions especially between rural and urban areas. The relationship between the two says much about the state of economic development since it is argued that the latter encourages considerable trade and migration between them as towns and countryside grow together. This brings us to a brief discussion of urbanisation. We shall consider the sense in which this process is said to be 'distorted' in the Third World.

5.3 URBANISATION

Modern industrial society is very much an urban society. The great majority of the population live, work and play in the great conurbations that sprawl across most of the advanced economies of the world in both West and East. Urban growth is clearly linked with population increase and industrialisation: but there is no simple direct relationship between these three processes.

First, large population growth in a country is not a necessary condition for large scale urban development. For example, if one looks at the growth of the city of London from 1650–1750 one finds that, despite a virtually static population level in England (about 5 million), London grew dramatically so that by 1750 it was the largest urban centre in Europe, with approximately 11 per cent of the English population. If, by some means, it had been isolated from the rest of the country it is unlikely that London would have grown, and indeed the reverse is more probable since there was an excess of mortalities over births in the city. What enabled London to grow was an inward migration from the Midlands where there was a substantial surplus of births over deaths. Thus, migration rather than population growth can be sufficient to generate large-scale urban development. Secondly, industrial expansion is not a necessary precondition for the appearance of large cities. Many large Third World cities have arisen unaccompanied by national industrial growth. Finally, large cities may exist without having an independent industrial character; for example, a rural settlement could grow sufficiently large for it to be endowed with city status as a political or administrative centre, or towns may be primarily merchant rather than manufacturing centres. Despite these qualifications, it is true that urbanisation is typically linked with industrial growth.

According to modernisation theory, the urban centre is the locus of population growth, mobility and integration. People living in close proximity in the towns create new lifestyles because of the need to accommodate each others' ideas, desires and interests. The town acts as a catalyst for social development producing new cultural orientations among its residents.

Weber saw the city, from the medieval period onwards, as the focal point for the development of a strong sense of individualism: in their business transactions people contracted to each other as theoretical equals, individuals of similar standing in the economic community with equal obligations and rights towards one another. As 'citizens' they become equal and 'free' members under the new town laws, shaking off the feudal burdens of traditional deference to the surrounding aristocrats on the rural estates.

A recent exponent of modernisation theory, Lerner (1964), sees the growth of the new urban centres in the Third World as similarly progressive, encouraging individualism and undermining the obstacle of 'traditionalism'. He argues that urbanisation is a force for increasing the level of 'participation' in communities: residents become more 'participant' as they develop new attitudes, a new openness and questioning that promotes 'psychic mobility' (see Chapter 3). Moreover, the requirements of urban living encourage specific features of modernity to develop such as literacy: people need to be literate to read timetables, street-signs, and so on if they are to move freely about the town or travel to work. The new ideas of this urban melting-pot are 'diffused' or 'trickle down' to the rural areas. In turn the rural regions become much more productive as farmers appreciate the ever-present and growing demand for food from the urbanites. Town and country grow together as material and cultural 'goods' are exchanged.

Many of these ideas which have become formalised into sophisticated models of urbanisation (for example Breese, 1972) depend, as is typical, on generalising from the historical experience of Europe. For example, in terms of rural–urban linkages, the growth of European towns is said to have sparked off a rapid rise in commercial farming. London is regarded as the foremost example of this process. Production for the London market was widespread from the mid-seventeenth century, extending as much as eighty miles outside of the capital. This led to the social development of new occupational groups to help in the production and transportation of the agricultural goods. In addition, London needed a large quantity of fuel – particularly coal – much of which came down the coast from Newcastle. This stimulated the development of the coal industry, shipping and allied technological innovation such as the steam engine and the railways. Subsequent growth spread from towns that furnished the technology of development, such as Birmingham. By the end of the nineteenth century however agricultural productivity had not kept pace with the rapid growth of industrialised urban centres, so much food had to be imported: by 1901 Britain imported over 70 per cent of her grain supplies.

While there is adequate evidence to indicate a strong link between urban growth, the commercialisation of agriculture and the development of industry, the modernisation thesis tells us relatively little about the social relations that inform these processes. After all, industrial production was not necessarily an urban phenomenon: as we noted in the preceding chapter, the first industrial factories were situated *away* from populous regions. Why were industrialists attracted to the towns in the nineteenth century? For many industrialists who did move to the towns conditions and some costs (for example fuel) were higher than in the rural regions from which they moved.

Mellor (1982) suggests a number of reasons why this relocation and concentration of industry in towns occurred. Of considerable importance was the availability of plentiful and cheap labour in towns, that was needed as business grew and became more competitive. In addition, *rural* industrialists had been obliged to provide some social amenities such as housing, water supply and basic education for their workers many of whom had been drafted in from other areas. Urban development was attractive inasmuch as it helped to defray these costs, which could only increase as the labour force grew, by spreading them more widely across all proprietors of business apart from some being met out of the public purse. Finally the capitalists found the town provided relatively convenient access to capital through the proximity of friends, relations, business-associates and bank and credit agencies. It also gave good access to information about the current state of the market, how competitors were faring, and new opportunities for capital investment. Despite its pollution, the drudgery of the workforce, the impact on health and mortality, urban growth suited private capital. Even workers appear to have been attracted to the towns: farm work meant very low wages and dismal housing conditions – 'bare-earth floors, crumbling plaster walls, sodden thatched two-roomed hovels' (Mellor, 1982, p. 19) – while in the towns, despite the rigours and poor earnings of factory work, life chances were marginally better for families. In general, then, the new towns and industry that grew up during this early nineteenth century period helped to break down what remained of English feudal culture. Once this had been achieved, however, the role of the town in sustaining capitalist development became secondary, because capitalist production was then strong enough to penetrate agriculture as well as industry. Clearly, according to this account, there was a strong link between the growth of industrial cities and the organisational and political power of the new urban classes.

Let us now turn our attention to urbanisation in the Third World. Under what circumstances has urban growth occurred? Are the ideas of modernisation theory relevant – Third World towns as cultural catalysts diffusing modernity throughout the rural hinterland – or does the growth of these cities indicate their increasing attraction to capitalist manufacturing? In fact both these accounts of urban industrial growth are in various ways inadequate descriptions of Third World urbanisation, and in character very different from the European model.

We must first recognise that the development of the Third World city was crucially influenced by colonialism. Different types of town grew under its influence, such as brand new settler towns established in virgin territory or colonial towns grafted onto existing towns and settlements. The latter had grown in the pre-colonial era as the commercial and political centres of indigenous kingdoms or empires. Benin, in West Africa, for example, was one such city much admired by the first Dutch travellers who visited it (see Rodney, 1972).

When established, the colonial city was very different from its European counterpart. It obviously grew to serve the needs of the colonial investors who used it as an administrative and commercial medium for the export of the raw materials needed in Europe as well as a 'home from home', a place where one could insulate oneself as much as possible from the local culture and sustain a life-style to which one was accustomed. Culturally, therefore, the town was relatively isolated from the surrounding regions, and economically it was used as a vehicle for getting produce out of the country rather than encouraging new commercial markets in the interior. Colonialism often only needed *one* town to serve its purposes and this became the 'primate city', a large, typically port-based urban centre unaccompanied by urbanisation elsewhere. Contrast this situation with that of, say, England in which, although London dominated, many other towns (like Manchester, Newcastle, Bristol and Hull) grew rapidly as well. The singularity of the colonial primate city was reflected in the pattern of road, rail and telegraphic links which served the export of raw materials and the import of goods from Europe. In terms of economic, cultural and political activities, therefore, the primate city had little competition.

This concentration of urban development has been difficult to dilute in the post-colonial era. Despite policies of urban resettlement, the primate city has remained the dominant feature especially in Africa. Indigenous manufacturing that has been established – often as a subsidiary of MNCs – needs access to port facilities to bring in machinery and components necessary to keep its plant going, transport and retail outlets for distributing its product, and a sufficiently prosperous consumer market that will purchase its goods. Given this, movement away from the primate city to the poor rural regions becomes highly improbable. Thus, town and country do not, as in the case of the London example, yet have a mutually beneficial relationship. The pre-colonial towns that did have such a relationship, such as Timbuktu in Mali or Kaumbi-Saleh in Ghana, were actually made uninhabitable or non-viable by colonial aggression similar to that displayed by the British against the West African Ashanti towns from 1820 to 1870.

Therefore, it is suggested that the colonial and neo-colonial periods have encouraged a process of skewed or 'distorted' urban development that does not conform to either the diffusionist or capitalist interest theories discussed earlier. The result is 'overurbanisation': this concept refers not so much to the actual density of population – which in most cases is not significantly higher than that found in cities in advanced countries – but to the condition of *insecurity* that the majority experience. Three main aspects of 'overurbanisation' can be identified.

The Circumstances of Migration to the Towns

Many rural farmers find that their land is either becoming too costly to keep as rents increase, or perhaps overworked so losing its fertility. Frequently, poorer peasants are encouraged to buy (through credit) farm equipment, fertiliser and new high yielding seed to push up their crop production for both their own consumption and for sale. This so-called 'Green Revolution' agricultural policy has had very limited success. Poorer farmers are unable to maintain this sort of farming which is relatively expensive and the crops that it produces are high in price, often much too high for sale on the local market. Either the government subsidises sale prices at great expense (as typified in India) or peasants gradually lose interest in production, and only those with the investible capital, the more affluent farmers, can stay in business. Where poor farmers have to repay loans it is usually the case that they will have to sell off part (or all) of their land. If they are tenant farmers, the extra yields and costs of Green Revolution farming tend to push up rents and thus make life more difficult for the small tenant. In short, poor farmers whether owners or tenants often become more insecure by certain agricultural 'development' policies. In response they and their families will seek what additional work they can get, perhaps on another farm or as servants in a more prosperous household. Many will decide that the best thing to do is to move to the town in search of work.

The condition of insecurity which often prompts people to migrate to towns means that urban growth occurs under highly unfavourable circumstances. Compare this with the circumstances surrounding Western European urbanisation: there, rural and urban regions were, as we saw in the case of London and its hinterland – mutually supportive, agricultural productivity meant a *lowering* of crop prices, and while it is true that people were displaced from the land through the enclosure movement this was not only a more gradual relocation of rural residents (over 150 years) but also one that was accompanied by a rapid growth in new jobs.

The Character of the Market

It has been argued that the market for many Third World commodities is primarily overseas while many local consumer needs go unsatisfied. This state of affairs has been called 'growth without development': while production in the Third World has increased, the economic system is geared to serve external interests rather than internal development. The physical fabric that accompanies this growth – the offices, factories, warehouses, motorways, telephone systems etc. – of the city has a commercial character which looks like that of any town or city in process of development. However, a number of differences have been identified.

(i) in smaller countries with relatively undiversified economies the commercial sector of the primate city deals with a wide range of goods but will tend to concentrate on a few commodities (often raw materials) for export, the value of which is subject to considerable fluctuation on the world market. This is particularly true of some Caribbean and African countries. Relatively few commodities enjoy the stability of price and demand that oil has, a situation exploited to the full by the OPEC group of countries. Some towns in the period of European industrialisation did rely on a thriving export market. This was true of London for example. But the export market handled a much wider range of agricultural and manufactured goods, and, most importantly, was accompanied by a thriving *domestic* market for similar goods;

(ii) many sociologists, particularly within the Marxian school, have argued that much commercial enterprise is not under the direct control of an independent business community as was the case in towns like London where the merchant community put its accumulating capital to productive use; instead, as Frank argues, the Third World community is typically subordinate to the interests and investment decisions of foreign MNCs – they are as suggested in Chapter 4, a 'comprador bourgeoisie';

(iii) there are, it is argued, few 'backward linkages' developed from activities in the Third World town, that is, associated industrial development in the *manufacturing* sector: the largest growth has been in the *service* sector, particularly, as noted in Chapter 2, in the 'informal' service sector;

(iv) finally it is often suggested that instead of enhancing local trades, Third world commercial activity often weakens craft skills since much of the expansion in commerce has been through importing technology and expertise. This is particularly true of large cities in Brazil such as Sao Paulo. While this clearly encourages workers to develop new skills – for example for the car assembly plant – imported technology creates comparatively few jobs.

Demographic Circumstances

As noted above, population growth has been much more rapid than was the case in Europe during its period of urban growth mainly because of a natural increase in Third World population as improvements in health care allow a greater life-expectancy.

These three factors combine to produce unfavourable urban circumstances: a condition of over-urbanisation occurs. Unlike the European experience, residents in the cities experience desperate housing problems and a highly limited labour market as a result.

The most evident sign of the unique difficulties connected with housing is the appearance only in the Third World of 'shanty towns' that skirt most primate cities. Was there nothing similar in the early period of European industrialisation?

If we look at the early stage of English industrialisation we find that, typically the working-class poor lived in 'one-up one-down' single family terraced houses with a communal muck heap or earth closet providing the only means of 'sanitation'. Although by modern standards such conditions would be deemed unfit for habitation, in comparison with the poor in American tenement housing, the English working class were better off. Conditions improved slightly during the nineteenth century when larger single-family houses to rent were built by private developers, some of whom formed themselves into 'building societies'. There were,

ILLUSTRATION 5.1 *The shanty town*

ILLUSTRATION 5.1 *The shanty town*

of course, many inner-city districts where conditions were atrocious. Citing Gauldie's (1974) survey of inner Leeds, Mellor (1982, p. 42) notes that,

> in 1833 (the year of a cholera scare there), 75 cartloads of accumulated night-soil (excrement) were removed from an infamous fever-spot – the Boot and Shoe Yard, then housing 340 people in 57 rooms. . . . In 1840 it was found that nothing had been removed subsequently.

Yet the mortality rates in the growing urban centres were lower than in previous generations, except for infants, where death rates of about 200 per 1000 were the norm throughout the nineteenth century for working class babies. Major improvements for all members of the working class did not come till the end of the nineteenth century when better housing, legislation to control public sanitation and higher wages appeared.

In the Third World the primate cities have very limited housing available for workers, so considerable overcrowding has occurred, with very high rents to match. Many have responded by constructing the shanty towns on waste land using whatever materials – wood, metal, polythene – that can be gathered together. Not surprisingly, these sites usually lack a water supply and provision for sewage disposal. In terms of living conditions, these homes have some similarities with the earliest slums of British urbanisation but there are crucial differences: first, the low income housing in Britain sheltered *workers* who although suffering hardship at least had a job; secondly, the houses were either purpose-built for workers by employers or private building associations; thirdly, while the public authorities showed some concern over the living conditions therein, they did not, as frequently happens in the Third World, demolish the housing and evict people as 'squatters'. Since the latter is a routine event for many poor shanty towns it is not surprising that the residents do not invest much effort in improving them. Nevertheless despite these extremely uncertain and deprived circumstances communities do develop among the poor in these settlements particularly those that have a chance of escaping the government bulldozer (see Gutkind, 1967).

Over-urbanisation also means a shortage of jobs in the towns for newcomers: unemployment and underemployment are the norm

'Enterprise' in the shanty town

Though residents of shanty towns experience serious deprivation this does not stop them trying to improve their lot through their own initiative. But if the poor are propertyless the only way to obtain something is often simply by taking it. Worsley (1984) describes what is no doubt a common practice within the shanty towns of the world:

> [The residents] organise themselves as pressure-groups to obtain water, electricity, a school, paved roads, sewerage, usually by invoking the aid of powerful brokers for whom their votes become the basis of their own standing within the political party. If they do not get these things, they simply take them wherever possible, and others show them how to do it. A wealthy colleague of mine in Mexico City, having failed to get the electricity corporation to connect his house to the mains, was rescued by his poor neighbours, who did for him what they do for themselves: hooked him up to a *telarana*, one of the spider webs of illegal cables plugged into the city's electrical supply-system which festoon the dwellings of the poor from Mexico to Hong Kong, and provide free electricity for rice-cookers, fans, TV sets and radios' (p. 214).

for those who lack education needed for work or family contacts that could help in finding a job. Singer (1970) has estimated that by 1990 urban unemployment in the Third World will range between 58 and 73 per cent. The limited size of the formal labour market has led as we saw in Chapter 2 to the development of the 'informal' sector of work. While an 'informal' sector is likely to have existed during European and American urbanisation these towns were usually places that provided jobs, sucking in people from the rural regions as well as soaking up the natural population increase within them. Towns of the neo-colonial capitalist economy have yet to function in this way.

In conclusion, rapid urbanisation has typically occurred without an improvement in the life-chances of the majority of the urban population. Many Third World governments are aware of the urban problems of today but often try to cope with them by tackling only their symptoms – that is stopping people from coming to towns or returning unemployed people to the countryside. For example, in the summer of 1983, the Mozambican government decided to give the urban unemployed two weeks to leave the towns, after which they were forced to go, sent back to their villages, state farms or work camps.

Urban planning in India

India has the fastest rate of growth in urban population anywhere in the world. For example, between 1971 and 1981, over 50 milion people were added to India's urban centres. This has occurred through both large-scale migration from rural regions as well as an increasing birth rate in the cities. Major metropolitan areas such as Delhi, Bombay, and Calcutta have had to develop planning policies to cope with this growth and the problems of housing and welfare provision, transportation and employment that it creates. The Indian authorities at state and national levels have proposed to reduce urban growth through promoting more development in the rural regions and limiting further industrial expansion in the cities. In practice, however, these proposals have been only partially implemented, and in-migration continues apace. At the same time, the urban planners have failed to cope with the growing numbers of shanty-town residents, focusing instead on 'Master Plans' for city centre development land use and traffic movement. This is in part because of the divisions within the Indian bureaucracy in which economic planning has been traditionally separated from urban planning. As Jha (1987) says, 'Physical and economic planning are carried out in complete isolation from each other with the result that even though new towns come as a result of the location of productive activities under the five year plans, there is no arrangement for physical provision of services and regulation of physical expansion' (p. 172). As a result the problems of squalor amid the skyscrapers and motorways are ignored: 'In Bombay, "Manhattan" is being recreated along Nariman Point along with sprawling ghettos in the form of *Jhopadpatties* and *chawls* proliferating at a faster pace than affluent neighbourhoods and prestigious commercial centres. People's priorities do not find any place in the planner's perception' (p. 173). With the urban population growing towards 320 million by the year 2000, social and political tensions are likely to increase.

In the majority of Third World towns urbanisation is not acting as an effective medium for the 'diffusion of modernity' to the surrounding countryside. It is true that capitalist industrial growth has occurred on a considerable scale in some areas, such as Brazil, Argentina, Nigeria, parts of India (for example West Bengal) and South-East Asia. Much of this growth is yet to be inner-directed; it is constrained from being so by the dominance of the export market and the primate city which tends to monopolise and contain large scale industrial, financial and commercial activity. Thus, Third World urbanisation does not readily conform to the two models of 'diffusion' or domestic capitalist expansion that were discussed earlier.

Those who tend to do best in the urban centre are the educated. Before seeing why this is so we need to consider the general relationship between education and development.

5.4 EDUCATION AND INDUSTRIALISATION

The General Relationship between Education and Development

The prinicpal thesis that has dominated the literature in this area is that education is a crucial factor (or even precondition) for 'development' since it promotes economic growth and enables the socialisation of new members of society into the dominant political and cultural value system. While educational institutions are an almost universal phenomenon, the way they go about their tasks differs considerably, particularly if one compares educational programmes in capitalist and socialist societies. Whichever country one looks at, it is certainly the case that education is given great importance in society, reflected in its massive budget, the large number it employs and reaches and the not inconsiderable influence that the education establishment can exert on government policy.

The sociology of education in the West has been heavily influenced by a *functionalist* view, which sees education as the provider of basic skills, such as literacy and numeracy, and the most specialised technical knowledge that modern methods of production and management demand. In addition, the reward system that structures educational careers is said to encourage a strong commitment towards self-discipline, hard work and achievement, attitudes which are not only conducive of educational success but also industrial productivity and innovation. Many of these arguments have been advanced by functionalists with a specific interest in modernisation theory. Apart from making an explicit link between educational growth and industrial modernisation, such theorists also believe that the specific direction of education is tied into the occupational demands of industry. For example, courses reflect economic needs and a rise in the required level of qualifications reflects an increase in the skills demanded to do the job. In short, increasing educational sophistication and increasing economic growth go hand in hand.

These ideas seem at first sight self-evident. However, they need to be questioned (see Bilton *et al.*, 1987, pp. 313–23). Berg (1970) argues that one cannot assume that the more qualifications a person has the more productive and proficient he or she will be at work. Instead, Berg shows how higher qualifications are needed today often only to make people *eligible* for jobs. They are typically insignificant for on-the-job proficiency which derives much more from work experience than academic training. The correlation that does exist between educational achievement and high wages does not necessarily reflect the increased technical proficiency of training; however a person with high qualifications can get a better paid job at the outset of their career. Secondly, as Johnson (1972) argues, educational qualifications often act to *restrict entry* to occupational specialities to ensure they obtain high reward and social status – this is especially true of the professions which require many years of costly training in skills which are not demanded on the job. Thirdly, as Willis (1977) shows, the education system does not encourage all who enter it to be high achievers: many working class pupils are actively discouraged, are told that they should lower their sights which are 'unrealistically high'. Finally, Collins (1977) argues that the functionalist approach presumes that there is a range of jobs in a society with specific skill demands for which education has to budget. This implies that the skills of such jobs can be clearly measured according to some objective technical standards, such that some jobs have more skill and are therefore more important than others. Collins argues that this distorts the way job demands and definitions of what is or is not 'skillful' are determined: it is not by the application of neutral technical standards but by the patterns of social negotiation and conflict between groups of people in the labour market. This negotiation is not some even-matched debate but reflects the inequalities of power between status-groups. Those who enjoy wealth and status in association with their high class position are likely to be able to set the standards of skill, training and social conduct to be rewarded: this is particularly true of professional and managerial staffs who are drawn from higher social classes.

The increasing priority given to 'vocational' courses in some industrialised countries such as Britain and France can be seen as an attempt to direct in a much more controlled manner the relationship between industrial need and educational training.

If one looks closely at such schemes they do not involve a major restructuring of the educational establishment nor challenge the way the system caters to elite status groups: instead they appear to be a means of checking youth unemployment primarily among the working class. Moreover, if one looks at the attempts that governments have made to find out what industry wants, the notion that education is geared to industrial needs becomes even more dubious. Many surveys show that industrialists are unsure about the specific skill demands of the jobs they offer and appear to be only certain that what they need is not more trained labour but access to cheaper raw materials (Berg, 1970). In addition, the new stress on vocational training implies a shortage of engineering, technical, and scientific skills when in fact there are many with appropriate qualifications unemployed. The notions that an economy will grow via the expansion of these skills through education or the corollary that unemployed skills are unneeded by the economy are then, simplistic. It *is* likely, however, that the development of basic skills such as literacy and numeracy *are* important in encouraging social and economic 'development' particularly in agrarian societies. There is little that one could find wrong with this claim which one finds in a variety of sociological models of change including that of modernisation theory.

If basic educational instruction on literacy and numeracy is of 'developmental' value it is important to have some idea about the *opportunity* people around the world have to receive training in these two areas. As one might expect, given the inequality between countries and thereby the resources they can make available for education, there is considerable variation in this regard.

Levels of Educational Provision, Literacy and Attendance

Universal primary education is not yet established throughout the world. While it has been provided for a number of decades in both capitalist and socialist countries in the North, it is far from being so for the children of the South. The Third World has seen a rapid increase overall in its educational institutions since the 1950s but there are only about 65 per cent of children in primary schools and many regions within the Third World with lower figures than this (for example Senegal with 42 per cent). In most countries in the North secondary level education is also extensive with about 90 per cent of the appropriate age group enrolled. In the Third World the equivalent average figure drops to just below 40 per cent, although this disguises a very wide range with a high of 82 per cent for the rich OPEC state of Kuwait and a low of 4 per cent for Tanzania (see *World Development Report*, 1988). For those who seek to draw comparisons with European development (as modernisation theorists do) the overall average for the Third World is similar to that of mid-nineteenth century Europe when industrialisation was proceeding rapidly. This indicates little if anything about the potential for comparable Third World development today. The expansion of European education was accompanied by an expanding national and overseas market, technological superiority, home grown industry and so on.

Levels of literacy have risen in the Third World, mainly through the expansion of primary schooling noted above such that by 1986 'only' 20 per cent were thought to be illiterate (UNESCO, 1986). While this figure is a great improvement on the 80 per cent estimate for the turn of the century, in *absolute* numbers the scale of the problem is massive and still rising. India alone has estimated her illiterate population to be over 250 million people. In the literate North most people can read and write though the official figures for illiteracy are likely to be an underestimate because of under-reporting: who likes to admit that they cannot read and write when literacy is supposed to be 'normal'?

Even if the provision of primary and secondary education places in the Third World expanded to match the population's increase it is unlikely that illiteracy would be reduced dramatically as many illiterates are adults outside of formal schooling. Moreover, even children's educational performance is unlikely to be dramatically improved since they are subject to a number of factors beyond their control. There are three which seem of particular significance: first, poor children who experience chronic malnutrition from birth are educationally at a disadvantage because of possible mental handicaps as malnutrition affects the development of brain tissue; secondly, the children, as we noted earlier, are an important source of labour for rural families, particularly daughters, who will be expected to leave school early, often at no more than seven or eight years old; finally, although primary schooling is now typically state funded, parents usually have to pay for books and almost always for secondary schooling, where school fees per term may be up to four times the average monthly wage of male manual workers: one can understand how difficult it is to keep just *one* of your children in school. Poor health, labour demands of the family, and costs will work against the ambitions of many Third World children and their parents, leading to early drop-out rates and low or irregular attendance.

Impact of Colonialism on Education Provision

Much of the expansion of education from the 1960s onwards was sponsored by the ex-colonial powers keen to sustain their cultural influence in the Third World. The direction this educational programme took had already been signalled in the colonial period, which in form and content installed a system of schooling that was essentially European. As with other institutions in the Third World education has been heavily influenced by colonialism. Watson (1982) has provided a valuable survey of the impact of the colonial administrations on education provision in several countries. A number of general points can be made by way of summary.

The colonial authorities were ambivalent towards spending money on education: not only was it an additional cost but it could also promote an ambition, confidence and knowledge among the colonised which could lead them to question the superiority of the European. At the same time, however, education was seen as a vehicle for the cultural assimilation of the colonised into European cultures (this was particularly true of French colonial policy). It was also a way of training local people who could be used by the authorities to help run the colonies, to supervise workers, and provide clerical and support staff. For those who got such jobs colonial patronage brought considerable advantages in terms of income and prestige. The indigenous culture was naturally weakened by this process of cultural incorporation and the European missionaries had a key role to play in this regard: for example, many condemned African religion as witchcraft, as pagan and evil and, as Mohiddin (1977) notes, encouraged the virtues of 'private property, frugality and the need to save and to accumulate', ideas which could have enhanced the capitalist penetration of the colony. In order to do well in the colony, the locals had to embrace the European culture, but even then, and even when successfully employed by the colonial administration the colonised had a subordinate status. As Daniel (1981) says:

> [The African] had to adopt the European's religion, master his language, acquire a knowledge of the rivers and mountains, kings and queens etc. of the European metropole – in other words, a knowledge of Africa became irrelevant to his acquisition of status. Yet even those who did acquire such status could not escape from the humiliating 'boy-girl syndrome' common to all colonial societies, whereby even adult and professional Africans were reduced to an infantile status of being described as 'boys' or 'girls'.

Those who went to the most prestigious colonial schools were usually recruited from the wealthier families of the local elite: the sons of chiefs. With few places available and recruitment limited to those from a higher social background, those who went to these schools enjoyed such advantageous circumstances as to be co-opted into the colonial regime with ease. It was these willing disciples who at independence received the political office of leader granted by the outgoing colonial administration to govern the newly 'independent' states. In the colonial period it was felt that people like this had lost touch with their 'true' culture and so were known as 'Afro-Saxons' or 'white-blackmen'.

For those in the poor rural region the schools were few and ill-equipped, but nevertheless keen to promote European culture, and the young children endeavoured to learn the languages of urban commerce – English and Mathematics – without learning the farming skills that they perhaps most needed for survival in the countryside. The European influence was particularly strong in Africa and remains so in the post-colonial schools of today. Very little has been done to direct the curriculum towards African needs and higher education is still available for only the privileged few (for example Kenya's 2000 degree students).

When changes have been made that favour the disadvantaged, dominant social classes have often opposed them, seeing them as a threat to their superior position. This is illustrated by educational policy in Bangladesh. There the authorities introduced a plan to make Bengali the sole language used in primary schools. This was partly a symbolic attempt to challenge the cultural dominance of English and a way of giving peasant children and their teachers, both poor English speakers, a better chance to do well as pupils and staff. The plan collapsed quite quickly, however, when prosperous English-speaking urban and rural elites combined against it, fearing that their own children's futures were in jeopardy. In 1978 the authorities reintroduced English as the language of instruction in primary schools: as Dove (1981) says, 'Children in schools which emphasise the teaching of English and use it as a medium of instruction will be advantaged throughout the education system while the children of the impoverished rural schools will be poorly taught and sooner or later "cooled out"' (p. 179).

The majority of aid that arrives in the Third World to develop education does not in fact go to the urban and rural masses despite the World Bank giving more attention to primary schooling recently, but to the higher education sector. This has created a group of people who now have high qualifications but, because of the limited labour market, limited job prospects. The result is that one needs more and more qualifications to have a chance of employment in the higher paid, more secure sectors of the professions, the civil service or national politics.

This situation seems to be a good illustration of Berg's (1970) argument that higher qualifications are today's norm if people want to be eligible for jobs. Dore (1976) has called this the 'diploma disease', rife in the capitalist and socialist societies of the North and increasingly so in the Third World; Collins (1977) treats educational qualifications as a form of 'cultural currency', and thus describes this situation as 'an inflated supply of cultural currency', and as inflation lowers the value of the 'currency' more is needed just to keep up.

Given the importance of education, it is crucial to ask whether the chances of obtaining this 'cultural currency' are equal in society. As already hinted at above, these chances are not equally distributed as those from a privileged social background can use their resources – both material and cultural – to stay on in the system through to the higher level. This is also true of most industrialised societies in the North (including the Soviet Union), as, for example, Halsey's (1980) study of British education shows. Gugler (1978, p. 165) notes, similarly, that in the context of West Africa,

> Elite children have been, and can be expected to continue to be, inordinately overrepresented for two reasons: only their parents can finance an extended education for all their children, and they are much better prepared for the severe competition in the educational system.

Just as educational opportunity is differentiated on the basis of socio-economic background, so is it on the basis of gender. In the Third World as in the North it is typically the case that girls and women do not have the same opportunities as boys and men. This has been rectified to some extent in countries that have experienced the cultural turmoil accompanying liberation struggles under a socialist leadership, such as Mozambique, Guinea-Bissau and Vietnam. In these cases women were involved in the war as party workers and active in formulating new policies of sexual equality after independence. Typically however in most countries females are under-represented at all educational levels, the more so the higher one goes. This means that women experience poorer job prospects in the towns, although if they do manage to get a position in the professional or technical sectors they will be considerably better off than the women remaining in the rural regions. The latter, of course, have no job 'problem': maintaining the house and small holding which most women do while their husbands go to town in search of work is a full-time job with little relief. As Hazlewood (1979, p. 186) comments with regard to Kenyan women in this position: 'In such households in particular, and in rural areas in general, there is no unemployment problem for women, no problem of underutilised labour, but rather a life of unremitting toil'. This is, in fact, the main reason for female under-achievement in education, for, as early as the end of their primary schooling, most young girls withdraw from the educational system because of the expectation that they will help their mothers in the house or in the fields to sustain the family while their fathers look for work and their brothers, cost allowing, continue at school. The onus of domestic labour leads to an abbreviated educational career and thereby reduces women's chances of getting proper wage labour. Even in societies where women's training and employment opportunities have improved domestic labour is still a female burden, as Ellwood (1982, p. 21) comments, 'Soviet women can fly to the moon. But they still have to do the ironing when they get home again.'

Educational Reform

Most Third World governments are aware of the inadequacies and irrelevancies of their educational institutions which remain from the colonial period. In recent years they have tried to introduce reforms to cater for a much broader section of the population, especially the rural poor. But financial constraints on government have meant that the new programmes have had to be designed with a self-help, community based concept in mind, drawing on existing resources without creating high budget demands. Such reforms have been made particularly popular through the work of Coombs and Ahmed (1974, p. 8) whose concept of 'non-formal education' dominates discussion in this area. They define this as,

> ... any organised, systematic, eductional activity carried on outside the framework of the formal system to provide selective types of learning to particular subgroups of the population, adults as well as children.

The sort of activities envisaged include the development of informal 'apprenticeships' where people with trade skills in villages teach others their crafts, encouraging those with literacy and numeracy to coach others in these skills, taking children and, especially male, adults to the fields to learn the science and art of farming, using school buildings round the clock to enable those not in formal education to have a chance to participate and learn, and so on. These reforms are to be applauded because they give some of the poor a chance to develop new life skills. Harrison (1980, p. 274) believes that, despite reaching only 10 per cent of the rural population, non-formal education is 'a real tool for individual and community development'.

It is clearly assumed by Coombs, Harrison and others that these reforms will develop new skills among the poor, so enhance their marketability and eventually raise their income and status. But this is too optimistic a view given that there is considerable evidence indicating that *without formal credentials* employers are unlikely to welcome people into the more secure, better paid jobs. To argue that non-formal education raises the skill level in rural regions so encouraging social mobility and community development implies that there is a strong relationship between technical skills and economic growth, an assumption very similar to that of the functionalist theory criticised at the start of this section. Hence bearing in mind those criticisms, the rural poor are unlikely to enjoy upward mobility as they do not have the cultural – let alone material – 'currency' whereby people obtain reward in the social structure, a structure dominated by members of the elite. Much wider social and economic changes are needed than mere educational reform to significantly improve the position of the rural poor.

5.5 CONCLUSION

We have seen in this chapter, albeit very briefly and schematically, how the growth of population, urbanisation and education typically associated with industrialisation in the Eurocentric models of 'development' is distorted particularly because of the impact of colonialism and current underdevelopment. The chapter suggests at various points how the experience of the Third World in these areas is distinct from that of the history of industrialised societies. This should warn us against proposing some general evolutionary model of 'development' with universal application. The difficulties of Third World societies in these areas are partly a matter of policy – for example overstressing higher education – but are more a reflection of the cultural and economic process of underdevelopment. Policies in themselves are unlikely to bring about major changes whether they concern family planning, controlling urban growth, or promoting non-formal education. These are useful in relieving some of the symptoms of underdevelopment. The problem ultimately lies in the relative weakness of the Third World economy in the world capitalist system. One possible source of change lies in the political realm. Can the Third World politically challenge the status quo or are its political institutions similarly under-developed? It is to these matters that we now turn.

6

Political Development and Social Class

6.1 INTRODUCTION

So far we have examined aspects of development and social change in the Third World without any detailed consideration of the political context in which these are found. As we have seen in previous chapters, many theorists have developed their ideas through using the historical experience of Europe as a blueprint for 'development'. One might wonder then whether the development of, say, capitalist relations in Western Europe was accompanied by a particular pattern of political development and whether this is to be repeated in the Third World because of capitalist penetration there. The reader should not be surprised to discover that there is no simple answer to this question since there are competing theoretical accounts of political change in Europe and the Third World, accounts which on the one hand come within the broad scope of modernisation theory and on the other derive from the underdevelopment school.

The substance of 'politics' is not limited to what goes on in government: it involves all situations in which one individual or group exercises power over others. To exercise power is to have at one's disposal some resource whereby one can control or coerce others: this could be derived from the control of economic resources such as private property and thus we should expect the analysis of power to refer to the property relations between *social classes*.

As Mann (1986) has also argued, power may be derived from *organisational strength* and a monopoly of coercive force, and here we should expect power to be closely tied to institutions that are patently powerful in this sense, for example, the military. Finally, power could be derived from the *status* that groups may enjoy due to the traditional, or charismatic authority they hold over others and so we might expect the analysis of power to be concerned with the strength of the political appeal of say nationalist or religious leaders and the cultural processes that sustain their attractiveness to the masses. This last point draws our attention to a crucial aspect of the exercise of power. We must examine the political perceptions or consciousness of those in subordinate positions since their compliance to the powerful may not depend on coercion by the latter but the subordinate themselves believing that the dominant have a right to rule. Keen to encourage this view rather than relying on naked force, the dominant encourage various ideologies – such as *noblesse oblige* – to persuade the masses that their subordination is right and proper.

Dominant groups rely on different sources of power: economic, organisational and so on, but at times these groups are likely to form an alliance to promote their shared interests: Mills (1959) writes of the existence of a dominant elite in the US made up of an alliance of big business, senior military personnel and senior politicians. To identify power blocs in any society is only the beginning of the analysis since we need to know what these dominant groups *do* with their power. As Therborn (1970) asks, 'What does the ruling class do when it rules'? To answer this we need to go beyond questions about *who* has power and to what degree, to questions about the social and economic context in which power is exercised and the sort of social relations it serves to maintain.

6.2 THIRD WORLD POLITICS: THE ANALYSIS OF INSTABILITY

In some societies it appears that the dominant group and the state administration are inherently weak. This is particularly true in the Third World. Political instability in the Third World seems to be an everyday fact of life. A formidable catalogue of political irregularities can be constructed by a quick look through the overseas pages of the Western press: stories about political assassination, military coups, intimidation, political bribery and corruption, rigged elections, the removal of opposition parties by dictatorial regimes, or a comparatively rapid turnover of governments, are commonplace. It may well be the case that political correspondents are *looking for* such news items and may thus 'over report' them, so that the Western reader gets a somewhat misleading picture of what is going on in, say Latin America. It may also be the case that the people who are supposed to be suffering from such political turmoil may not have realised it. Nevertheless, it would be foolish to suggest that Third World instability was all a fabrication of journalists justifying their existence in the ex-colonies. Instability does exist.

Clearly, though, instability in the Third World can only be said to exist because we have some model of what a 'stable' political system looks like. Two important but very different models of political systems are those developed by pluralist and structuralist writers. Each model has a different answer to the question 'what causes instability?'

The Pluralist Account of Instability

Drawing on its conception of the democratic nation-state as the paragon of political stability, the pluralist account of the troubles of the Third World stresses the latter's political immaturity compared with the 'mature' political culture of Western society. How is this maturity measured? Its principal features have been identified by Finer (1974). First, it is a political system in which the public interest is paramount, pursued through its wideranging participation in mechanisms of democracy (parties, trade unions, pressure groups and so on), and its highly developed sense of an individual's rights which no government should infringe: the 'silent majority' knows when it is time to raise its voice and remove any political regime abusing its power. Secondly, public opinion is politically informed and articulate, willing to make rational compromise rather than being factionalised or polarised around extremes. Thirdly, the two preceding features ensure the development of a strong *national* identity built on a democratic civil order. We should note that 'maturity' is measured here not in terms of the mere presence of institutional structures like parliamentary houses and elections; these are just the enabling mechanisms whereby democracy operates. The crucial criterion of maturity is a strong sense of political action being pursued through *legitimate* channels such that conflicts or disputes are subject to the restraints of a political framework that is basically consensual.

Notwithstanding the fact that these alleged principles of Western democracy are difficult to find on the ground, the pluralist modernisation theorists use them to show how the Third World political system is immature and thus unstable. Hence, it is suggested that the Third World 'political public' is very limited because of a comparative lack of bodies like mass political parties and national trade unions, through which participation and a sense of the independence of the civil order from the government is developed. The public is polarised around right and left, or broken into warring factions based on ethnic or tribal loyalties. Finally, there is little by way of a national identity as leaders have to contend with ethnic and regional disunity, particularly in those countries whose national boundaries were established according to the convenience of colonial authorities, rather than a reflection of the territorial provinces of the indigenous people.

Immaturity on these counts, it is argued, leads to instability since governmental authority and the legitimacy of national politics is weak. In these circumstances, the capacity of the political leadership to build a sense of 'nationhood', to create political integration, is limited. The immaturity in the political sphere is symptomatic of the broader undeveloped socio-economic structure of the Third World. The 'traditional' society generates a thoroughgoing traditionalism in all institutions: the people and their leaders cling to the past as a source of security, and fail to see beyond their immediate local, regional or ethnic concerns. Political rivalry and failed national policies reflect this parochialism. Thus, any governmental authority typically relies on a populist appeal in an attempt to unite these factions, an appeal which is usually backed up by the aggressive use of force against any opposition groups. The pluralist believes that the only way to overcome this undemocratic state of affairs is by education, changing people's values and attitudes to life through the diffusion of ideas from the developed to the undeveloped cultures, slowly building up social expectations that will promote economic modernisation and the development of a democratic nation-state. All of which sounds familiar, and is of course a refrain last heard in the tradition-modernity thesis discussed in Chapter 3.

The Structuralist Account of Instability

The structuralist explanation for Third World instability is very different from that of pluralism. While it accepts many of the empirical details of instability noted by the pluralist such as military coups, division along ethnic and regional lines etc., it does not account for these in terms of an alleged *undeveloped political culture* but in terms of a more fundamental factor, the *undeveloped class structure* of the Third World, with particular attention given to the *comparative absence of a dominant economic class* in most Third World countries.

According to Marxist political sociology, the State functions in such a way as to serve the interests of the dominant economic class which need not actually be the *governing* but is the *ruling* class. In the Third World, however, as we saw in Chapter 4 (section 4.4), the indigenous bourgeoisie is seen by writers such as Frank (1981) and other dependency theorists to be subservient to the demands of the true dominant capitalist class located in the metropolitan centre. It is often the case that the local commercial class has been weakened by the penetration of foreign capital. Moreover, little attempt has been made in the past by indigenous classes to strike up alliances – say between the agrarian landed elite and the small commercial elite – that could lead to the formation of a strong state serving their interests. Instead there is often a situation of competing economic factions. This fragmentation among the potentially dominant classes encourages dependency as each vies for access to the wealth of overseas capital, access best achieved by controlling the state agencies. As Roxborough (1979, p. 124) says,

> Partly because of economic underdevelopment . . . there is very rarely a complete dominance within the power bloc of any single class or fraction. It is much more usual to find several classes or fractions sharing state power among themelves in an uneasy equilibrium. The state becomes a focus of struggle, and no class is able to develop a hegemonic (or dominant) position within the society as a whole.

This struggle for access to state power and the fight to influence state policy leads to a situation in which political support is bought through a system of *patronage* and *clientelism*. That is, privileged social groups may use ties of kinship, ethnic or regional loyalties etc., to ensure that the political and bureaucratic administrations of the state develop policy – such as the provision of large commercial grants – that serve their interests. In return, this patronage buys the support of the 'client' groups. But clientelism has an international dimension too: foreign interests will use a similar strategy of patronage to co-opt the indigenous commercial, political and bureaucratic groups. This incorporation of high ranking indigenous groups can of course go to such an extreme that the Third World state becomes little more than the puppet regime of an overseas power. Powerful American MNCs as well as the US government itself have co-opted regimes in this way, especially in the Caribbean.

There is, however, considerable variation in how the social classes of Third World societies relate to the economy, the polity and thereby to each other. In some regions of the Third World it seems that classes are well-developed, perhaps, as in Latin America, because of the associated strengths of industrialisation and commercial agriculture. Where classes have developed strong economic interests which class members *identify as shared* interests, it is likely that they will use whatever resources they can to ensure that the State acts on their behalf. In this sense, *class interests lie behind and orchestrate political practices and conflict*. The *degree* to which this occurs can vary. For example, as Cammack (1988, p. 79) says:

> Class constitutes a more important basis for interest-group appeals and for political cleavage in the industrialised countries of Latin America than in the predominantly agricultural societies of Africa and the Middle East; in Africa especially, only the middle-class is well-developed and there is not yet in the majority of states a strong sense of urban or rural exploitation.

Moreover, the *way* in which interests are pursued in relation to the State is also varied. For example, even where class interests are sufficiently developed such that one could speak of an emergent 'class structure', members of classes may still find that the most appropriate means of defending these interests is through sustaining a system of patronage, clientelism and communal loyalties and obligations that *cut across* class lines. We need, then, a model through which we can make sense of the *strength* of social classes within a country and how this affects the way they relate to the State.

Class-divided Societies

Perhaps one of the more useful sociological models we could use here is that which has been developed by Giddens (1981, 1987). Giddens identifies two forms through which class and polity (the State) are related: he distinguishes between 'class societies' and 'class-divided' societies.

The first of these concepts refers to societies in which the economic relations of class are the primary basis of social stratification. Class interests determine and are in turn regulated by the activities of the State. In advanced capitalist class societies the *nation state* emerges as an important political framework through which class interests are organised and expressed.

'Class-divided' societies, on the other hand, are those in which one finds distinct economic classes but in which the networks of alliance, lines of conflict, and political forms of expression and control are not organised around, or simple expressions of, the existing classes. This is one way of apprehending the persistence of clientelism in Third World societies. The question arises as to why class-divided societies can be found.

Giddens argues that class-divided societies exist where there is no single, dominant economic system around which class interests could crystallise, organise and find primary expression at the political level. In these circumstances, those who seek to dominate, to act as a dominant group, clearly have to use whatever access they have to communal, political and perhaps military institutions in order to maintain their superiority.

Feudal societies were ones that Giddens characterises as 'class-divided' inasmuch as the economy was limited in the extent to which it could orchestrate class interests. Instead, the aristocracy, baronial lords and other dominant groups had to defend their local, regional and national interests through (fairly crude) political and military means. While circumstances, most importantly the arrival of a global capitalism, have changed since feudal days, Third World countries' elites could also be said to preside over societies in which economic relations have been inadequately developed, where capitalism, as we saw in Chapter 4, though present, is itself underdeveloped, weak and so failing as a vehicle through which the class interests it embodies could be integrated and expressed economically and politically at the national level. As we saw in the structuralist account above, we are more likely to see the prevalence of competing economic and bureaucratic factions, with the State being, as Roxborough said 'a focus of struggle'.

Economic factionalism, clientelism and the Indian State

While India has experienced economic expansion in some sectors, many people experience chronic poverty, in both rural and urban areas. At the same time, the dominant economic groups have been incapable of developing a shared identity of interests as factionalism, political patronage and corruption create splits and divisions between the powerful business groups. The government, caught up in this system of patronage and corruption ('black money'), reinforces the divisions among Indian capitalists such that policies for 'capital as a whole' are difficult to pursue. Rubin (1985) describes the situation in the following terms:

> Business ... receives protection from competition from both foreign capital and new entrepreneurs who cannot negotiate the bureaucratic hurdles.... This system of interconnected bargains creates vast numbers of conflicts requiring arbitration. These conflicts are so many opportunities for political leadership to step in and appropriate part of the benefits generated, either for clients of the politicians or for the politicians themselves.... Private deals negotiated among politicians, bureaucrats, and industrialists, closed with licences and black money, render difficult the pursuit of policy in the interest of 'capital as a whole' or, for India, the dominant coalition as a whole.... Protests by those outside the dominant coalition may create some disorder, but resistance from the dominant groups themselves to crack-downs on inefficiencies institutionalised in various forms of patronage, subsidies, and corruption, if the government indeed attempts such crack-downs, will be a more difficult challenge. The will or capacity of the political leadership to meet the challenge is especially questionable since political parties ... have relied on such arrangements to fund many of their activities (pp. 946–55).

Source: B. R. Rubin, 'Economic liberalisation and the Indian state', *Third World Quarterly*, October 1985.

In most Third World countries, then, we would expect to find factions using a range of strategies which, while defending their economic (class) interests, are organised and expressed in non-class terms. This is not to say that there are no Third World countries where social groups have appeared that are primarily integrated along class lines (that is via their occupational and property relations). This has tended to happen in those countries which have experienced a longer and more substantial industrial growth in recent years, the so-called 'newly industrialising countries' (NICs). In Latin American NICs, such as Brazil and Mexico, we find agricultural and industrial elites often sharing class interests through marriage and family ties.

Moreover, in many Third World countries a large, salaried middle class based in white-collar jobs attached to state bureaucracies, health and education services has grown. In other parts of the Third World which have experienced a more faltering industrialisation process, such as in Africa, social classes are 'still in the process of formation' (Babu, 1981, p. 126). Here the development of social classes is tied to the emergence of a smaller post-independence State: in these contexts, as Raikes (1988) notes, the more privileged social groups sustain their position 'through "straddling", that is, using funds accruing through state employment or connections for investment in private enterprises both agricultural and other' (p. 245). For example, those who manage state grain monopolies may pay low prices to peasants and use the 'surplus' to enhance their own standard of living. Raikes is quick to point out, however, that the members of this privileged social stratum are unlikely to become a progressive, modernising *social class*, investing the 'surplus' in capitalist enterprise: their advantages derive from their control of the peasantry via price or rent control rather than via an expanding productive commercial agriculture.

Studies of the development of a working class in Africa suggest that it, too, is still being formed, being relatively undeveloped. Hence, the display of integrated or shared class interests among industrial workers – say through radical trades unionism – has been less frequent and less sustained than in the history of First World industrialisation. Moreover, many workers may harbour individualistic rather than class ambitions, believing they can improve their life chances by hard work: as Sandbrook and Arn

(1977) note, 'Social mobility, after all, represents a personal solution to the generic problem of poverty for the most able and ambitious. In Greater Accra [Ghana] a popular view prevails among the poor that the class structure is indeed open.'

At times, class orientations that do prevail may well be cut across by ethnic ties. Many sociologists have pointed to the economic support that ethnic networks can provide for their members, especially in assisting the passage from rural to urban residence and work. Indeed, at a more political level, it appears that ethnicity can be at least as if not more important than class as a mobiliser of social change: clearly, when expressed as a religiously inspired nationalist struggle such as has been the case in Islamic states recently, ethnic loyalties and their attendant conflicts can be very significant indeed.

In more general terms, Hyden (1984) has explored what he calls 'the economy of affection' that he believes prevails in many African countries where ties and obligations of ethnicity, kin and community determine the pattern of economic reward in the society, their influence felt 'from the grass roots to the apex of society'.

While the economy of affection may be strong, state agencies and institutions are correspondingly underdeveloped. Precisely because economic integration by class is limited, so the political strength of state institutions as mechanisms for integrating the entire population, for overcoming factionalism, is limited. Even if party leaders and civil servants try to promote a sense of citizenship, nationhood and loyalty to the State, many people – especially those in the countryside – are likely to regard the state, if not with suspicion, as something to be avoided. At the local village level, social groups may prefer to organise and even to defend themselves through their own devices. Abrahams (1987) has, for instance, examined the growth of neighbourhood networks and vigilante groups (*sungusungu*) in Tanzania which grew out of traditional communal associations, and towards which the Tanzanian government has had a rather ambivalent attitude.

Given the argument so far, the only effective way of strengthening the state is through a strengthening of social classes to remove factionalism and patronage. This would entail, in other words, a shift from a class-divided to a class society. Hence Hyden's claim that Third World development can only occur through the de-

Class-divided Nigeria

Dress gives a valuable guide to the complex nature of the class system ... particularly on the naming ceremony, marriage and funeral circuits. Until recently it was relatively easy for poorer Nigerians to cut a dash as expensive imported cloth was available and local tailors ran up garments for knockdown prices.

Unfortunately, post-oil boom austerity has now widened both class differences and dress differences.... [D]ifferences between the classes on the basics of living have widened.... Education, the essential element of the Nigerian dream is on the chopping block – school fees have been introduced in many formerly free schools and private schools have hiked their fees.... The class system is under strain. Traditional social distinctions have widened in some areas and have been eroded in others. Plutocrats, the super rich, the governing class – whether military or civilian – remain in a hermetic zone which seals them off from more humdrum and sordid realities. But the middle class is disintegrating at the seams. Its upper reaches are either contracting out of the country or trying to get standing room in the plutocrat class, while its lower reaches are melding into an undifferentiated low income urban and rural mass.

Source: *Guardian*, 29 October 1988.

velopment of integrated class interests throughout the economy in order to displace 'the economy of affection'. While the dominant groups would become more closely integrated, the subordinate peasantry, fragmented and tied to clientelism itself, would similarly assume a more uniform working-class identity perhaps by being incorporated into industrial or commercial agricultural sectors. Understandably, as Worsely (1984) has argued, the peasantry is likely to resist this process. The shift towards a class society is likely to be a slow process.

It will be particularly prolonged if one accepts recent arguments advanced by Vogler (1985). She believes that the capacity of any country to become or prevail as a class society depends as much on *what is happening in the world economy as it does on processes occurring within its own territory*. Like many others within the neo-Marxian school, Vogler, argues that global capitalism has undergone a period of major restructuring primarily through the activities of multinational corporations (MNCs). As MNCs have sought to increase their flexibility for global investment (see chapter 4, p. 91) all nation states have been under pressure to meet the new demands of a more mobile international capital. Some have been able to respond to this pressure better than others. Vogler believes that Britain, even though a 'First World' nation, has experienced severe difficulties in this regard, being unable to sustain itself as one of the stronger *class societies* of advanced capitalism. Clearly, if one can find First World countries in such difficulties, one would expect the already fragmented class-divided societies of the Third World to be in at least as difficult a position.

The Third World State: Recent Marxist Views

Given the argument so far, it would appear that the Third World state cannot be understood as serving the interests of a unified ruling class precisely because of the absence of such a class. What then *is* the state? Some would say that instead of a dominant class there is a ruling elite which is recruited from the well-educated members of professional families (Lloyd, 1967). Most Marxist writers believe however that this ignores the way in which access to political power can allow people to pursue their own economic interests and *over time constitute themselves as a dominant capitalist class*. The classical Marxist thesis is reworked here by arguing that economic power derives from access to state power rather than the other way round. As Miliband (1977, p. 109) notes,

> It is rather political power (which also means here administrative and military power) which creates the possibilities of enrichment and which provides the basis for the formation of an economically powerful class, which may in due course become an economically dominant one.

It is crucial to note Miliband's point that the dominant class can become so *both economically and politically*, in contrast to the notion that in advanced capitalist states the ruling class sustains its economic interests *without* having to hold political office.

A number of Marxists identify the emergent political structures of Africa, Latin America and the Middle East as 'state capitalist'; that is, the government acts as the principal agency of development, provider of capital (through foreign loans and local taxation) and director of economic planning. Those in positions of bureaucratic and political power who administer the state can

Corruption within the African State

Patronage may lead to an abuse of office, and is, therefore, not very far from corruption. An African Marxist, Onimode (1988), sees this as a serious obstacle to the emergence of nation-state legitimacy – and so progressive state capitalist development in Africa. He writes:

> The political problems associated with the abuse of office in Africa have increased to the extent that people now assert that in Africa, it is not simply that officials are corrupt, but corruption is official, and that many African states operate a 'lootocracy' or government-by-looting of the state treasury. Nigeria's political refugees in Western Europe and the USA thus looted their country of billions of dollars and stacked the money abroad.... By breeding apathy and cynicism among the masses, such official corruption also operates to erode the legitimacy of government, and this has been a persistent element in the crisis of legitimacy in many African countries (p. 231).

Source: B. Onimode, *A Political Economy of the African Crisis* (London: Zed Press) 1988.

accumulate wealth through their control over and access to the capital resources that are available for 'development'.

For some Marxists, such as Mafeje (1977) *state capitalism* is likely to be the principal vehicle through which Third World societies begin to shake off their underdevelopment, a view which would presumably have some bearing on Warren's ideas about the possibility of capitalist development in the Third World, although Warren himself does not discuss the political context in which this would occur.

Nevertheless, Mafeje and others also argue that in those countries where an emergent dominant class is beginning to build state capitalism, the chances that it will be successful are remote. This is for two reasons:

(i) the regime usually seeks to legitimise itself via an appeal not to the particular class it represents but to 'the people', a populist strategy to win broad support. In Africa, some political leaders, even though officiating over what is in reality an underdeveloped capitalist system, have proclaimed their cause to be *socialist* in order to attract mass support from the victims of underdevelopment, the chronically disadvantaged rural population. They do not have the economic or political resources to deliver their promises to the people. Consequently, as Mafeje (1977, p. 417) writes,

> Sooner or later (the government) falls victim of rising but unfulfilled expectations. As all citizens are not equally placed, disillusionment among certain sections becomes rife and the government is called upon to make an unavoidable choice as to what class interests it is going to sponsor. More often than not the dice are cast in favour of the educated middle classes who, practically, control the instruments of government.

(ii) the regime clearly may pose a threat to overseas capital and foreign political interests in seeking to establish greater control over the investment of any surplus generated by capital. In response, foreign interests may attempt to destabilise or disrupt the economy through such tactics as economic blockade, foreclosure of debts, removal of technology and expertise and so on.

These two factors explain the chronic weakness of the Third World state that lacks an economically independent dominant class, and go a long way to explaining the persistence of the instability noted earlier.

While both the pluralist and the structuralist accounts draw attention to the forms of instability in a similar fashion, the structuralists offer a stronger analytical framework since they account for at least two crucial matters which the pluralists ignore. First, the pluralists fail to give any indication of the basic weakness of the Third World polity and economy at an international level while the structuralists highlight this through their investigation of the distribution of power in the world capitalist system. The pluralist conception of power as the capacity to influence decisions on policy in one's own interests clearly has some merit as a *description* of the activities of Third World groups using the State institutions to serve their competing, particularistic ends, but it does not identify the fragmentary class character of this competition nor does it recognise that the *institutional* forum in which it occurs is subordinate to the international structure of power.

Secondly, if the structuralist analysis of politics in terms of class relations has any merit we should be able to find evidence for the development of subordinate classes paralleling and challenging the emergent dominant economic class in Third World societies. One way of identifying an increase in class politics is by seeing if there is an intensification of class struggle, through a strengthening of working class solidarity in face of the bourgeoisie. Much evidence has indeed been found for this in recent years (for example Sandbrook and Cohen, 1975) though there is still debate over the strength of the indigenous working class, particularly in Africa given the relatively small industrial development that has occurred there. Some have argued that the small industrial workforce is not concerned to challenge the unequal socio-economic order: in terms of pay and conditions they are better off than their rural counterparts and so are more interested in getting whatever improvements they can out of the existing arrangements in which they have a material stake. On this view the working class are seen as a conservative rather than radical political force. Yet while it is true that working class politics is undeveloped it is not the case that this is so throughout the entire Third World. Capitalist penetration is uneven as we saw in Chapter 4, so the process of working class formation is also uneven: in some contexts the working class *has* been able to establish itself as a radical, revolutionary force where the division between labour and capital has been more clearly drawn, as has been the case in a number of Latin American countries such as Bolivia, Chile and Mexico.

There is a very different path of development from state capitalism that the political leadership of the Third World could take, and that is the road of *state directed socialism*. Progressive socialist government has been established through nationalist struggle as in China, Nicaragua, Mozambique and elsewhere. As we shall see, the success of this socialist reform or revolution depends on the existence of a *strong* state, to mobilise resources and administer policy in the face of attack from the privileged middle classes and those in senior administration, as well as from overseas interests. It appears that development, whether of capitalist or socialist direction, can only occur in the Third World if there is a cohesive, centralised state (as in South Korea, for example).

The political weakness of the Third World state often leads to economic crisis as the uneasy alliance between the more advantaged social classes breaks down. In these circumstances the military have often staged a coup, taking over the running of the state from the civilian authorities and establishing their control over the law, the economy, the media, education and so on. Military intervention is a commonplace phenomenon in the Third World; for example, between 1930 and 1966 there were 81 coups in Latin America. Political sociologists have offered a variety of opinions on the military; let us consider a few of them.

6.3 MILITARY INTERVENTION IN THE THIRD WORLD

The nature of military intervention has been the subject of considerable dispute among political sociologists. Odetola (1982) provides a valuable summary of the literature of this debate. He suggests that there are three principal intrepretations of the military and its contribution to 'development'. The first sees the military as an 'apolitical' institution, that intervenes in circumstances of social disorder solely for its self-interests, is not trained in government rule, and is thus an unstable agency of modernisation and economic development. A major exponent of this position is Huntingdon (1968) who has given particular attention to military coups in Latin America. The second viewpoint, represented by those of Marxian persuasion such as Petras (1968) and Murray (1977), argues that the military is an obstacle to revolutionary change, particularly in its tendency to ally with the privileged middle classes and with external superpowers who typically provide military and financial support for the regime. Finally, there are those who believe, as does Johnson (1962), that the military is no obstacle to change, but on the contrary the best trained and most well organised agency for bringing about the major changes that are needed for development.

We do not have the space to discuss the merits of these different approaches in detail here. While there is substantial divergence between them on the role of the military, there is broad agreement as to why it is the military rather than any other social group that tends to take over when the dependent state is in crisis. First, its command structure gives it the organisational strength to assume office quickly and in a disciplined fashion. Secondly, it has the firepower to back up its actions which do not however, have to be extensive since control of the primate city, usually the capital, is all that is normally required for an effective coup d'etat. Thirdly, the officers and the rank and file soldiers are often highly motivated to flex their organisational muscles to promote their interests: for many, a military career is the only hope of attaining high social status and material reward, this is particularly true of those who are neither members of the landed nor commercial classes. Fourthly, the military can often present themselves to the populace as free from the corruption that the comprador bourgeoisie and bureaucracy indulge in. As Murray (1977, p. 387) says,

> The military elite is to some extent insulated from these high-living social circuits by its separate institutional and social setting (camps). It is thus relatively immune from the popular condemnation of waste and excess. It may easily put itelf forward, or be propelled forward, in these circumstances as the only valid national force capable of cleaning up and restoring lost dignity.

It is not surprising then that the military often claim to be the guardians of the social and economic order capable of restoring national pride, and they will draw on all the traditional symbols of the 'warrior', 'hero' and 'liberator' to press their claims most forcefully. Finally, it is suggested that the military are most likely to intervene because they are most susceptible to outside prompting from other countries (usually the advanced states) keen to remove the sitting government from office. Chomsky and Herman (1979) detail the way in which the US has poured millions of dollars in armaments and military and police training to support some of the most violently undemocratic regimes. Over 25 per cent of US foreign aid goes to the Third World military directly.

Once the military has successfully carried out the coup d'etat it soon faces problems. While it may have got rid of an unstable government presiding over a weak state, it has itself an inherent weakness that makes sustained stable rule (whether progressive or reactionary) exceptionally problematic. First, the military lacks a clear political basis of popular or class support: in other words it has no evident political constituency, it has to try to create one once in power. Consequently, when the coup has been completed, the new military regime seeks allies among the senior ranks of the bureaucracy. This can open up the channels of corruption once again as the military attempts to purchase loyalties, leaving the regime open to the charge of having 'sold out,': eventually cynicism replaces populism.

Secondly, 'the military' should not be regarded as a homogenous grouping: it may well be internally divided along ethnic lines or have major differences of political belief among its members, as was true for example of the soldiers who overthrew the Portuguese government in April 1974. The military regime that followed was riven by infighting between the more radical rank and file and the more conservative officers.

Thirdly, the military are unlikely to have the skills of government needed to put together and implement social and economic policies, particularly in a period of social disorder. They often try to overcome this problem by withdrawing to a position of indirect rule, that is 'inviting' civilians and bureaucrats to establish a new administration while the real power remains with them. Obviously though during the coup the military has created enemies among just these civilian groups and it is likely that given the chance, the latter might try to regain real power and attack the military. If the military elite tries to civilianise *itself*, to substitute the suit for the uniform and promise new elections and the restoration of party politics, it has to somehow be seen to be using democratic means rather than coercion: this of course means that all those who were suppressed during the period of the coup and its aftermath, such as lower ranking white collar workers, wage labourers, intellectuals and students, now find they have the room for manoeuvre to challenge the authority of the new government, in the campuses, factories, offices, and on the streets. Political instability appears once again.

As noted earlier, Johnson (1962) has argued that the military could be a progressive force inasmuch as it frequently gives priority to a programme of industrial expansion (albeit through overseas capital). Johnson thus believes that the military regime can be a force for 'development.' A similar argument has been advanced more recently by Philip (1984), based on his observation of the political endurance of military governments in Latin America. He argues that the military may be the only effective organisation for social and economic development and industrial growth.

However, this begs the question as to the *character* of this industrial growth: as we saw in Chapter 4, there is as yet little evidence to indicate a growth of inner-directed industrialisation. It would seem that, given their reliance on overses capital, military governments are likely to encourage rather than reduce 'dependency.' Moreover, given the political weaknesses described above, the military are unlikely to promote a strong state, which as we have noted appears to be an important requirement of Third World development. Most commentators argue that one is likely to see a cycle of instability set in motion as one military coup gives way to indirect rule, which in turn is checked by a further military coup and so on. Finer (1974, p. 567) concludes that,

> The most likely outcome of one military coup and one military regime in the Third World is a second coup and a second military regime, separated by bouts of indirect military rule, monopartism, and feebly functioning competitive party politics – an alteration of these three types for a considerable age to come.

6.4 CONCLUSION

In this Chapter we have looked briefly at two important theories that provide general analyses of political development and specific interpretations of Third World politics. On both counts the structuralist analysis seems to be of greater value than the pluralist account. We have seen that democracy is not inevitably connected with capitalist economic growth, and that to understand political processes we have to pay close attention to the play of class relations that lie behind the state. It also seems to be the case that *if* the Third World is to 'develop' industrially it needs a strong state.

If state capitalism is the objective (as in South Korea or Brazil) the government needs to develop the strength and unity of the indigenous business class. It is also possible that state socialism is the broad aim. Apart from some discussion of this in Chapter 8 where we look at developments in Tanzania, we shall in Chapter 9 look at the viability of three distinct forms of state socialism that derive from mass populist appeal (Tanzania), democratic election

(Chile), or revolution (China). As we shall see it appears to be only the last of these that has any chance of success in establishing an alternative to underdevelopment. We have seen in this chapter that Third World governments can often be unstable bureaucratic states reliant on overseas capital, much of which comes from the metropolitan centre via official 'aid' programmes. The role of foreign aid and national development programmes is the focus of Chapter 7.

7

Development Planning and Aid

7.1 INTRODUCTION

At the start of the International Monetary Fund's 1988 Annual Conference held in West Berlin 40 000 anti-IMF demonstrators marched against the Conference demanding fundamental changes to the Fund's investment and aid policies for the Third World. Rather than relieving Third World poverty the IMF's programmes were attacked as being the very cause of this poverty.

Such protests are not uncommon, and they are part of a wider critique of international development programmes that have been managed and sponsored by very powerful agencies in the capitalist First World. Development planning within Third World nations has been subject to similar attacks from those it is supposed to help. There appears, at least superficially, to be neither rhyme nor reason to a situation in which, though aid and GNP increase, they are accompanied by a massive insoluable debt problem and a rapid growth in the numbers in poverty. Something, somewhere has 'gone wrong'.

When many Third World countries failed to 'develop' or did so only slowly after formal independence, new funds and new agencies were set up at national and international level to contribute towards the rebuilding schemes mapped out by the willing but inexperienced Third World governments. Hydroelectric power, rural development projects, transport and telecommunications, all were to be supported in some way. Rural schemes have been given considerable attention precisely because of the rapid population growth: food provision, whether through local agriculture or international food aid, has been a priority at a time when almost

500 million experience severe malnutrition. Yet the offical national and international programmes seem not to have been working as intended, one reason for the mushrooming of alternative, popular, charity-based assistance, epitomised in Bob Geldof's 'Band Aid' organisation.

In theory, official assistance should be very effective in stimulating development. Those in the Third World encouraged to borrow or obtain capital from institutions like the IMF and World Bank have often seen such funding as more suited to their needs than raising finance from commercial banks. Offical assistance is preferred because (in theory):

(i) it can be used for the development of social utilities which would be unlikely to attract money from private investors who would gain no return; utilities might include schools, hospitals and other non-commercial establishments;
(ii) it can be more carefully controlled by officials in the field to ensure that those who are supposed to receive it actually do;
(iii) it can be obtained from donors in various forms and on varying terms and so is a much more flexible source of funds than private investment, and usually, of course, is much cheaper because of interest-free loans or straightforward grants.

More generally, aid overcomes the shortage of investment capital and provides the foreign currency to pay for the necessary technological imports the Third World country needs for manufacturing and commercial agriculture. Aid acts as a 'pump-priming' mechanism according to this view, triggering growth in the modern sector the effects of which will 'trickle down' to the relatively backward sectors of the economy.

Western providers of official aid packages have been prepared to lend vast amounts not merely for humanitarian reasons but also as a way of sustaining their influence in ex-colonies, or building new influence in new territories – as the United States has done since 1945. National governments on both sides of the Atlantic also see great benefit for their own indigenous industries which can be contracted to provide whatever expertise and technology is needed for specific projects: as much as 70 per cent of British aid has a direct commercial benefit to private corporations in Britain itself. In 1987 the British government provided 'aid-contracts' for firms, which had a total export value of £1082 million.

However, although loans from official sources have been provided at relatively low cost to Third World borrowers, there is now a very large debt-burden carried by most Third World economies. This debt-burden is a unique feature of the process of 'development' as experienced by the Third World. And it is attended by hunger, sickness and poverty.

The debt-crisis

Susan George (1988) has recently described the emergence of and reasons for the 'debt-crisis' in the Third World. While official and commercial banks have been prepared to lend increasing amounts to the Third World (in fact almost two-thirds comes from private banks), the ability of countries to repay these loans looks increasingly unlikely. Although Third World countries are repaying their debts, most owe more in interest and capital repayments than they earn each year from exports. To keep going, they have to borrow more, and so the debt burden increases, where it now stands at $1.217 billion, or about 40 per cent on average of the Third World's total GDP (for the poorest 15 countries the equivalent figure is 60 per cent). The IMF encourages 'austerity' measures, believing that these will remove the conditions that create debt in the first place. However, as Bryant and Portes (1988) and the 40000 Berlin demonstrators argue, these policies have not only been counterproductive but have actually led to increasing indebtedness.

The impact of IMF policies

Hunger
In one third of recent cases countries were required by the IMF to reduce badly needed food subsidies. The result was a dramatic increase in malnutrition:

In Peru it rocketed amongst under six year-olds from 41% to 68% between 1980 and 1983; Ghana saw pre-school malnutrition swell from 35% to 54% between 1980 and 1984; and in Botswana child malnutrition increased from 25% to 31% between 1982 and 1984.

Sickness
Government spending on health was cut in nearly half the African countries and in 60% of Latin American countries where the IMF was involved from 1980 to 1985:

The money spent on an individual's health plummeted by 85% in Ghana between 1974 and 1982; by 78% in Bolivia from 1980 to 1982; and by 32% in El Salvador from 1980 to 1984. The grim harvest of these cuts was an increase in preventable diseases and hence child deaths – especially in Ghana.

Poverty
Between 1980 and 1985 inflation soared, and wages crashed by 9 per cent in Latin Ameria and 15 per cent in Sub-Saharan Africa from 1980 to 1985:

In Mexico they fell by 30% between 1981 and 1984; in Ghana by 22% between 1979 and 1984; and in Sri Lanka by 18% between 1978 and 1983. The number of people below the poverty line increased by up to 75% in parts of Ghana between 1974 to 1984.

Source: *Adjustment with a Human Face*, a study by UNICEF 1987.

Aid Donors

The major international agencies that distribute aid to 'developing' countries include the United Nations, the Organisation for Economic Co-operation and Development (OECD), the IMF, the World Bank, and the Development Fund of the European Economic Community (EEC). There are also various national bodies such as the US Agency for International Development (AID), the UK Overseas Development Administration and the West German Ministry for Economic Co-operation. Western aid programmes are selective inasmuch as most support those countries which are friendly to western interests. In effect, this means that any country that adopts an anti-Soviet, anti-communist policy and which opens its doors to western investment is a potential recipient of aid. There are some exceptions to this general practice: a number of countries still receive aid despite periods of conflict with dominant western interests. For example, the British government in August 1983 endorsed a $100 million cheap loan from British banks to Argentina despite failing to declare a formal cessation of hostilities over the Falkland Islands dispute. Although official western policy is to allocate aid to countries that operate as 'democracies', in practice a number of right-wing military governments have been able to attract both financial and military aid, for example Pakistan, Chile and Argentina. In terms of the ex-colonial powers most of their assistance goes to their former colonies; for example, 90 per cent of UK aid goes to India, Pakistan, Bangladesh and Kenya.

Direct Soviet involvement in the Third World in the form of financial aid did not appear until relatively late, the first major investment occurring in 1956 in Egypt and the Soviet backed construction of the Aswan High Dam, after France, Britain and the USA had decided against supporting Nasser's government and this project in particular. The Dam became a symbol of the new Soviet interest in Africa, which subsequently became firmly established in Angola in the west, Ethiopia and Mozambique in the east and Libya to the north.

As is evident aid transfers are highly political especially in regard to competition between the two superpowers. The political nature of aid is well-illustrated by the following remark made by a deputy administrator of US AID, a Mr Coffin:

> Our basic, broader goal is a long range political one. It is not development for the sake of sheer development. . . . An important objective is to open up the maximum opportunity for domestic private initiative and to ensure that foreign private investment, particularly from the US, is welcomed and well-treated. . . . The problem is . . . to evaluate the manner in which the program can make the greater contribution to the totality of US interests.

7.2 THE FAILURE OF DEVELOPMENT AID

The continuing failure of official international aid to encourage the emergence of a self-sustaining growth in agricultural and industrial sectors, geared to local needs, has led many to question the appropriateness of aid *per se*. A number of problems with the current system of aid assistance have been identified.

(i) Since some of the aid is in the form of loans rather than direct grants poorer countries may find themselves getting into increasing debt.

It is the poorest countries that are in most serious difficulties even though they may actually owe a comparatively small amount to the aid agencies. Since they do not have the political influence of some of the bigger states, African countries like Uganda, the Sudan, and Malawi may find it virtually impossible to attract extra money for the relief of basic subsistence needs and thereby increasingly difficult to prevent more of their people falling into a state of absolute poverty. These countries rely on exports of single commodities to earn revenue: for example, Uganda depends on coffee sales to earn 96 per cent of its export revenue. When commodity prices fall on the international markets, as they have done in real terms for the past four years, it is clearly very difficult for countries reliant on one or two items to generate sufficient revenue from exports to repay loans. This problem of repayment is of course heightened inasmuch as a good deal of the aid that is received is used to fund projects such as school-building, which do not generate revenue for the country. The irony is that in these difficult circumstances, some Third World countries have been tempted to use their aid capital to try to *increase* production of that very commodity on which they are very dependent as a source of export revenue. As we saw in Chapter 4, many (for example Frank, 1981) argue that this tends to encourage their dependency on overseas 'metropolises', a weakening of 'inner-directed' growth and the possibility of an increase in landless labourers in the rural areas.

(ii) A considerable proportion of any aid package is swallowed up in payments to technical experts, the field-staff of the donor countries, or on the costly housing, transport, and diet arrangements made for them in the host country. As the *New Internationalist* (1981, p. 9) noted:

> Up to 25% of Western aid budgets is spent on experts. After salary, airfares, school fees, various perks and home based overheads are covered, the average British expert costs $150,000 a year.

Experts typically receive tax-free salaries usually paid directly into their home country bank account as they have a living and transport 'allowance' to cover their needs while working in the host country. Thus the salary is unlikely to be used to buy host country products, a potential source of demand that is sorely missed.

(iii) An important form of assistance to Third World countries is food aid. The first country to establish a food-aid programme was the United States after 1945. The context in which this programme was formulated reveals yet again the way that aid has been of considerable value to the actual donor country. American agricultural productivity in the 1950s was exceptionally high due to increased use of large-scale farming techniques and support prices from the government. Productivity outpaced American consumption and huge grain surpluses were created which had to be stored at a cost of hundreds of millions of dollars each year. Given the social status and political strength of the farming community of 'middle America' they were successful in their demand that the stocks should not be released on either the domestic or international market, since this would put downwards pressure on the sale price of grain and the exchange value of the dollar. Instead, the grain was made available to Third World countries who could purchase it in their own currencies (until 1971) so unaffecting the market value of the dollar. Whereas previously such countries had not been a significant part of the US market, they became a valuable outlet for US produce, not only food crops but also the storage and transportation technology needed to handle them. This policy became more ambitious as US corporations moved into Third World countries to process and refine the foodstuffs for both human and animal consumption. The speed of this food aid penetration was quite dramatic: for example, in 1967 Korea imported only 3000 tons of US wheat; by 1972 this had risen to 450 000 tons.

In the long term food aid can have serious social and economic consequences. Economically it tends to undermine the Third World agricultural sector by depressing local markets and so discouraging local production. Despite farmers' desire to work and cultivate successfully, local economic conditions mean that there is limited opportunity to get an adequate return on one's business (Mann, 1969). Socially this can lead to farmers going out of business adding to the huge volume of under-employed and unemployed landless labourers. Politically it can also encourage a subservience to donor states by Third World governments such that they may be obliged to buy surplus donor goods when they are unwanted: for example, Pakistan has had to take surplus US cotton when it had sufficient of its own. The boxed extract from *New Internationalist* is an excellent illustration of the social, economic and political effects of food aid.

From hand to mouth?

Advertising posters of the big relief organisations invariably carry the portraits of skinny infants clutching a tin cup of milk or gruel. But, if Bangladesh is anything to go by, it is debatable whether the food aid actually reaches those empty bellies. Despite the 4.5 million metric tons of grain and cooking oil received from the US since independence from Pakistan in 1971, Bangladesh still seems no closer to being able to feed itself. In fact, that massive amount of imported food may be one of the main causes of stagnating production.

According to *Wall Street Journal* reporter, Barry Newman, grain imports have tripled since the 1960's, while malnutrition has increased from 45 to 60 per cent of the population: the average Bangladeshi plate holds even less than it did 20 years ago.

Needless to say it is the middle class in cities and rich landowners in the countryside who have prospered. Most food destined for the 90 per cent of Bangladeshis who live in rural areas is instead sold in local markets by the government which then uses the money as it chooses. Ration cards meant to enable the holder to purchase foreign grain at subsidised prices are dealt out as political rewards. So those with power and clout – civil servants, police, the military and employees in big factories – end up with the lion's share. One World Bank study discovered that a rural resident gets an average 14 kilos of food aid grain a year while his city cousin grabs more than ten times that amount.

Because most spare cash is siphoned off by government-run ration shops, incentive for local food production is badly undercut. Why grow more food if there is no-one to buy it? But by now food aid has become so much a part of the political landscape that any efforts to dismantle the system would run into stiff opposition. 'To be very frank,' Food Minister Abdul Momen confided to reporter Newman, 'political aspects must be taken into consideration. If the price is suddenly increased or subsidised foods are withdrawn, this may lead to discontent.'

President Ziaur Rahman has ambitiously pledged food self-sufficiency by 1985. He hopes to increase grain production from the present 13.1 million tons to 20 million tons, with a guaranteed production of 18 million even in bad weather years. Most observers wish him well. But his chances of success are virtualy nil unless he grasps the nettle of land reform. Otherwise large farmers would turn their attention to feeding the city and those with neither money nor land would be no better off.

Over half of the people in Bangladesh are landless. Another 25 per cent are tenants farming small plots in return for half the harvest. But the 15 per cent which controls over two thirds of the land carries considerable weight in the ruling party and the opposition. And they are rather prickly about moves to erode their holdings. 'They talk of removing property markers. I will kill you if you move my property markers one inch' warned one Dacca resident whose family owns 50 acres in his ancestral village.

And it appears that the President is unwilling to step into this political quagmire: 'We are working towards land reform', he says, 'but it must be done quietly. 'It's not something you can beat a drum about.'

Source: *New Internationalist*, June 1981, p. 6.

(iv) Aid often increases dependency by being loaned to a country on condition that it is used to purchase goods from the donor country: this is known as *aid-tying*. Almost 70 per cent of

British aid is loaned on these terms, which means in effect that aid provides an important market for British manufacturers. As King (1975, p. 9) says,

> Aid creates *more* jobs and leads to the establishment of *more* industries in the developed than in the developing countries. The main beneficiaries of aid are those countries which provide the bulk of international expertise to developing countries and which export equipment, through direct links with aid agencies and projects, to them.

Presumably however, official aid agencies would reply that King's remark clearly implies that *some* jobs and *some* industries are being created in the Third World through aid transfers. To this extent at least, aid has a 'development' effect. A similar position would be taken by Warren, the neo-Marxist, thereby suggesting an intriguing convergence of radical and establishment views.

(v) Aid beneficiaries in the Third World tend to be urban centred – the bureaucrats, entrepreneurs, politicians, and industrial workers, as the extract on Bangladesh above indicates. The poorest in the rural sectors, those that one might think are supposed to benefit most from aid, particularly food aid, usually end up seeing very little of it.

The system of aid transfers is still very much dominated by the commercial interests of the donor economies. This is also true of the Soviet Union which in some cases exploits Third World economies by receiving its loan repayments in the form of commodities which it then re-exports at a profit to other countries. Nevertheless lobby groups have developed some pressure within the aid agencies, such as the World Bank, to try to reduce the practice of aid-tying, to encourage instead untied grants for the satisfaction of 'basic needs'. As we saw in Chapter 2, this concept has been developed into a policy giving priority to the provision of basic physical, social and political needs of people, particularly those in the poor rural regions. While on paper this is a significant step forward in thinking since it is not a slave to GNP as the criterion of development, in reality it has had relatively little impact on donors' assistance programmes: apart from paying lip-service to the philosophy of the 'basic needs' approach, donors prefer to give assistance with commercial priorities first. As van der Hoeven (1988) notes, donors (like the IMF) have also been over-preoccupied with aid programmes geared towards economic reform and political stabilisation. He argues that a 'basic needs' approach is the only genuine way in which economic growth will occur in the Third World.

7.3 RURAL DEVELOPMENT PROGRAMMES

Many people would argue that aid problems are connected with mismanagement of funds or the local corruption of bureaucrats who administer it in the Third World: that is, that in principle aid is a good thing, it is merely the way it is delivered and utilised that needs more attention. There is some evidence (Hartmann and Boyce, 1980) of misdirection of funds and 'creaming-off' of monies by members of the local political and landowning elites. Many of the richer farmers corner the aid-inputs – the new tubewell or pump for example – by bribing local officials. According to the official documentation and reports these inputs are widely used by the poorer farmers in the area, but in reality, they are typically under the control of the richer farmers, sited on their land, their benefits, such as irrigation, only made available to poor neighbours at a high price. So long as aid capital is given initially to bank officials and local bureaucrats it is very likely that the more affluent farmers will be its prime beneficiaries.

To those that have. . . .

There is very little evidence that recent World Bank agricultural projects have benefited the poorest farmers, or have even been intended to do so. There is evidence that the benefits of World Bank loans have accrued to the rich rather than to the poor, and that some projects have excluded the poor from access to productive resources and redistributed assets and incomes to the rich. Where projects have been directed to smallholders, they have been dictated by the requirements of agro-industrial firms and the fiscal requirements of the state.

Source: G. Williams, 'The World Bank and the peasant problem' (1981).

Richer farmers are likely to have a long-standing business connection with local banks who prefer extending credit to those who own rather than merely have access to land. Gibbons (1981) has estimated that the Asian Third World is largely made up of small farms less than 1 hectare (2.5 acres) in size. Excluding China, 45 million farms are of this size or less, and Gibbons argues that government priority in Asia should set in motion land development and redistribution programmes so that each farming family has sufficient acreage to allow it to cultivate enough to bring it above the poverty line.

Kinsey (1987) extends this argument further, by calling for rural policies that incorporate the poorest rural peasantry into the local farming and business sector, rather than, as often happens, exclude them. One of the most important ways this can be achieved is by introducing farm practices that are labour- rather than capital-intensive. In addition agribusiness enterprise that uses farm products should be encouraged to obtain them from small farm producers. Rural development programmes based on the needs and resources and affordable inputs of the local community are seen as being much more appropriate than large-scale cash crop agribusiness whose benefits, whether in terms of wage-income or foodstuffs tend, as Lipton (1977) argued, to be distributed towards the more prosperous rural and urban social classes.

There has, however, long been a tension between those policies that require central direction and management of rural activities and those which emerge from the grass roots upwards. This is particularly true of Indian development planning, as a recent text by Mehta (1984) shows. Mehta argues that rural policies for growth ought not to be imposed from above, but emerge through self-directed peasant initiative – an expression of the democratic culture which Mehta believes is 'ingrained' in India. However, at the same time Mehta, as many other writers, appears to have little regard for the poor's abilities to do this:

> The poor in the rural areas are dependent on the national government as they lack adequate knowledge, skills and appropriate attitudes to take the initiative on their own.... Their socio-economic status has fostered apathy, lethargy and 'poor work ethics' in them (p. 167).

Self-reliance now appears to be a pious hope and one is not surprised to find Mehta urging the government to take a more interventionist position. The poor should be educated, he says, to accept the state's programmes. Others, however, such as Chambers (1983) argue that the poor do not need training from above but education to inspire confidence in order that they can use the farming skills they already have.

The top-down rural development policy is perhaps best illustrated by programmes which together have been the basis of the so-called 'Green Revolution'. These internationally sponsored and nationally managed rural development schemes have a history stretching back thirty years, inspired originally by the attempt to produce high-yielding varieties of crops for the Third World. A revolution in agricultural production would be a 'green revolution' that would not merely solve the problems of food supply but also weaken the appeal of radical political activists challenging the status quo.

Much as been written about the impact of the green revolution technology on Third World farming. Most of its critics have argued that it is a landlord-biased form of agriculture: since the higher-yielding seed needs a range of expensive inputs to work – fertiliser, irrigation, pesticide and herbicide – only the richer farmers have been able to afford the new technology. Where poorer farmers do get involved they often find they have to borrow money to pay for these inputs at excessively high levels of interest – perhaps 200–300 per cent per year. In these circumstances any crop failure will create severe financial problems for the poor farmer: to meet any debts, rural families may have to sell some of their land to the rural rich, thereby reducing their chances of self-sufficiency for the following year.

Although richer farmers have usually welcomed the new technology, Bhaduri (1977) has argued that in some circumstances they may well resist its introduction. This he says has happened in some parts of India because the landlords' dominance over the poorer peasantry is thought to be threatened by green revolution technology. Traditional farming relations mean that many peasants are dependent on and in debt to the landlord, precisely because their own meagre landholding will not support their families. Landlords will use this relationship to suit their own ends, maintaining the dependency and subservience of the peasantry.

Clearly, were green revolution technology to allow peasants to grow more crops the whole basis of the relationship would be undermined, as peasants would be able, at least in theory, to grow enough crops for themselves. Hence, Bhaduri claims that richer farmers may in certain contexts fend off the arrival of the new technology in their area. This is not some sign of 'backwardness' but, on the contrary, a carefully calculated resistance which in the eyes of the landlords makes good economic sense.

In response to what are often seen as expensive, relatively inefficient national development policies, many groups at local and community level have tried – despite Mehta's misgivings – to introduce self-reliant, cheap farming practices that will enhance agricultural productivity. Many of the non-official, international charities have played a leading part in helping to foster such work. Oxfam, for example, has had considerable success in restoring arid land to a state on which crops can again be grown through the simple – and in the opinion of local farmers sensible – technique of 'stone-lining'. This involves placing stones in a line to match the contours of the terrain in order to trap rainwater more efficiently. The method has reportedly boosted crop yields by an average of 50 per cent, without the attendant costs that green revolution farming would have meant.

Throughout Africa, Asia and Latin America, voluntary associations and charity groups, increasingly helped by national government, are devoting considerable efforts to this type of peasant-based, collaborative farming. Harrison (1981) goes further, arguing that the peasants should take priority over the agricultural professionals that are supposedly employed to implement development plans. He urges that the power of the professionals should be continually challenged by the grassroots organisations that now flourish: 'with a very modest amount of specialised knowledge, almost anyone can deal with the major problems that crop up. Through the local committees that support and guide them, the professionalised experts should remain under the control of their clients' (p. 345).

Harrison is obviously an advocate for the 'basic needs', 'bottom up' development school. We shall see in the next chapter how this position has a long pedigree and an increasing importance through the 'alternative technology' movement. The fact that there is a tension between this approach and the top-down, state-sponsored approach to rural development indicates the way in which development planning ultimately involves *political* decisions and choices. As we saw in Chapter 6, however, political power in the Third World is typically fragmented across clientelistic networks. This means that whether one tries to introduce initiatives from above or below, they are likely to run up against social, economic and political factionalism which is likely to weaken their efficacy.

While those international, national and local agencies that are directly involved with development planning and assistance may be concerned about how best to initiate and manage aid packages, there are a number of economists and sociologists who have challenged the whole aid enterprise itself. Such critics reserve their strongest attacks for international aid which they believe is fundamentally harmful to the Third World. The reasons for this argument vary considerably. Let us first consider the right-wing 'liberal economic' critique of aid.

The Liberal Economic Critique of Aid

'Liberal economics' is a school of economic theory that can be traced back to the classical writings of Adam Smith (1776) and David Ricardo (1817) who sought to explain the rapid growth of the British economy during the latter part of the eighteenth century. They claimed that it was the development of 'free market' enterprise that was most conducive of growth, ensuring that the 'factors of production' – land, labour and capital – would be most productively used under competitive circumstances. They argued that the government should not interfere in the market which, through the laws of supply and demand, self-regulates the economy to ensure the best use of resources. Free trade without intervention enabled the ambitious entrepreneur to develop a successful enterprise – at home and overseas.

Despite the fact that the so-called self-regulation of the market apparently means that a state of 'full-employment' in Britain for example requires a structural unemployment level of about a million workers, the basic philosophy of 'free trade' and market 'regulation' is still a strong ideology today. It is a philosophy which most western leaders in the late 1980s hold dear and champion publicly even though most of the time government intervention and support for private capital is the order of the day.

One of the strongest adherents to the liberal, free trade thesis is Peter Bauer. He believes that growth, whether in the UK or the Third World, can only come through liberalising the market, removing trade restrictions so encouraging capital to find its most profitable outlet. That inequality in the world economy exists merely reflects the relative failure of some countries to provide the right conditions for entrepreneurial capital investment. The notion that economic development involves increasing *equality* through, say, the redistribution of land and income is dismissed as a delusion, as is implied in the very title of one of his more recent books, *Equality, the Third World and Economic Delusion* (Bauer, 1981). That the Third World does not prosper in comparison with industrialised countries of the west is nothing other than a reflection of the inefficient use of resources and lack of entreprenuerial motivation in poorer countries. Their claim that they should be given aid to help them should be dismissed says Bauer, since it depends on the fallacious notion that they are in some way a special case, countries that can hold the west in some way responsible for their problems. They proclaim a shared identity as the exploited, calling themselves 'the Third World' in order to 'extract resources from the west' particularly through foreign aid. So long as aid is given they will continue to peddle the myth of their collective identity and milk it for all it is worth: as Bauer (1981, p. 87) claims, 'the Third World is the creation of foreign aid: without foreign aid there is no Third World.'

Clearly, Bauer's ideas would find considerable support among economists who belong to the modernisation school of development, such as Rostow (1960), and the stress he puts on entrepreneurial motivation recalls the claims made by McClelland (1961) and Lerner (1964). Like them, he has a Eurocentric view of development. He argues for example, that foreign aid is not necessary in the Third World since the poor countries of seventeenth century Europe did *not* need it to grow; moreover, European countries did not have the advantages which the Third World enjoys. Hence Bauer's (1981, p. 99) claim that,

> Western societies progressed in conditions far more difficult than those facing the Third World, which can draw on huge external markets, on external capital markets, on a vast range of

technology and on diverse skills unavailable before. Plainly, official aid is not indispensable for progress.

What then, one might ask, of the wealth brought to Europe through the exploits of merchant capitalism and colonialism? Surely Bauer cannot have forgotten this? Indeed not; he argues that (1981, p. 100)

> such bonanzas as the discovery of precious metals, or their acquisition by conquest . . . are windfalls which accident or the play of political forces has conferred on the owners or controllers of potentially valuable resources. By themselves, such occurrences have not hitherto led to sustained development.

What sustains development is the right motivation (1981, p. 100):

> Economic achievement depends on people's attributes, attitudes and motivations, mores and political arrangements. In many countries the prevailing personal, social and political determinants are uncongenial to material progress: witness the preference for a contemplative life, opposition to paid work by women and widespread torpor and fatalism in certain countries.

Foreign aid is itself an obstacle to material progress. Bauer argues that it is a most unproductive and inefficient use of capital, particularly when used for projects 'unrelated to development' such as overcoming poverty. It creates dependent, parasitic local elites who have little interest in encouraging real economic growth in their countries. Aid does not create the cutting edge of competition needed to make good use of scarce resources. Instead of relying on aid-capital, Bauer claims that poorer countries should try to develop projects that will attract commercial loans from private investors or banks since it is in the latter's interest to ensure that they get a good return on their investment. Even if much of the capital invested and profits generated – as much as 70 per cent – finds its way back to the industrial North, this still means that the remaining 30 per cent of commercial capital is at work building enterprise and employment. In this, Bauer's argument comes close to that of Warren (1980, p. 175) who, in his Marxist critique of dependency theory speaks of 'the ridiculous notion that because the outflow of profits and dividends exceeds the original investment, the host country has lost'. This is similar to Bauer's argument except that for Warren the expansion of capitalism in the Third World though 'progressive' is also by definition *exploitative* of labour in its appropriation of their 'surplus value' through profit (see Chapter 4, section 4.2), whereas Bauer would regard profit-taking as the 'fair' return to employers for 'risking' capital.

Bauer also challenges the view that aid acts as a valuable subsidy for domestic industry in donor countries through loans being tied to the purchase of goods from the donor. He argues that if the government wants to use taxpayers' money effectively for its own economy it should give subsidies *direct* to domestic industry rather than using the medium of aid deals in which some of the capital is given over to the Third World recipient. Aid transfers are neither especially productive for donors nor for the Third World. For the latter the only contribution that aid makes is that it cheapens the cost of borrowing since loans are not normally charged at commercial interest rates. But this small advantage is heavily outweighed by the deleterious effects aid has on economic growth.

Bauer's argument is highly controversial since it attacks the very principles on which aid policy has been built and, more concretely, threatens the employment of a considerable number of aid personnel. As we shall see in Chapter 9, Bauer is realistic enough to recognise that the aid industry is not about to be dismantled, so he makes a number of suggestions about how aid could be used more effectively even though in principle he is opposed to it.

Bauer's thesis is a powerful argument which makes some cogent criticisms of certain aspects of aid particularly with regard to mismanagement and corruption. Some of these are also found in the radical critique of aid discussed below. There are, nevertheless, a number of general remarks that need to be made by way of criticism.

First, Bauer's ideas suffer from a Eurocentric view of economic growth by which he judges all other societies. This is historically a weak approach to understanding patterns of change since it treats specific features of the development of certain societies as having general applicability. To put this more abstractly, 'contingent' features are given 'necessary' status. Thus Bauer speaks of the individual entrepreneurial ambition and 'free trade' of the British developmental experience as though they are *necessary* conditions for economic growth. This can easily be challenged by showing that countries have experienced industrial development by very different means: for example Japan and the Soviet Union were both industrialised primarily through strong *state intervention*, as more recently was South Korea.

Secondly, Bauer underplays the material importance of merchant capitalism and colonialism for the industrialisation of Western Europe. In suggesting that the control of material resources have not 'hitherto led to sustained development' he ignores the qualitative difference between capitalist imperialism of the late nineteenth century and the booty and tribute extracted from territories by pre-capitalist empires such as Rome. The wealth extracted by the former was used directly to promote capitalist industrialisation bringing great changes in the social and economic structures of European and colonial society, particularly through the introduction of 'free' wage labour. The wealth of the Roman empire was based on slavery and supported a ruling aristocracy in prestigious urban comfort.

Thirdly, Bauer like all modernisation theorists, places great stress on the motivational aspects of growth, arguing that poor societies are likely to be deficient in this regard compared with more prosperous ones. We have already considered important evidence in Chapter 3 that challenges the view that pre-industrial societies lack ambitious or entrepreneurial people: when economic opportunity has presented itself poor people have engaged in commercial activity with considerable success.

Fourthly, Bauer claims that direct subsidies to domestic industry would create more exports and employment than using the medium of aid-tying. While there could be circumstances when this is true, it is possible that small aid-transfers with the addition of recipient country capital enable the start of large projects which would otherwise never have got off the ground and which generate employment in the donor country *at a much higher level* than if the equivalent aid capital had been directly invested in the donor's economy.

Finally, while there may be some truth in his view that capital is more profitably invested within the context of a commercial rather than aid venture, it may well be the case that people's social and economic needs are not met even when commercial capital is invested – radicals would say *because* commercial capital is invested. There are indeed many commercial schemes in the Third World that have relied primarily on private capital but which have been detrimental to Third World development precisely because the schemes' priorities are to serve the manufacturing interests of capitalist enterprise in the centre – the Volta Dam project in Ghana is a classic example of this (Lanning, 1979). Moreover in some circumstances it is possible that capitalist enterprise is *less* productive in its use of resources – such as land and labour – than non-capitalist enterprise. For example, peasant family farms that produce for local markets as well as for their own subsistence are likely to *increase* their production of cash crops when the market price for them drops in order to maintain their income: this, of course means working all hours they can possibly find; a capitalist farmer on the contrary, would be likely to *cut back* production by laying off labour to defray costs. As Kitching (1982, p. 50) says, 'under certain circumstances peasant farmers may be able to compete with large-scale capitalist enterprises and be successful'.

Most of the criticisms of Bauer's thesis are similar to those we advanced against modernisation theory. As noted earlier, Bauer's views receive considerable implicit support in the current policies of industrialised western countries which are less willing to continue to advance aid and which seek outlets for private commercial capital in the Third World. Yet they do *not* in practice hold to the other crucial aspect of Bauer's thesis, namely, free trade with Third World economies. Although often attacked by Bauer, it is ironic that many Third World governments are pushing for more liberal trade policies and less protectionism by the industrialised North. The latter, especially the USA, wants to promote private capital investment in the Third World but not open its economies to cheap imports from it.

This suggests that aid and trade policy are in reality designed to serve the needs of the capitalist centre. Such a view lies at the heart of the second critique of official aid that comes from a point on the political spectrum diametrically opposed to that of Bauer, the radical left.

The Radical Critique of Aid

The radical critique of aid was given its first detailed presentation through the work of Theresa Hayter (1971) and subsequently by contributions from Payer (1974), Griffin (1976) and others. As the title of Hayter's first text, *Aid as Imperialism*, indicates, these radical theorists see aid as merely another vehicle for continuing the underdevelopment of the Third World by the capitalist centre of the world economy. Hayter (1971, p. 7) calls aid 'the smooth face of imperialism'. Whereas for Bauer aid results from the demands made by idle, corrupt governments of poor countries who call themselves 'the Third World', Hayter sees it as an enabling mechanism for sustained capitalist penetration in the neo-colonial period, although she says that it has not been as effective in this as envisaged, hence its recent decline.

Hayter's major claim is that aid acts as a form of 'leverage', as an instrument that has a strong influence on the direction in which Third World economies will go, a direction most suited to the interests of capitalism. The way it does this is by donors specifying certain conditions to which the recipient country must agree before any grant or loan is given. These conditions supposedly serve to put the recipient's economic house in order; in fact they weaken the economy in the long term ensuring its increasing dependency on foreign capital. The most important institutions which act as the intermediaries for this form of 'imperialism' are the World Bank and the IMF. Hayter herself was working for an aid organisation part-sponsored by the World Bank, the Overseas Development Institute, which not surprisingly, refused to publish the original highly critical report which she submitted to the ODI in the late 1960s on the performance of aid in Latin America. This became the manuscript published as *Aid as Imperialism*. Let us look briefly at the way the IMF conditions help to weaken and destabilise the Third World economy.

The IMF functions as an international credit agency sponsored by developed capitalist states. All contributing states may veto investment and loans to a country if the applicant does not agree to conform to IMF conditions. That is, the IMF will only grant credit if the borrowing country institutes a 'stabilisation programme' to control inflation, the assumption being that inflation generates a balance of payment crisis. The conventional IMF conditions include:

(i) anti-inflationary policies – such as reducing government spending and bank credit;

(ii) the devaluation of the borrower's currency – to promote exports;
(iii) the development of 'incentives' for foreign investment by such policies as anti-strike legislation, tax benefits, and guarantees regarding profit repatriation.

As Payer (1974) shows however, the combined effect of these conditions is to increase the dependency on traditional primary product exports, which she argues convincingly is the real cause of instability in the first place, inflation being merely a *symptom*. Thus, deflation reduces government investment in domestic businesses which rely on public finance and hence may be forced to sell to foreign capital; secondly, the devaluation of the currency increases the costs of inputs that accompany foreign business and immediately raises the cost of repaying the IMF loan. Payer points to many cases where IMF aid has actually increased economic dependence and so instability. Hence it is difficult to see the logic of theorists such as Bauer who argue that aid makes the local population complacent and idle receiving 'benefit' from an international system of social security. Clearly in many cases the advent of aid exacerbates social and economic insecurity. A more recent study (Williamson, 1983) of the current impact of IMF conditions on the Brazilian economy confirms Payer's earlier argument.

Other criticisms made by the radical theorists concentrate on the social and political effect it has in the Third World. They argue that aid is used as a short-term prop to support unstable governments whose continued existence is to the strategic interest of the West. A recent detailed study of the funding by the World Bank of the Marcos dictatorship in the Philippines over the past decade provides a clear discussion of how this support can be provided (Bello *et al.*, 1982). Aid is said to create a subservient bourgeoisie who, in their dependence on foreign investment become political allies of capitalist states in the North and so provide a strong (though not insurmountable – as in Nicaragua) barrier to any attempts by poorer people within the Third World to challenge the status quo. That is, they are counter-revolutionary elites. Moreover, the local elites will use their access to aid capital not only to line their own pockets and sustain their power but will buy off subordinates in the government and civil service as well, as we noted earlier, consolidate their relationship with the richer farmers by directing most rural aid capital or technology in their direction. Thus, in short, as Hayter argues in a later text (1981, p. 95):

> It is exceedingly unlikely that any government in an under-developed country will act to eradicate poverty except under pressure.

This later text by Hayter is an attack on the first 'Brandt Report' (1979) that recommended a doubling of aid and increased lending facilities for the Third World to draw capital from the World Bank and IMF. The Brandt commission argued that it was in the interests of both North and South to encourage development in the Third World. Hayter saw the process more one-sided in the interests of the North, aid itself simply creating more world poverty.

The radical critique of aid has become conventional wisdom for most *dependency* theorists today. It has much to commend it particularly in terms of its situating the development of aid in the context of neo-colonialism thereby linking it to other aspects of neo-colonialism such as the exploitation of the Third World surplus by private MNC capital. Furthermore, like Bauer's argument previously, it draws attention to the political patronage and corruption aid engenders in Third World countries and the disadvantages experienced by those without power, the rural masses. Its strongest point is its detailed analysis of the actual operation of aid organisations and their destabilising economic influence. This is something that Bauer's argument lacks. It is quite clear from Payer's contribution that IMF treatment of the Third World can be, and is indeed likely to be, exceptionally damaging to its social and political structure.

However as with dependency theory the radical critique leaves little room for the prospect of Third World industrial or rural workers actually doing something about their disadvantages. While Hayter (1971, p. 192) argues that 'under socialism, and with the principles of international solidarity operating in full vigour, things will be different', it is not clear how or where (in the centre or Third World?) such principles are to be established. A similar criticism has been made of Frank's (1971) earlier analysis. In addition, the radical critique tends to suffer from the same problem identified in dependency theory, namely, the implication that the Third World economies will remain *stagnant* in their underdevelopment. There is no room here for a 'progressive' even though exploitative role for capitalist penetration which Warren perceives.

We have seen that for different reasons both Bauer and Hayter see aid as an obstacle to Third World development. For Bauer it works against the efficient use of capital, for Hayter it is another means whereby Third World resources are extracted by western capitalism. Both could be right: that is, one could argue that as a form of neo-colonialism aid does work on behalf of the capitalist industrialised centre but not as effectively, or to use Warren's term, 'progressively' as it could do were it to become more directly involved in capitalist production in Third World agriculture and industry, promoting new capitalist markets in the poor countries of today. This, of course, would have major implications for the present structure of economic and political power in the world. We shall return to this in Chapter 9.

7.4 CONCLUSION

Despite continued attacks by right and left on aid, it continues to arrive in and be requested by the Third World. The problems of aid are seen by the donors as matters of mismanagement rather than anything to do with the workings of a world capitalist economy which exploits the Third World. Indeed, the EEC Development Agency sees the economic and political divisions in the world, particularly those that surface in the perennial North–South conferences, as petty minded and childish bickering, which obscures the 'real issues' and closes the door to 'true growth'. Perhaps though, rather than disguising the real issues, political disputes about economic inequalities between North and South *are* a direct indicator of the real divisions that operate within and sustain the world economy. The progressive notion of texts like the Brandt Reports, *North–South* (1980) and *Common Crisis* (1983), that we can create the conditions for interdependent development is a highly appealing but perhaps misconstrued basis for action to alleviate world poverty. It may be much better to argue that aid should be given as advice/training for subsequent self-reliance so that rural and urban workers can *regain* control over their livelihoods.

It is this notion of 'self-reliance' which is an important element of the philosophy behind the movement for the introduction of 'intermediate' or 'appropriate technology' that is gaining momentum in the Third World. It is hoped that this cheap self-reliant technology will help poorer countries to security without incurring more of the problems – such as increasing debt – which have bedevilled them to date. This movement is also linked to a general ecological critique of industrialisation and the goal of unlimited economic growth. The following chapter looks at the background to this movement and the impact it has had on the Third World.

8

Critique of Industrialisation

8.1 INTRODUCTION

This chapter examines, briefly, a range of related ideas or schools of thought that could in terms of conventional thinking be described as 'anti-development', that is if 'development' is to be conceived of as the expansion of industry, capitalism and urban growth. This critique of industrialisation has taken a number of forms. We first look at the emergence and current appeal of a *populist rural socialism* that has its roots in early nineteenth century Europe, even though it was not to flourish there. Its principal impact has been in Tanzania and to a lesser extent in China and these two countries provide the focus for our discussion of populism which draws on the exceptionally valuable analysis of Kitching (1982). We then move on to our second critique of industrialisation, that which comes from the *ecological movement*, which in its attempt to defend the environment from the ravages of modern industry has within it an implicit critique of capitalist development. Its many recommendations for improving the quality of the environment often require a check on further capitalist industrial growth and even a complete end to the environmentally most damaging forms it takes. What is offered as an alternative is the construction of a less wasteful, less polluting and less 'soul-destroying' system of production based on 'intermediate' forms of technology. This becomes the focus of the discussion in the third section of the chapter which looks at the philosophy behind *alternative technology* and gives some examples of it in action in the Third World where some hope that its low cost and labour-intensive character will allow a system of production that is affordable and geared to high employment and local needs, suggesting the possibility of self-reliant (dependency-free) 'development'.

8.2 THE POPULIST CHALLENGE TO INDUSTRIALISATION

Wherever nineteenth century capitalist manufacturing sought to establish itself it met resistance, not only from the traditional landed elite threatened by the new power of the industrialists but also and more concertedly from the lower social classes whose labour power it sought to harness and exploit. The state and employers combined to control the opposition from the workforce which was most acute in the first half of the nineteenth century particularly in Britain, involving mass demonstrations against low wages, the wrecking of machinery and the burning of mills. The army, police and law were used as weapons to quell this working class opposition, many workers being killed, seriously injured or imprisoned as a result. Liberal and early socialist intellectuals were alarmed by the social disorder, deprivation and urban squalor that accompanied the onset of capitalist manufacture. Some argued strongly in favour of small scale industrial enterprise sited in rural communities under the communal control of 'free and equal' workers. Theorists of such rural co-operatives certainly envisaged a growth in economic wealth but this was to be redistributed equally throughout the workforce. 'Development' could occur then, under the control of village artisans and farmers rather than through the anarchy and horrors of rampant industrial capitalism or through the bureaucratic excesses of central government. In this context populist socialism meant the development of small-scale enterprises under the control of the (primarily rural) people who worked them.

Some of the more prominent early nineteenth century representatives of this populist socialism include Robert Owen in Britain, Proudhon in France, and Herzen in Russia. Owen's ideas are in many ways typical of them all inasmuch as he proposed – and made a start in building in New Lanark – villages of co-operative production, 'the co-operative Commonwealth', that would avoid the evils of urbanisation and unchecked factory production. Owen envisaged a number of industrial villages characterised by humane management, good pay and reduced working hours, decent sanitation and housing, village children being educated by members of the community. Such was the appeal and innovation of Owen's work that as many as 20 000 visited New Lanark including politicians, administrators and benefactors from Britain and elsewhere. For the villagers Owen's ideas raised the possibility of a new, egalitarian industrial order on a human-scale; as Tawney (1966, p. 39) says,

> In the eyes of thoughtful wage-earners Owen was the prophet who had laid his finger on the mystery of iniquity, and had preached a fraternal gospel by which the capitalist demon could be brought to heel.

But Owenism gradually lost any hope of becoming a national populist movement in face of the onslaught of capitalist manufacturing and the comparative indifference of the British government to support its principles. Social opposition to the 'capitalist demon' could only become effective when emergent from the ranks of ordinary workers themselves, whose early militancy against employers led to the formation of the first trades unions. Owen's policies represented the tradition of enlightened individualist philanthropy against social ills, except that it took on a force or 'demon', namely capitalism, which was beyond any one individual's control. Owen and most other European populists were proposing something that was not possible given the dramatic change in the social and economic relations of production then occurring: they sought to 'develop' society through raising productivity but within the social constraints of village life.

Yet ideas of this sort were not to be completely lost to history. Even outside populist socialist thought one still finds traces of anti-urbanism, and anti-industrialism. Current planning policies for new towns favour restricted industrial zones neatly screened from green suburban residential areas. Similarly, elements of anti-industrialism can be found in most children's books which make virtually no reference to industrial settings and tend instead to romanticise the countryside: as Mellor (1982, p. 67) neatly summarises,

> From their earliest years children are brought up with fairy

> stories from pre-industrial cultures, rural whimsy and farmyard fantasy, and tales of children exploring rivers, fields and moorlands rather than urban parks, canals, cleared sites or derelict railways.

The favoured image in the industrial society is of a 'green and pleasant land'.

In the Third World, it *is* the countryside, the rural village life of predominantly agrarian societies that is the routine reality for many people. For most however life is also harsh and indeed virtually unsustainable as absolute poverty overcomes entire communities – there is no room here for a romanticised version of country living. Yet clearly, for many post-independence leaders the rural nature of their societies is the fact which has to be uppermost in their minds when formulating their 'development' policies. There are some governments, such as those of India and Brazil, that have responded to this state of affairs by promoting commercial agricultural programmes in rural regions while investing heavily in the construction of modern industrial centres hoping that the latter will provide the principal impetus for development. There are a few others however that have explicitly adopted a rural-based populist socialism that is not far removed from some of the nineteenth century ideas we saw above.

Tanzania in East Africa is the best example of a country that tried to take an anti-capitalist, anti-urban road under the charismatic leadership of Julius Nyerere, President, 1961–86. One might suggest that Nyerere had the political power that a figure like Robert Owen would have liked, to establish a national programme of co-operative socialism. Apart from Tanzania, it is often claimed that China provides another important example of self-reliant rural development along populist socialist lines. While there is some truth in this, as Kitching (1982) correctly observes China's road is not in essence populist but instead heavily reliant on the direction of the people by a strong central state. While Tanzania has recorded some important advances such as the universal provision of primary education, in comparison with China its self-reliant policies for development have failed. This indicates that much can be learned from comparing these two countries about the sort of conditions that will make self-reliant rural based socialism a viable programme for 'development'.

Independence for Tanzania (in 1961) did not usher in a period of economic prosperity. By the mid-1960s the growth-oriented development model it had adopted in common with many other ex-colonies created more problems than success for the economy. Revenue from cash-crops had declined as world prices fell and in the urban regions there were too few jobs available for the students from prosperous families. The students' discontent was something Nyerere had to deal with. Instead of capitulating to the interests of this privileged minority, Nyerere and his party (TANU) called for a completely different approach to 'development', outlined in the policy document issued in 1967 as the *Arusha Declaration* and Nyerere's text *Socialism and Rural Development*. These laid out the principles for a policy of rural-based populist socialism built through village co-operatives, the '*ujamaa*' or 'familyhood' village scheme. The principles established the need for state control over industry to forestall the emergence of an exploitative industrial class, the need to place the agricultural resources of the country in the hands of the peasantry, and abandoned the pursuit of 'development' requiring heavy capital investment particularly through foreign aid, which led to indebtedness and sustained dependency; as the *Arusha Declaration* said, 'We made a mistake in choosing money – something we do not have – to be the big instrument of our development.' Instead, the basis for a self-reliant development became 'the people and their hard work, especially in agriculture'.

Much of Nyerere's policies rested on the proposition that the rural socialism he advocated was in fact no more than what was 'natural' to the African: it was a mere extension of the traditional, pre-colonial way of doing things communally in kin-based villages which had been temporarily lost or displaced during the colonial era. He was basing the whole viability of his policy on the success of his appeal to an African communalism which needed no instruction or political education to emerge. This was Nyerere's populist claim, the *inherently* socialist character of traditional African people. The class divisions of capitalism that appeared during the colonial phase were an aberration and distortion of the African people's true class-free social bond. The *ujamaa* village system would be the means of recapturing this lost heritage, a village system in which people would respect each other, share communal property and the produce and income it yields, work hard, and accept low standards of living for many years to come. For Nyerere, this path was the only one open to Tanzania, whose poverty and external dependency could only be overcome by an approach that could rekindle communalism mobilising the only resources available, land and labour. In his call for Tanzanians to recapture their native socialism, Nyerere explicitly moved away from the classical Marxist theory that proposes that socialism is born out of the class conflict of capitalism. Nyerere's approach depended on the peasants realising socialism through their own local initiatives and not through organised class action nor through strong state direction.

The *ujamaa* scheme created many thousands of rural settlements comprising at least two hundred and fifty households on average, each house having a small private plot of land while a communal farm area was established in a central clearing. By 1976 virtually all (about thirteen million) of the peasantry were resident in these villages, some of which had been purpose-built, while others were established by the simple act of designating existing residential areas as either co-operative *ujamaa* villages or just 'villages'. Each village is supposed to have had a full-time manager to help co-ordinate production and to ensure that the children receive proper education. Produce is sold to village agents working for the government marketing board.

Has this policy of rural socialism been successful? Most commentators such as Saul (1977) and Kitching (1982) do not think so. There have been a number of factors which have not encouraged a smooth implementation of the *ujamaa* scheme and which have seriously weakened the Tanzanian economy in the past decade or so, such as a period of falling coffee prices in the early 1970s, bad harvest due to adverse weather and increasing oil prices after 1973. These the politicians have had little or no control over. But Kitching also argues that the government's whole strategy has been doubly flawed. First, he argues that Nyerere's faith in a resurrected African socialism was naive: there is little to suggest that it ever really existed, and the speed of the *ujamaa* programme meant bewilderment, bad organisation and under-resourced settlements, circumstances hardly conducive for realising 'community'. There were very few signs of peasants taking the government's lead and initiating village communes. Those who did set about this task were mainly, though not exclusively, urban people who had

had experience of industrial labour and trade union organisation. Kitching suggests that without this sort of industrial experience to draw on, or without strong state direction, the communal socialism of Tanzania is not likely to grow.

Secondly, Nyerere's settlement scheme depended on a widespread distribution of resources to meet the primary farming requirements of the villages. Basic tools like spades, hoes, ploughs (plus oxen), and seed and fertiliser were all needed for the communal plots especially in less fertile regions. Most villages did not receive adequate supplies. In addition many who were resettled as 'farmers' lacked farming knowledge despite the rural development official's advice being available. In such conditions little real progress could be made: as Kitching (1982, p. 113) remarks,

> As a result ... the experience of communal production was almost totally negative, and rapidly productive of either hostility, or, more frequently, indifference, and a speedy return to concentration on private plots.

Shortages in basic items arose because of Nyerere's commitment to sharing on an equal basis whatever resources Tanzania had. This meant spreading out a very low resource base such that, according to Kitching, 'critical minimum levels, necessary for any effective impact, have not been obtained anywhere'. As a consequence, the Tanzania of the 1980s has found itself turning back to the international financiers to purchase necessary imports for the agricultural settlements. As in the early 1960s, Tanzania is now dependent on overseas capital and foreign aid. Self-reliant populist socialism is very far from the reality in Tanzania today.

How, then, does the Tanzanian experience compare with that of China? We do not intend to offer a detailed answer to this question here, but we can identify two aspects of China's socialist programme that distinguish it from Tanzania and which have been of great importance in enabling the state to employ, house, feed, and physically care for a population now in excess of one thousand million. First, unlike Tanzania, China has developed and used the agencies of a strong state – the army and party workers – to mobilise, train and work with rural peasants without assuming the latter to be 'naturally' inspired by a co-operative socialism.

Secondly, and again in contrast with Tanzania, China does have a productive and relatively large industrial sector, found primarily in the Manchurian region constructed with Soviet aid in the 1950s. This has not only encouraged a wider spread of skills which have been taken into the countryside but also provided the implements, fertilisers and other technology needed by the agricultural communes to maintain production while the population has increased.

The comparison with China is instructive, suggests Kitching, for it implies that *socialist* development policy in the Third World, while avoiding the deprivations of capitalism, can only hope to overcome rural poverty through *strong state intervention and the establishment of an effective industrial sector*. Populist socialism which as we have seen turns away from state collectivism and industrialisation is unlikely therefore to be an effective instrument in the alleviation of Third World poverty. As Kitching says, we should not glibly dismiss Tanzanian efforts since 1967 as total failure: the country has at least developed a sound primary education service for all, and, were coffee prices on the international market to improve, more revenue would be forthcoming making it more feasible to provide resources for the village settlements.

Since Nyerere's retirement in 1986, the loss of his charismatic leadership has created difficulties for the ruling political party. Without a strong state bureaucracy and party structures – such as used by China to carry the country forward after the death of the charismatic Mao – Tanzania is likely to experience a period of considerable political instability. At the same time, the interlocking political, bureaucratic and military authority of a state such as China can militate against the gradual process of economic and political reform, whether initiated 'from above' or 'from below'. The danger then is that reformist movements, such as that inspired by China's students in 1989, have no institutional forum in which to register their views and suffer repression at the hands of a state hostile towards institutional change.

8.3 THE ECOLOGICAL CRITIQUE OF INDUSTRIALISATION

One of the features of the populist rural strategy in Tanzania has been the stress placed on using basic, inexpensive forms of technology to produce the country's needs in working towards self-reliance. The concept of self-reliance not only implies breaking the tie of dependency on the industrial centre but also an acceptance of the need to use available resources as efficiently and frugally as possible. Similar principles underlie the Chinese approach to production.

In the case of Tanzania and China this careful use of resources is seen as an economic necessity. There are many people who now argue that all countries, rich and poor, should regard their resources and the environment as precious because they will not last forever, so care in their exploitation is not only an economic but also a social and ecological necessity.

The demand for ecological awareness has become a significant political issue in advanced industrial societies. The new 'green movement' in politics has played an important part in recent European elections, and government policy makers have to attend to the environmentalist lobby in planning decisions.

In Germany as many as 10 per cent of voters voted for the Green Party in 1987, and in European elections in 1989 the Greens secured thirty-two seats in the European Parliament. Pressure groups such as Greenpeace and Friends of the Earth have highlighted the environmental degradation caused by nuclear power, chemical pollution and agribusiness.

The literature on environmental issues is vast and no attempt can be made here to discuss the depth or range of the debates: all we shall do is look at some of the themes that seem to crop up most often. Three have been selected which bear most directly on the critique of industrialisation that interests us in this chapter.

The first theme is that the world cannot physically sustain present rates of economic growth and industrial development since the resources this requires are simply not available. This is true even though the Third World is relatively undemanding of resources, in particular, of energy. If the Third World were to industrialise along capitalist lines, as Warren suggests is possible, the strain on world resources would increase dramatically. This would cause not only excessive ecological damage but also political instability as currently dominant states would seek to preserve their access to raw materials in the Third World. That these resources are crucial for any sustained industrialisation of the West is evident from statistical data: for example, although the Caribbean as a whole accounts for almost 40 per cent of world bauxite production little of the aluminium that this produces (less than 1 per cent) is actually consumed within the Caribbean: the United States however, consumes about 33 per cent of world aluminium even though it mines only 2.8 per cent of world bauxite (see Girvan, 1976).

Independent of these problems in the future there are those who argue that further industrial development, wherever it may be, brings the world closer to that point at which economic expansion means global ecological disaster, unrestrained growth bringing a sudden ecological collapse in the capacity of the planet to sustain humanity. The message here is that the ecological system cannot tolerate increasing growth: there must therefore be 'limits to growth'. Meadows (1972) provided one of the first detailed expositions of this view, and the same year saw the editors of *The Ecologist* produce the now famous *Blueprint for Survival*. Both studies make exceedingly alarming – some would say alarmist – projections about the depletion of resources, such as Meadows comment that 'within 50 years, at rates of consumption most valuable minerals and metals will be completely exhausted'. There are alternative scenarios which doubt that access to resources will be a major problem in the future. For example, critics of the limits to growth thesis argue that there are new sources of energy – such as nuclear or solar power, and materials – such as fibre optics to replace copper wiring, that make doom-laden forecasts unnecessary. Whom are we to believe? Each side has apparently firm scientific data on which to base its projections, yet such data clearly does not speak for itself or we would presumably have a relatively clear scientific consensus on the issue. Each side of course interprets data differently and stresses those factors it thinks suits its particular case. The debate over resources is well summarised by McCutcheon (1979) and will not detain us here. What is significant is that this ecological concern over resource use has had relatively little impact on the actual way production is accomplished in most industrial economies. No state to date has yet formulated a policy for monitoring or overseeing the use and processing of natural resources. Priority for resource use is given to the self-determined interests of commercial manufacturing rather than being established according to a long term national plan that balances commercial interests against a caring use of resources. Much of the conservation measures now seen such as bottle banks only appear when they can be made into commercial, profitable ventures. Many of these ventures are locally rather than nationally inspired: at the national level little is done. In the United Kingdom, for example, despite there being a Department of the Environment and numerous parliamentary select committees of inquiry into energy, there is effectively no national energy policy at work, as recent work by Sweet (1983) has shown.

While the ecological critique of industrial development is, therefore, of value in drawing attention to resource depletion it has had little to offer by way of a sociological or political analysis of the way decisions are made about resource use. It is this arena of often *ad hoc* policy making that needs to be investigated if one wants to understand and influence this aspect of 'development'.

A second theme that figures in the environmentalist literature is that the world cannot tolerate the levels of pollution now associated with large scale industrial production. For example, an apparently clear blue sky carries increasingly harmful levels of carbon monoxide and sulphur dioxide, the latter falling as 'acid rain', polluting land, vegetation, lakes and rivers. It also appears that the 'clear blue sky' has a large and growing 'hole' in it located over the Antarctic region, as the ozone layer is rapidly depleted there due to the impact of chlorofluorocarbons (CFCs) in the stratosphere. First developed in the 1930s as 'hazard free', chemically stable substances, CFCs have been used as propellents in aerosol cans, for refrigeration and certain forms of plastic foam. They are now seen as the source of increased skin cancer as more ultraviolet light penetrates the thinner ozone.

Pollution is also to be found in modern agriculture with the increasing use of herbicides and pesticides in intensive farming. Ecologists argue that often the expansion of food production by such farming methods is wasteful and harmful. Intensive farming has overworked the fertility of the soil and meant that farmers resort to more and more fertiliser and pesticide to sustain their yields. Moreover, there is some evidence that indicates that the energy used to make all these chemical inputs and to drive modern farm machinery is greater than the energy or calorific value of the resultant crop: more energy input for lower energy output. Intensive arable farming – such as the 'prairie farms' of the US – is said to be particularly wasteful since the grain produced is typically

The oft-quoted statistic ...

The often-quoted statistic that one American farmer now feeds forty-eight other people also ignores the economic costs, especially now that the epoch of cheap oil is over; the equivalent of 80 gallons of fuel to produce an acre of corn, and an even more wasteful use of energy to produce meat. Paradoxically, while farm exports pay for more than half US oil imports, for every dollar's worth of farm exports in 1980, American agriculture used the equivalent of 25 cents of imported oil. To this global irrationality, there has to be added energy-production ratios which make Western agriculture 'one of the least efficient in history':

> Asian wet rice cultivation yields 5 to 50 food calories for each calorie of energy invested. The Western system requires 5 to 10 calories to obtain one food calorie

Source: P. Worsley, *The Three Worlds* (pp. 164–5).

processed to become feedstuff for animals, especially beef and dairy herds: twenty pounds of grain protein are needed to produce one pound of meat protein. In addition, the use of pesticides is criticised inasmuch as many pests are becoming increasingly resistant to pesticides and the latter are building up in the food chain, threatening other animals including humankind. Finally, environmentalists point out that the occupational hazards associated with the production and use of these chemicals are often unacceptably and unnecessarily high: for example, an important herbicide, 2-4-5T is sometimes manufactured according to a process which gives off a highly toxic by-product, dioxin; it is possible to produce the chemical more cleanly without the dioxin waste and without extra expense. The dangers of dioxin contamination are well known to the residents of Seveso in Italy who in 1976 were exposed to it following an explosion in a neighbouring factory.

A third theme found in the environmentalist critique is that industrial development has spawned a type of technology that has a dehumanising effect, in the workplace and beyond. The critics argue that the technology of the productive system is indifferent or even callous with regard to people's needs, destructive of the human spirit, and alienates people from their work and each other. This critique has a long pedigree: similar comments were made by liberals and radicals of the past such as Adam Smith and

Karl Marx. While the first and second criticisms of industrial development concern its destructive impact on *nature*, this third criticism highlights the damage it does to the *cultural* realm.

For some, modern technology seems to take on a life of its own; thus Reich (1979, p. 26) argues that, technology is 'a mindless juggernaut, destroying the environment, obliterating human values, and assuming domination over the lives and minds of its subject'. This 'juggernaut' seems to have little purpose: simply because the technology is developed it is put to work without asking whether it serves any social purpose. The technological means take precedence over social ends. At a general level many of the problems of today's society suggest a lack of control over technology and its practitioner experts, where decisions taken are often done so on a piecemeal basis where the increasing technical specialisation of knowledge makes it more difficult to co-ordinate as part of a coherent plan. More importantly, because of the fragmentation of expertise, no one group of specialists believes itself to be responsible for unanticipated and unwelcome results of its work. It is in response to this lack of ethical concern about the direction of science and technology that a minority of scientists have formed liberal and radical organisations such as the British Society for Social Responsibility in Science.

The ecological critique of industrialisation highlights the problems of declining resources, environmental destruction and cultural alienation. It argues for the use of renewable resources, conservation of finite ones, a reduction in pollution and a technology that is once more under people's control. This has led to calls for a more 'appropriate' form of technology, which is cheaper, and environmentally and socially 'non-violent'. It is argued that this alternative technology should be gradually introduced in advanced societies as they wind down their economic growth, and more rapidly installed in the Third World before it suffers the environmental and social harms of full industrialisation. Let us look briefly at this alternative technology in the final section of this chapter.

8.4 ALTERNATIVE TECHNOLOGY

'Simplicity, cheapness, smallness, and non-violence': these are the features of an alternative technology as identified by one of the most important advocates for radical technological change, E. F. Schumacher whose book *Small is Beautiful*, (1973) has become a virtual bible for the growing alternative technology movement.

Schumacher's ideas were developed after visiting India in 1961 to advise its government on the establishment of small scale industrial concerns that could be set up in rural regions to generate employment. Subsequently Schumacher formed the Intermediate Technology Development Group (ITDG) based in London whose brief is to identify and develop forms of technology that will be most appropriate for the Third World where capital is scarce, labour abundant and resources finite. Despite Schumacher's death in 1977 the Group has continued to develop and now has many hundreds of people in Britain and overseas contributing ideas for action which are then made available to Third World organisations and governments. As a charity it relies on support from many sources, though the British government contributes each year about £2 million to its funds.

Instead of the destructive and ecologically violent system of mass production, Schumacher proposes a 'technology of production by the masses', which is, as he says (1973, p. 143),

> conducive to decentralisation, compatible with the laws of ecology, gentle in its use of scarce resources, and designed to serve the human person instead of making him the servant of machines. I have named it intermediate technology, to signify that it is vastly superior to the primitive technology of bygone ages but at the same time much simpler, cheaper and freer than the super-technology of the rich.

Accordingly, he urges the development of small scale industrial enterprises which have four features:

(i) Workplaces should be created in areas where people live;
(ii) Workplaces should need neither large capital investment nor costly imports to operate;
(iii) Production techniques should be fairly simple so demands for high skills are kept low;
(iv) Production should try to use local materials and be for local use.

As we saw in section 8.1, similar ideas have been advanced by the populist socialist critique of industrialisation: both favour decentralised small-scale enterprise, location in rural areas, under local control and non-destructive use of the environment. Schumacher's thesis also shares with the populist approach a critique of capitalism although he never explicitly advocates its removal by radical revolution. Instead he offers a sort of compromise that gives a degree of control over the direction of capitalist production. He suggests that large scale industrial corporations should allow 50 per cent of their share capital to be held publicly by what he terms 'Social Councils', locally appointed groups made up of trade unionists, employers, and other community members, who would use the share dividend revenue to invest in the 'vital social needs' of the community, something which private capital could never be relied on to do. There would be no compensation for this partial change in ownership: insted, companies would have to pay no taxes to the state. Moreover, Schumacher dismisses any possible complaint that this places an excess burden on the private sector since the latter already gains substantial material benefit from the public provision of 'infrastructure' at comparatively little (and often no) real cost – that is, roads, energy services, educated personnel, and so on. Private management would still run the company but would have to allow members of the 'Council' to inspect their books and observe Board meetings. He argues that this policy is as applicable in developed as it is in the Third World countries.

That this claim is not entirely utopian can be demonstrated by examining the work of the ITDG whose activities have been summarised by McRobie's book *Small is Possible* (1980). Research centres based on an approach similar to that of Schumacher have been established throughout the world. For example in Britain the Centre for Alternative Industrial and Technological System (CAITS) provides an important locus for the development of 'socially useful technologies' combining the skills and knowledge of industrial workers and academics. It was founded by workers from the Lucas Aerospace Corporation (which has major interests in military technology), who, threatened with large scale job losses, developed a highly detailed Plan for the corporation, proposing new, socially useful (as well as commercially viable) products, which would ensure employment. The Plan comprises over 1000 pages of technical details, costings, drawings and other information for the development of over 150 products, including heat pumps, solar units, deep sea diving gear, windmill energy sources and so on. The foundation of CAITS in 1978, as Wainwright and Elliott (1983) show, was very much a result of the rejection by the Lucas management of the workers' proposals, in particular their desire to have a greater say in the direction of the company, an increase in worker control seen as a direct threat by executives.

In the Third World, however, much has been done to implement forms of intermediate technology. There are numerous examples to be found of cheap, labour intensive devices which as Harrison (1980, p. 142) notes, have meant

> improving an existing traditional technique, modifying a modern machine, inventing a new one from scratch, digging out a piece of antique Western technology from industrial archaeology, or finding a particularly ingenious bit of indigenous wisdom working in a small area and spreading it abroad.

One of the most important needs in the Third World is a good water supply. When water shortages occur the result may be failed harvests, food shortages, and as we have seen when linked to low income, famine. Large, expensive dams are not the appropriate technological answer to this problem since they carry economic and social costs which poor countries cannot bear. Small water collection tanks holding up to 100,000 gallons are more useful as are the cheap water pumps that are available to move the water to where it is needed. Some pumps are of old design others more recent: one of the recent types developed through the ITDG is the 'underwater windmill' – a form of water turbine whose blades lie horizontally in a river turned by its flow. The pump is inexpensive and easy to make locally and has astounding power: a 3 foot diameter underwater turbine has as much power as a 60 foot diameter traditional water wheel.

Nevertheless, the introduction of alternative technology is no simple technical matter, however apparently suitable it is to local needs. Social factors intervene; for example, some of the proposals cut across class boundaries so making implementation very difficult where it threatens class interests. The development of cheap biogas plants using animal waste to produce pollutant-free methane gas and fertiliser relies on a steady supply of cow dung; often only richer farmers own cattle and many have been reluctant to provide the animal waste that will benefit poorer classes in the community. In Africa, farmers have tended to buy the technology for their own use, and the dung, which was once freely available and dried as a fuel for cooking, now has commercial value, and like water for those in shanty towns, has become an expense many find difficult to meet. In the context of the subsistence resources of poor families fuel costs are high: as McRobie (1980, p. 54) says, in some communities 'what goes under the pot costs more than what goes inside it'.

While social factors need, then, to be considered, Clark (1985) argues that there may be circumstances prevailing which economically may limit the value of 'appropriate technology'. For example, although appropriate technology presumes that labour-intensive technologies are always to be desired, Clark points out that 'even if labour-intensive techniques do exist and could be adopted, policies promoting them would lead to technological stagnation since the potential for improving on them is strictly limited' (p. 187).

The introduction of new forms of technology has therefore to contend with prevailing socio-economic conditions. Harrison (1980) argues that any attempt to promote development in the Third world, whether using intermediate technology, will only be successful if it meets the basic social requirement of encouraging local people to participate as fully as possible in the direction, planning and benefits of projects, though he adds that people still need 'material and technical help from above' and, we may suggest, political support and direction from the state, if our comparison of Tanzania and China is to be instructive. Schumacher himself recognises the need for considerable state activity in the enactment and enforcement of the necessary legislation associated with the transfer of corporation property to the 'Social Councils'. As he correctly observes, technological changes of the sort envisaged here are *political* as well as economic in the implicit challenge they pose to the distribution of power in society.

8.5 CONCLUSION

The three critiques of industrialisation outlined in this chapter, populist, ecological and technological, have made valuable contributions towards a policy for a more 'human', less destructive process of 'development'. Yet, as we have indicated, they have had relatively marginal impact as either economic theory, political philosophy, or social movement. This is perhaps because they all fail to give sufficient attention to an analysis of the *social relations* of production that lie behind the industrialisation process. What Tawney (1966) said of Owenism in Britain is true of all three critiques of industrialisation, that is, they, in their different ways, promise to bring 'the capitalist demon' to heel without actually squeezing the life out of it. Capitalist relations essentially remain intact in the analysis. The populist socialism of Tanzania has thus failed to check the re-emergence of dependency on overseas capital and overcome poor economic performance; ecologism seeks a reduction in the environmental damage of industrialisation without going sufficiently far in its analyses of the potential national and international socio-economic implications this would have if the current pattern of resource control and usage was fundamentally altered. Finally, the Schumacherian proposals for an intermediate technology are unlikely to be widely implemented unless wholesale rather than partial changes in the structure of property and work relations are made, as is evident from the failure to implement the Lucas Workers' Plan in Britain. It is perhaps the comparative failure of intermediate technology in the advanced countries that has led many of its proponents in the West to have greater hope for its establishment in the Third World. However, they have yet to give proper consideration to the possibility of this being a viable developmental alternative, given the international context of dependency and multi-national corporation influence.

Despite, then, the exceptionally valuable analysis of the social, economic and environmental problems of our time, these critiques do not go far enough in their diagnosis of the source of such problems: to borrow a remark from one of Osborne's plays, they seek the removal of 'the symptoms of the disease but not the disease itself'.

For such a diagnosis we have to return to the major accounts of 'development' discussed in the book. This is the task of the final chapter which summarises these accounts and their views about the possibility for 'development' in the future.

9

Conclusion

9.1 INTRODUCTION

This book has explored different conceptions of 'development' and explanation for world inequality and Third World disadvantage. Accounts vary as to the 'problem' of development and what solution might be appropriate. We saw, for example, differing conceptions of the 'problems' of population, development planning, political instability and limited industrial growth. Modernisation theory and underdevelopment theory (in its various forms) have framed much of the analysis. We have also seen how a third approach, that of the ecological, populist critique of industrialisation, shapes the development debate, raising vital environmental and social problems ignored by the first two.

The central question running through all of this is, of course, whether the Third World can 'develop' and if so, what direction it should take? As we have seen, the Third World is made up of very different types of society, some better placed in both global and national terms to industrialise according to their own development plans. Some of the most successful countries include Mexico, Brazil, South Korea and India, where, for example, growth in manufacturing has been sustained over many years. It has been suggested, for instance, that the South Korean economy will continue to grow such that by 2010 its GNP (both absolute and per capita) will be greater than Britain's.

Yet even this development success has been accompanied by continuing political instability, by massive borrowing (Mexico, Brazil and South Korea are the world's most indebted countries) and severe poverty for many of the local people.

Development, then, seems to carry continuing costs for many in the Third World. Are these temporary or chronic? What is the best way of dealing with them? In this final chapter we shall explore the different strategies for development advocated by the three 'development' models discussed in the book, and conclude by considering the relative strengths of capitalism and socialism as alternative routes to development.

9.2 DEVELOPMENT MODELS AND POLICIES

The Models

The Tradition/Modernity Model of Modernisation Theory

This model was discussed and criticised in detail in Chapter 3. Among others, theorists such as Parsons (1966), Eisenstadt (1966), Lerner (1964), and Bauer (1981) advance the view that modernisation is primarily a *cultural* process which involves the adoption of values and attitudes suited to entrepreneurial ambition, innovation, rationality, and achievement orientation in place of the contrary values and lifestyle of 'traditional' society. Societies are at different stages of development according to the extent to which they have institutionalised, that is established as expected behaviour, the sort of social action these modern values dictate – for example, achievement rather than ascription as the basis for the allocation of reward. Thus, poorer, less developed societies are so because of the comparative absence of modern value-orientations. Third World development is said to occur through both the *diffusion* of ideas and values from the West and through the '*logic of industrialism*' which will push aside the cultural obstacles of traditionalism and so make the Third World 'modern', which also means 'Western' in character.

The Model of Capitalist Underdevelopment

This model was discussed and criticised in Chapter 4. In fact it carries a number of versions of Marxist and neo- (even post-) Marxian analyses. The dependency theorists, especially via the work of Frank, Furtado, and Cardoso, argue that the Third World remains in a state of 'dependent' underdevelopment because its resources and 'surplus capital' is continually syphoned off by metropolitan states in the developed capitalist First World. The only way of shaking off these imperialist chains is through the peasantry and industrial working class removing the comprador bourgeoisie in the Third World and the subsequent establishment of a self-reliant socialist state.

Another version of underdevelopment theory has been provided by the neo-Marxian articulationist school which is critical of the dependency thesis. For articulationists (such as Taylor, Alavi and Wolpe) Third World underdevelopment can only be explained in terms of the structural relationship between First World capitalism and indigenous non-capitalist systems in the Third World. This relationship, or 'articulation', varies and determines the extent to which capitalism penetrates and displaces local economies. This articulation has cultural, political and economic effects within the Third World which are extremely varied. 'Dependency' is much too simplistic a notion to describe this state of affairs.

Lipton's work that we also saw in Chapter 4 represents in some way a bridge between underdevelopment theory and the 'alternative development' model which follows. He clearly accepts many of the arguments advanced by both schools but argues for an approach to development that cannot be placed neatly into the one or the other. His future image of a self-reliant mass-based agriculture with an attendant industrial sector is a recipe which many theorists regard as unworkable in the current global context.

The 'Alternative Development' Approach

This approach to the 'problem' of development was examined in the preceding chapter. The concept 'alternative development' is a 'catch-all' label for a range of ideas that differ in their focal concerns but which all propose alternatives to the capitalist, mass-production form of industrialisation that is currently established. This third approach, represented by the work of Schumacher (1973) in particular, is unlike the previous two schools of thought inasmuch as it is less an attempt to account for the passage of 'development' that has so far occurred, and more a prescription for what 'development' *should* be like. Clearly though, its recommendations are based on an assessment of the current 'problems' associated with unrestrained industrialisation and so it does offer a number of theoretical and historical propositions about 'where we went wrong'. The 'mistakes' have been, and continue to be, made on a number of fronts: industrial enterprise is too large, and its technology mind-numbing; the people lack control over their productive labour and suffer from the environmental and social damage the production system engenders; non-renewable resources are washed into the sea or disappear into thin air. This approach offers an alternative to industrialisation that would involve a significant *de-industrialisation* of the mass-production economies of today and the introduction of self-reliant, small scale technological systems in the Third World.

All three accounts offer very different diagnoses of the major problems and sources of strain facing the world today. What answers do they provide? What are the strategies for development, what one might loosely call the 'policies' for change that these three accounts recommend? Again we shall give a schematic, summary presentation of them for the sake of clarity.

The 'Policies'

The Policy of Modernisation Theory

Since modernisation theory is an advocate of the diffusion of competitive industrialism and its entrepreneurial ethic as the driving force of development its principal recommendations would be as follows:

(i) Give priority to encouraging international trade and foreign investment in the Third World and so gradually reduce aid programmes;
(ii) Encourage the development of 'modern' attitudes and entrepreneurial ambition to create an appropriate cultural medium in which modern economic institutions would thrive;
(iii) Promote development in the South since it is a crucial long-term market for goods manufactured in the North.

This model and its policies clearly presuppose that the world can tolerate an expansion of capitalist industrialisation, so long as this is done in a 'responsible' fashion, helping out those who are most unfortunate in times of serious difficulty. This approach can be said to fall within the broad pluralist perspective which seeks to combine a free-market capitalism with responsible government intervention at a national and international level to check any imbalances that might occur in the world economy. One text which epitomises this view is the Brandt Commission Report (1979). It argues that the relief of world poverty and thus the enhancing of world peace can only come about through increased trade on improved terms for the South; interdependence is the keynote:

> The South cannot grow adequately without the North. The North cannot prosper or improve its situation unless there is greater progress in the South (Brandt, 1979, p. 33).

The Policy of Underdevelopment Theory

i) Dependency Theory

Dependency theory rejects entirely the arguments advanced by Brandt of the need for greater co-operation between North and South as completely spurious, since an increase in trade and investment will drive the capitalist wedge deeper into the Third World and promote an *even greater* surplus transfer to the North. As underdevelopment is the *result* of ties with the capitalist metropole, the recommendations from dependency theory are:

(i) The Third World should break its links with capitalist metropolises;
(ii) That it should do this by challenging international capitalism, mainly by the working class removing the domestic comprador elite;
(iii) There should develop a policy of international solidarity between Third World countries in order to help each other to build an effectively *independent* industrial base in the South.

The policies advocated here are derived from the Marxian structuralist thesis that world capitalism is inherently contrary to people's real needs. Any expansion of trade and investment from the North merely accentuates the division between rich and poor not only on a world scale but also within the Third World itself, where the privileged commercial and white collar classes would simply enjoy even more prosperity. The Brandt recommendations are dismissed since the strategies they invoke 'are not designed to be translated into basic products and services for the moneyless poor, but rather for the moneyed spenders of the South' (Frank, 1980, p. 674). There is no conception here of some harmonious global future within a world capitalist system. The only way of removing poverty and satisfying people's needs is by a complete removal of this system. Until this is achieved, a policy of *collective self-reliance* should be pursued by all Third World countries. This policy is the official aim of many Third World 'socialist' governments, though many in reality find it exceptionally difficult to extract themselves from the capitalist world economy.

ii) Articulationism

According to this approach, the weakness of dependency theory is its failure to consider the growth, character and future role of social classes within the Third World. Frank and others are criticised for presenting an over-general world system perspective that ignores the local political and economic circumstances that prevail in the Third World, which in some conditions, foster the growth of capitalist structures, including most importantly an emergent bourgeoisie and working class. It is through the action of and conflict between such classes that further progressive development will occur, rather than awaiting the arrival of an internationally based socialist revolution.

Articulationism recognises the limited nature of Third World development, as we shall see in more detail in the discussion of Taylor's views below. But, unlike dependency theory, it avoids the *stagnationist* position of writers such as Frank. Some transitional capitalist development appears possible, as does thereby the emergence of a local working class that can constitute the basis of a local socialist movement against national and multinational capital. However, as we shall see below, the evidence for this actually happening is very limited.

The Policy of Appropriate Development

Unlike the models and policies of the preceding two theories that argue in their different ways for the industrialisation of the Third World, this third approach seeks to check industrial growth, arguing that many of the development problems in the Third

World are due to the introduction of unsuitable technologies from the North. Its 'policies' would include:

(i) A reordering of the priorities of production to ensure that the character and output of the enterprise is geared towards the interests of the whole community and the natural environment;
(ii) A reduction in the 'standard of living' in the affluent countries, especially the US, in order to achieve a redistribution of world resources in favour of the 'have-nots': the US with 6 per cent of world population should not be consuming 40 per cent of world energy supplies.
(iii) A major slow down in growth throughout the world economy for without this massive long term damage will result.

This model and its policies assumes that the world *cannot* continue to grow in the manner it has done till now. Its main proponents include environmental pressure groups, political parties of the 'green movement' and those who have established alternative technology centres in both the North and South.

Possible futures

What then of the future? Is the Third World likely to follow one rather than any other of the three models of development sketched out above? We shall focus our attention on the first two models, the capitalist and socialist paths, since the third, the Schumacherian vision of 'appropriate development', has policies but little by way of a proper analysis of how these might be implemented, which is a major weakness since it seems clear that they would require some significant social-economic and political changes. What circumstances, for example, would lead the advanced capitalist state to inaugurate 'Social Councils' and a major reform of the property rights of large corporations? Since no answer is to be found in Schumacherian texts it becomes impossible to assess the merit of this third account as an indicator of future trends. What then of the other two: what are the chances of capitalist or socialist development?

A Joke (?)

President Reagan asks God whether there will ever be Communism in the United States and is told 'Yes, but not in your lifetime'. General Secretary Gorbachev asks God whether Capitalism will ever come to the Soviet Union, and gets the same answer. Finally, President Sarney asks whether Brazil will ever be able to pay back its debts. 'Yes', says God, 'but not in *my* lifetime.'

Source: Susan George, *New Internationalist*, November 1988.

Is Capitalist Development Possible in the Third World?

Those of the pluralist persuasion clearly believe that an expansion of industrial capitalism Southwards is not only likely as the influence of Western technology and investment is felt but is also of great importance as a necessary fillip to the market for manufactured Northern goods. There are, it is recognised, problems that must be dealt with along the way, such as the attitude of traditionalism or an immature political culture, but given that the leadership of the South wants capitalist growth, these problems can be overcome in the long term. This vision of capitalist expansion depends on the willing compliance of Third World elites to open their countries to capital, technology and expertise from Western countries and to offer incentives to attract capital from overseas, including tax concessions, low wages and a range of public utilities such as transport, communications and health facilities etc., for the use of the foreign personnel. In short, the government tries to ensure the most favourable conditions to attract capital. A number of countries in Africa, such as Kenya, and in Latin America, such as Chile, have deliberately adopted this strategy with the long term hope of encouraging the growth of an indigenous, strong bourgeoisie, who, purely in pursuit of their own interests, can be relied on to push the country forward towards the prosperity bestowed by industrial growth. Hardship may prevail for the poorer rural sector who are not in the vanguard of this development, but this is to be tolerated as in the end *all* will benefit from the eventual establishment of a thriving domestic capitalist industry.

The structuralists of course reject the view that long term capitalist growth is possible by this strategy: they argue that it will always be distorted, uneven or abortive in character. Thus they argue that at present the world economy is split between North and South in ways indicative of abortive development. The North has the capital for investment, the technology for production and the monopoly of large scale manufacturing while the South is the market for Northern goods, the provider of cheap labour, and the cash crop producer. Moreover, those countries that are supposed to be moving down this capitalist road are the very ones that are amassing huge debts to world banks: Latin America as a whole owed over $500 billion by the autumn of 1988. Total Third World debt has now passed $1000 billion.

World trends in Production

One way of determining whether significant economic growth is likely to occur in the future is to inspect data from the recent past on relative shares in global production between different parts of the world economy. Any expansionary trends within the Third World could then be identified.

Gordon (1988) shows how, in Table 9.1 below, the share of Third World production has stagnated over the period 1948–84, whereas Japan and the Centrally Planned Economies (CPEs) have increased their relative share dramatically over the same period. The growth in the Third World (i.e. Less Developed Countries [LDCs]) during the 1930s resulted from their need to develop local industries in face of a world recession and their ability to supply raw materials to First World states during the subsequent World War. Presumably, one would not want future Third World development to depend on more of the same, especially if the next world war is likely to be nuclear.

TABLE 9.1 *The composition of global production, 1896–1984 (%)*

	DMEs*	Japan & CPEs	LDCs
1896–1900	91	6	3
1913	91	5	4
1926–1929	89	7	3
1938	76.7	12.9	10.4
1948	76.0	10.0	14.0
1966	65.8	22.0	12.2
1973	58.7	27.3	14.0
1979	54.5	30.9	14.6
1984	52.8	33.6	13.9

*DMEs = Developed Market Economies

We have seen however that writers such as Warren (1980) believe that these are short term policy problems which will be overcome in the future as industrial growth geared towards domestic needs gathers pace. For Warren this will lead to the ending of the domination by the old imperialist powers, as the newly industrialising countries such as India and Brazil begin to fashion their own *independent* industrial infrastructure.

As we noted, despite its Marxist pedigree, Warren's thesis is very strongly criticised by other Marxists, who, like Petras (1974) and Taylor (1979), claim that the *character* of industrial enterprise in the Third World does not point towards long term industrial growth.

On the face of it, however, it does appear that some leading NICs have begun to establish a manufacturing base in their own right that can be sustained and developed over the longer term. During the 1960s and 70s manufacturing production and export trade grew rapidly in Korea, Singapore, Malaysia, Brazil and Mexico. Thus, while core industrialised countries still dominate global manufacturing, these NICs have taken a significant minority share in it. Accompanying this growth in industry has been a growth in the industrial workforce: in Brazil, for example, the proportion of the labour force involved in manufacturing grew from 15 per cent to 24 per cent between 1960 and 1980. Some larger companies within NICs have grown to the point that they have begun to act as MNCs themselves, though compared with the range and scale of First World MNCs, they are still insignificant on a world scale. As Dicken (1986) says, the pattern of investment of these MNCs is very different from core country companies:

> The geographical pattern is heavily dominated by investment in other developing countries and especially in countries in close geographical and cultural proximity. Developing country [MNCs] tend to be small, to be involved in low-technology sectors with relatively high labour-intensity and to have close involvement with domestic firms in the countries in which they operate (p. 85).

Despite such developments, the NICs have in the past five years experienced a rapid slow down in the growth of their GDP with a number experiencing a negative growth rate between 1985–9. One reason for this is that NICs have relied very heavily on exports (mainly to Japan, the US and the EEC) to sustain their economies with local, domestic demand for goods being a smaller proportion of total demand. A few countries, most notably Korea, have been able to tie their export-led growth with a protectionist policy which has artifically restricted the import of foreign goods and services, unless they form part of export products to be. Latin American NICs have not been able – either politically or economically – to adopt protectionist measures and have seen a smaller overall growth in their indigenous industries while foreign MNCs have retained a substantial hold on their manufacturing base (almost 50 per cent in Brazil, for example).

We should be wary therefore of regarding NICs as countries that have 'solved' the development problem and are now set fair for sustained growth. Many have suffered a collapse in exports as the global recession of the mid 1980s led to a loss of First World demand. Moreover, as Gordon (1988) has shown (see Chapter 4), MNCs' global investment strategies suggest that they no longer regard Third World countries as most likely sources of profitable investment. MNCs will evaluate investment in countries like Malaysia, Brazil or Singapore against similar investment in the US, UK, Spain or wherever. Real labour costs and trade union power in the latter have been declining in recent years: in the UK real wages declined by over 30 per cent over the 1980–5 period (Singh, 1988).

Given these constraints on the sustained growth of NICs one should be cautious about accepting Warren's thesis of expansionary capitalist development in the Third World.It seems very unlikely that the Third World could independently industrialise and begin to consume resources in the same way that the North has done. Not only would this be ecologically disastrous, it would also be practically impossible. The US, the great consumer, spends considerable amounts of money militarily defending its access to scarce mineral resources, such as oil and uranium. It is not about to hand these over to any Third World state keen on independent growth.

Warren's reply to these various arguments about distortion, unevenness and constraints on capitalist growth is to argue that similar features can be found throughout the history of capitalist development in the West. For example there is nothing new about comparatively advanced technology locating itself in rural areas, using cheap labour and producing for markets elsewhere: such 'distortions' can be found during the early period of capitalist expansion in Britain. Hence, Warren remains unconvinced of the underdevelopment thesis and concludes his text with the words:

> Whatever the new world being created in Latin America, Asia, and Africa is to be, nothing can be gained from a refusal to recognise the existence of the developing capitalist societies already there. (Warren, 1980, p. 255).

What most of the structuralists, including Warren, agree on is that the expansion of capitalism in the Third World depends on the development of the class structure, and in particular, of the emergence of an aggressive, bourgeois class that can dominate the economy and influence the state (see Chapter 6). If industrialisation is to occur through the classical capitalist route then the rural peasantry has to be effectively eliminated as it was in Western Europe (Moore, 1966). Only then can agriculture be fully commercialised while the dispossessed peasants have to become 'free' wage labourers for the growing industrial and agricultural enterprises. Given the size of the Third World peasantry, numbered in hundreds of millions, such a route is indeed an awesome prospect, and it will only add to the deprivation that the rural poor already experience. This may, of course, prompt the masses into resistance, rebellion or outright revolution, which may take on a socialist character as the only real alternative to capitalism. Marxists believe that the socialist route is the only way in which Third World inequality can be overcome. It is argued that it is the only mode of production that can establish the conditions for a 'humane' industrialisation, that is, growth without inequality or deprivation. Is, then, the socialist route a real alternative?

A Socialist Alternative in the Third World?

The classical Marxist theory held that socialist revolution would be inaugurated by the industrial working class in the advanced capitalist states. Many socialist nations are in countries that are primarily agrarian. Some Marxists (for example Caldwell, 1977), revolutionary leaders (for example Guevara) and academics (for example Wolf) have argued that this indicates that it is likely to be the *peasantry* that is the most important revolutionary force in the Third World. The victories of Chinese and Cuban socialists has led some to believe that socialism need not be born of the struggle between the proletariat and the bourgeoisie in advanced capitalism. It can be installed in agrarian societies through a guerrilla war led by a socialist Party that has the physical support of the peasant masses (Cabral, 1969). However, this understates the political importance of the industrial and rural working classes that are growing in size in the Third World (see Cohen, 1979).

As we saw in Chapter 6, the vehicle for capitalist development has taken different forms, such as the strong German state or the liberal bourgeoisie of England. In a similar fashion, socialism in the Third World has been introduced by various means. Thus, we should not think that states declaring themselves to be 'socialist' are all alike. They differ in their origins, in the degree to which they have institutionalised socialist principles, and consequently in their capacity to prevail against all odds, in particular with the capitalist world economy.

Many states in the Third World are now officially designated as 'socialist', particularly in Africa and Asia. As such we should expect them to pursue policies which seek to abolish private ownership of the means of production and the exploitation of labour power in favour of the regulation of the economy by the state, priority being given to a redistribution of income and wealth. These countries vary however in the extent to which they have implemented these policies. While many, for example, Vietnam, Zimbabwe and Mozambique, have their origins in a nationalist, anti-imperialist struggle, as China and Cuba experienced, they face considerable difficulty in *continuing* the revolution and building socialism: no formal declaration of state is sufficient to bring about the fundamental economic and cultural changes socialism requires. In office, socialist governments have to contend with major problems with limited resources. It is no surprise then to find the Marxist, Paul Baran (1973, p. 14) remark, 'Socialism in backward and underdeveloped countries has a powerful tendency to become a backward and underdeveloped socialism'. It was pointed out in Chapter 6 how many so-called 'socialist' countries in the Third World are little more than quasi-state capitalist societies whose leaders use the rhetoric of socialism to garner popular appeal. What though of those few states that *have* attempted to bring about basic socialist reforms? Let us look, very briefly, at the inauguration of socialism in China, Tanzania, and

Chile. These three are chosen because they illustrate alternative paths to socialism that are more or less likely to lead to 'success', and since China is regarded as the most successful we shall give it most attention in our discussion.

The global conditions which prevailed when, in 1949, Chinese socialism was first established are not likely to be repeated. The Red Army under Mao's leadership fought its battles against the corrupt Chinese government and Japanese occupation, without having to contend with any external military threat from the centres of advanced capitalism, mainly because these very centres had just experienced the debilitating effects of the Second World War, 'victors' as much as 'vanquished'. US capital was more interested – through the Marshall Aid programme – in restoring the fortunes of Western Europe in order to capture the potential post-war market there, than what was happening in the Far East. Thus, China was relatively isolated in world affairs. Working with the peasantry in the rural regions over a number of years, Mao's army won the support of the peasantry from the landlords. When the Red Army finally triumphed against the government and the Japanese in the 1949 'War of Liberation' Mao had not only won the support of the rural classes he had also established an effective political and military machine that could be and was used to implement the major changes he wanted. In short he found himself with a unified country under the direction of a strong centralised state, whose agents, the Party workers and soldiers, were used to remove the remnants of the traditional local elites, control the movement of agricultural and industrial labour, ensure proper use of available resources, and hold down people's consumption to ensure a surplus for investment. Subsequently, as noted in Chapter 8, the Chinese received important assistance from the Soviet Union in the construction of large scale industrial enterprise in the Manchurian area which has been used to provide the technological inputs needed for *both* agricultural and industrial development. China is now one of the world's major powers and is beginning to come out of its relative isolation. However, it is still a predominantly agrarian society, with agricultural tasks soaking up almost ten million new members of the working population every year. Yet these who work in the agrarian communes are not peasants in the traditional sense of being individual, atomised small-holders; instead they are people working in the fields very much under the direction of the state. As Kitching (1982, p. 136) remarks:

> To put the matter paradoxically, the Chinese peasantry appears to have been 'saved' by being abolished. A total loss of individual peasant autonomy (in the use of land and labour power) has been the price of a continual rise in living standards and of greater equality both among peasants and between peasants and others.

Comparative isolation, class support, revolutionary struggle and a strong state machinery: these are four of the more important features that have accompanied the successful establishment of socialism in China.

What then of Tanzania? From our brief commentary in Chapter 8, it seems that Tanzanian socialism suffers from a virtual absence of the four aspects just noted. Tied into world capitalism economically, lacking a coherent power base among the rural masses, initiated through a radical shift in policy rather than revolution, and administered through a weak bureaucratic and Party structure: such factors do not bode well for the institutionalisation of socialism in the country. On top of which, we have already noted the absence of an industrial sector comparable to that of China which could provide the necessary inputs for *agricultural* as well as manufacturing growth. In short, socialism via populist reform lacks the structural strength that a fundamental socialist change requires.

What then of a democratic route to socialism? The democratic election of the Marxist government in Chile in September 1970 has a double significance: first, it clearly has something to say about the possibility of socialism via the ballot box; secondly, it might have some lessons for the socialist parties that currently hold power in Europe, such as in France. The fourth of September Presidential election saw Salvador Allende's Marxist Popular Unity party elected to office with 36.2 per cent of the vote. Electoral support for Allende was in fact slightly less than in 1970 when his party had polled 38.6 per cent of the vote. In 1973 however, the dominant right wing vote was split by two candidates, Alessandri and Tomic, allowing Allende to squeeze in to office with a slim 1.3 per cent greater electoral vote. Democratically, Allende's Popular Unity government had the constitutional right to *govern* Chile for the next six years. However unlike the Communist government of China, it did not have the *power* to rule. On the 11th September 1973 Allende's government was overthrown by the armed forces in a coordinated military coup. Why was it that Chilean socialism suffered such a fate as this?

One of the most detailed and careful studies of this period of Chilean history is that of Roxborough *et al.* (1977, p. 264). In it they argue:

> the working class cannot simply lay hold of the ready made State machinery and wield it for its own purposes. In practice, Allende's faith in bourgeois legality was suicidal: it was responsible for his death and for the death of some tens of thousands of other men, some of them supporters of Popular Unity, some of them not. The prospect of a coalition of Communists and Social Democrats taking the same road in Europe is not encouraging.

Why was Allendes's trust in 'bourgeois legality' so misplaced? Allende's task was to introduce a range of radical socialist policies that would favour the poor majority of the Chilean population through the use of the existing political institutions of the Chilean democratic State. Thus, although his powers as President were considerable they were largely circumscribed by the Chilean legislature, the Congress: this controlled taxes, ministerial appointments, had power to approve or disapprove of the budget, and of course was the only body which constitutionally was empowered to pass legislation. The Congress was controlled by the right wing parties whose leaders had been narrowly defeated at the Presidential election. Radical socialist proposals ran up against this concerted right wing opposition. The problem of 'bourgeois legality' is immediately evident: it effectively ties the hands of the radical left even when in office. Allende's proposals met with the combined opposition of the parties in Congress and the large private corporations, as well as the petit-bourgeois self employed who are of a significant number in the population. Thus as De Vylder (1976) says:

> Allende's position was ... precarious. He was elected on a programme which was radical enough to provoke determined resistance from the domestic and foreign economic establish-

ment, but his government was not strong enough to assume the direction of the economy and force the private sector to obey.

The fragility of socialism in Tanzania and its demise in Chile contrast strongly with the strength of China's socialist state. Both Tanzania and Chile, in different ways, have lacked the class support for socialist reform, and have failed to establish strong state administrations to implement policy. In addition, their peasant masses are still intact as smallholders with fairly strong individualist political consciousness and do not promise to become rural-based insurgents as they did in China. Last but by no means least, both Tanzania and Chile are much more exposed to overseas influence than China has ever been; Allende's government was particularly vulnerable to US economic and strategic interests in Latin America which perhaps explains why the US Ambassador to Chile should have said:

> Once Allende comes to power we shall do all within our power to condemn Chile and the Chileans to utmost deprivation and poverty (Roxborough *et al.*, 1977, p. 277).

9.3 CONCLUSION

In this final chapter we have summarised the three theories and policies of development discussed in detail in the book. The possibility of development via a capitalist or a socialist route was then discussed. Both seem to have major obstacles to negotiate concerning class and state structures. Capitalist expansion seems inherently limited due to weaknesses in the indigenous capitalist class and state, 'enclave' development and resource deficiencies. For its part, socialism can only be built through revolutionary class action and the formation of a strong party machinery that can mobilise resources and stave off foreign intervention: both requirements seem lacking in many underdeveloped countries. It is also the case that if socialism is to work as an alternative to capitalism its proponents in the Third World should not pursue an anti-industrial policy. As Kitching demonstrates convincingly through reference to China, centrally planned socialism can only work within a predominantly rural economy if it can draw on the technology and inputs of a healthy industrial sector. As we saw in Chapter 8, without this all Third World countries will remain vulnerable to foreign capital. Kitching draws the general conclusion that the transformation of society from rural to industrial structure is needed if one is to relieve world poverty. *If* this industrialisation occurs, and *whether* it occurs through the capitalist or socialist models, it will demand a high price in human suffering. As Moore (1966, p. 410) points out:

> Barring some technical miracle that will enable every ... peasant to grow abundant food in a glass of water or a bowl of sand, labour will have to be applied much more effectively, technical advances introduced, and means found to get food to the dwellers in the cities. Either masked coercion on a massive scale, as in the capitalist model ... or more direct coercion approaching the socialist model will remain necessary. The tragic fact of the matter is that the poor bear the heaviest costs of modernisation under both socialist and capitalist auspices.

Utlimately, perhaps, the global economy is structured not into 'three worlds' but two: the poor and non-poor. As Dube (1988, p. 113) says:

> There really are only two worlds – a small world of the rich and a much larger world of the poor – although within this bipolar world some other poles can also be identified. All projections appear to suggest that if the prevailing trends persist the gulf dividing these two worlds will have been considerably widened, not narrowed, as we enter the 21st century. The prospects for sub-Saharan Africa and South Asia are specially bleak. It is fashionable to talk of one planet and one environment: it is about time we began to think of one humanity.

Bibliography

2 MEASURES OF INEQUALITY AND DEVELOPMENT

I.-S. Abdalla (1978) 'Heterogeneity and differentiation – the end for the Third World?', *Development Dialogue*, 2.

R. Chambers (1973) *Rural Development: Putting the Last First* (Harmondsworth: Penguin).

M. Harrington (1969) *The Other America* (London: Macmillan).

N. Harris (1987) *The End of the Third World* (Harmondsworth: Penguin).

K. Hart (1973) 'Informal income opportunities and urban employment in Ghana', *The Journal of Modern African Studies*, 2, pp. 61–89.

R. van der Hoeven (1988) *Planning for Basic Needs: A soft option or a solid policy?* (Aldershot: Gower).

ILO Mission (1972) *Employment, Incomes and Equality: A Strategy for Increasing Productive Employment in Kenya* (Geneva).

M. Lipton (1977) *Why Poor People Stay Poor* (London: Temple Smith).

A. L. Mabogunje (1988) *The Development Process* (2nd edn, London: Hutchinson).

R. Matthews (1977) '"I'd sooner be here than anywhere": economic viability versus social vitality in Newfoundland', in S. Wallman (ed.) *Perceptions of Development* (Cambridge University Press) pp. 119–36.

H. Newby (1987) *Country Life* (London: Weidenfeld & Nicolson).

New Internationalist (1988) 'Native peoples and their future', August, p. 5.

D. Seers (1977) 'The new meaning of development', *International Development Review*, 3.

P. Streeten (1978) 'Basic needs: some issues', *World Development*, 6, pp. 411–21.

Y. Singh (1987) 'Rural development: rhetoric and reality', in K. S. Shukla (ed.) *The Other Side of Development* (London: Sage).

P. Townsend (1979) *Poverty in the United Kingdom* (Harmondsworth: Penguin).

Commission of the European Communities, *The Courier* (1982) (Brussels: Dieter Frisch-CEC).

S. Wallman (ed.) (1977) *Perceptions of Development* (Cambridge University Press).

World Bank (1982) *World Development Report* (New York: Oxford University Press).

3 MODERNISATION THEORY

M. Anderson (1971) *Family Structure in Nineteenth Century Lancashire* (Cambridge University Press).

P. Bauer (1976) *Dissent on Development* (London: Weidenfeld & Nicolson).

J. C. De Wilde (1967) *Experience with Agricultural Development in Tropical Africa* (Baltimore: Johns Hopkins Press).

M. Dobb (1983) *Studies in the Development of Capitalism* (London: Routledge).

E. Durkheim (1984) *The Division of Labour in Society* (trans. W. D. Halls) (London: Macmillan and New York: The Free Press).

S. N. Eisenstadt (1966) *Modernisation: Protest and Change* (Englewood Cliffs, NJ: Prentice-Hall).

S. N. Eisenstadt (ed.) (1970) *Readings in Social Evolution and Development* (Oxford: Pergamon).

A. G. Frank (1969) *Latin America: Underdevelopment or Revolution* (New York: Monthly Review).

J. Gusfield (1973) 'Tradition and modernity', in A. Etzioni and E. Etzioni-Halevy (eds) *Social Change* (New York: Basic Books).

E. E. Hagen (1962) *On the Theory of Social Change* (Homewood, Ill: Dorsey).

A. M. Hoogvelt (1976) *The Sociology of Developing Societies* (London: Macmillan).

D. Lerner (1964) *The Passing of Traditional Society* (New York: The Free Press).

N. Long (1977) *An Introduction to the Sociology of Rural Development* (London: Tavistock).

L. Mair (1984) *Anthropology and Development* (London: Macmillan).

G. Marshall (1982) *In Search of the Spirit of Capitalism* (London: Hutchinson).

B. Moore (1969) *Social Origins of Dictatorship and Democracy* (Harmondsworth: Peregrine).

D. McClelland (1961) *The Achieving Society* (New York: van Nostrand).

S. Ortiz (1970) 'The human factor in social planning in Latin America', in R. Apthorpe, *People, Planning and Development Studies* (London: Frank Cass).

T. Parsons (1951) *The Social System* (London: Routledge).

R. Penn (1986) *Skilled Workers in the Class Structure* (Cambridge University Press).

P. Roberts (1981) '"Rural development" and the rural economy in Niger 1900–75', in J. Heyer *et al.* (eds) *Rural Development in Tropical Africa* (London: Macmillan).

K. Polanyi (1944) *The Great Transformation: the Political and Economic Origins of Our Time* (Boston: Beacon Press).

W. W. Rostow (1960) *The Stages of Economic Growth* (Cambridge University Press).

I. Roxborough (1979) *Theories of Underdevelopment* (London: Macmillan).

R. F. Salisbury (1962) *From Stone to Steel* (Cambridge University Press).

M. Weber (1971) *The Protestant Ethic and the Spirit of Capitalism* (London: Unwin University Books).

P. Willis (1977) *Learning to Labour* (Westmead: Saxon House).
P. Willmott and M. Young (1971) *Family and Class in a London Suburb* (London: New English Library).
P. Worsley (1984) *The Three Worlds* (London: Weidenfeld & Nicolson).

4 THEORIES OF UNDERDEVELOPMENT

G. Adam (1975) 'Multinational Corporations and Worldwide Sourcing', in H. Radice (ed.) *International Firms and Modern Imperialism* (Harmondsworth: Penguin).
C. Ake (1981) *A Political Economy of Africa* (Nigeria: Longman).
S. Amin (1976) *Unequal Development* (New York: Monthly Review Press).
D. Apter (1988) *Rethinking Development: Modernisation, Dependency and Postmodern Politics* (Newbury Park: Sage).
A. M. Babu (1981) *African Socialism or Socialist Africa?* (London: Zed Press).
D. Booth (1985) 'Marxism and development sociology: interpreting the impasse', *World Development*, vol. 13, 7.
T. J. Byres (1979) 'Of neo-populist pipe-dreams: Daedalus in the Third World and the myth of urban bias', *Journal of Peasant Studies*, vol. 6, no. 2, pp. 210–44.
M. Caldwell (1979) *The Wealth of Some Nations* (London: Zed Press).
P. Cammack *et al.* (1988) *Third World Politics: a Comparative Introduction* (London: Macmillan).
F. H. Cardoso (1979) *Dependency and Underdevelopment in Latin America* (Berkeley: University of California Press).
T. Dos Santos (1973) 'The crisis of development theory and the problem of dependence in Latin America', in H. Bernstein (ed.) *Underdevelopment and Development* (Harmondsworth: Penguin).
D. Ernst (1981) *Restructuring Industry in a Period of World Crises* (Vienna).
J. Fielden (1836) *The Curse of the Factory System* (London).
D. K. Fieldhouse (1967) *The Theory of Capitalist Imperialism* (London: Longman).
A. G. Frank (1967) *Capitalism and Underdevelopment in Latin America* (New York: Monthly Review Press).
A. G. Frank (1969) *Latin America: Underdevelopment or Revolution* (New York: Monthly Review Press).
A. G. Frank (1981) *Crisis: In the Third World* (London: Heinemann and New York: Monthly Review Press).
A. G. Frank (1984) *Critique and Anti-Critique* (London: Macmillan).
A. G. Giddens (1985) *The Nation State and Violence* (Cambridge: Polity Press).
N. Girvan (1976) *Corporate Imperialism* (New York: Monthly Review Press).
D. Gordon (1988) 'The global economy', *New Left Review*, 168.

G. Kay (1975) *Development and Underdevelopment: A Marxist Analysis* (London: Macmillan).

G. Kitching (1982) *Development and Underdevelopment in Historical Perspective* (London: Methuen).

E. Laclau (1971) 'Imperialism in Latin America', *New Left Review*, 67.

V. I. Lenin (1966) *Imperialism, The Highest Stage of Capitalism* (Moscow: Progress Publishers).

C. Levinson (1980) *Vodka-Cola* (London: Gordon & Cremonesi).

A. Lipietz (1982) 'Towards global Fordism? Marx or Rostow?', *New Left Review*, 132.

A. Lipietz (1987) *Mirages and Miracles: The Crisis of Global Fordism* (London: New Left Books).

M. Lipton (1977) *Why Poor People Stay Poor* (London: Temple Smith).

N. Long (1977) *An Introduction to the Sociology of Rural Development* (London: Tavistock).

K. Marx (1976) *Capital*, vol. 1 (Harmondsworth: Penguin).

M. Mann (1986) *The Sources of Social Power* (Cambridge University Press).

K. Nkrumah (1965) *Neo-Colonialism: the Last Stage of Imperialism* (London: Nelson).

P. O'Brien (1975) 'A critique of Latin American theories of dependency', in I. Oxaal *et al.* (eds) *Beyond the Sociology of Development* (London: Routledge).

J. Petras (1969) *Politics and Social Forces in Chilean Development* (Berkeley: University of California Press).

P. Raikes (1988) *Modernising Hunger* (London: James Currey).

W. Rodney (1972) *How Europe Underdeveloped Africa* (Dar es Salaam: Tanzania Publishing House).

I. Roxborough (1979) *Theories of Development* (London: Macmillan).

R. Sandbrook and J. Arn (1977) *The Labouring Poor and Urban Class Formation* (Montreal: McGill University Centre for Developing Area Studies).

R. Stavenhagen (1973) 'Changing functions of the community in underdeveloped countries', in H. Bernstein (ed.) *Underdevelopment and Development* (Harmondsworth: Penguin).

G. Therborn (1979) 'Caudillos and elections', *New Left Review*, 113–14.

I. Wallerstein (1979) *The Capitalist World Economy* (Cambridge University Press).

W. Warren (1980) *Imperialism, Pioneer of Capitalism* (London: New Left Books).

G. P. Williams (1978) 'Imperialism and development', *World Development*, 6, 7/8, pp. 925–36.

5 POPULATION, URBANISATION AND EDUCATION

S. Amin (1977) 'The dynamic and limitations of agrarian capitalism in Black Africa', in P. Gutkind and P. Waterman (eds) *African Social Studies* (London: Heinemann).

I. Berg (1970) *Education for Jobs: the Great Training Robbery* (Harmondsworth: Penguin).
B. Bernstein (1971) 'A critique of the concept of compensatory education', in *Class, Codes and Control*, vol. 1 (London: Routledge).
A. Bilton *et al.* (1981) *Introductory Sociology* (London: Macmillan).
E. Boserup (1965) *The Conditions of Agricultural Growth* (London: Allen & Unwin).
G. Breese (ed.) (1972) *The City in Newly Developing Countries: Readings on Urbanism and Urbanisation* (Englewood Cliffs, NJ: Prentice-Hall).
R. Collins (1977) 'Some comparative principles of educational stratification', *Harvard Education Review*, 47, pp. 1–27.
R. H. Coombs and M. Ahmed (1974) *Attacking Rural Poverty: How Non-Formal Education Can Help* (Baltimore: Johns Hopkins Press).
J. Daniel (1981) 'The culture of dependency and political education in Africa', in D. L. Cohen and J. Daniel (eds) *Political Economy of Africa* (London: Longman).
C. D. Deere (1976) 'Rural women's subsistence production in the capitalist periphery', *Review of Radical Political Economics*, 8.
R. Dore (1976) *The Diploma Disease* (London: Allen & Unwin).
L. Dove (1981) 'The political context of education in Bangladesh, 1971–80', in P. Broadfoot *et al.* (eds) *Politics and Educational Change* (London: Croom Helm).
W. Ellwood (1982) 'Two steps forward, one step back', *New Internationalist*, no. 118, pp. 21–2.
E. Gauldie (1974) *Cruel Habitations* (London: Allen & Unwin).
S. George (1976) *How the Other Half Dies* (Harmondsworth: Penguin).
D. Gibbons (1981) *Agricultural Modernisation, Poverty and Inequality* (Farnborough: Gower).
J. Gregory and V. Piche (1978) *The Causes of Modern Migration in Africa* (Van Binsbergen).
J. Gugler and W. Flanagan (1978) *Urbanisation and Social Change in West Africa* (Cambridge University Press).
P. C. W. Gutkind (1967) 'The energy of despair: social organisation of the unemployed in two African cities: Lagos and Nairobi', *Civilisations*, 17.
N. Hafkin and E. Bay (1975) *Colonialism and Women's Roles* (Stanford: University Press).
P. Harrison (1980) *The Third World Tomorrow* (Harmondsworth: Penguin).
A. Halsey *et al.* (1980) *Origins and Destinations* (Oxford: Clarendon Press).
A. Hazlewood (1979) *The Economy of Kenya* (Oxford University Press).
F. Hosken (1979) 'The Hosken Report – genital and sexual mutilation of females', *Women's International Network News* (Lexington).
G. Jha (1987) 'Urban development: aspirations and deviations', in K. S. Shukla (ed.) *The Other Side of Development* (London: Sage).
T. Johnson (1972) *Professions and Power* (London: Macmillan).
F. Lappe and J. Collins (1977) *Food First* (Boston: Houghton Mifflin).
D. Lerner (1964) *The Passing of Traditional Society* (New York: The Free Press).

M. Mann (1986) *The Sources of Social Power* (Cambridge University Press).

R. Mellor (1982) *The Urban Perspective* (Milton Keynes: Open University Press).

M. Mies (1986) *Patriarchy and Accumulation on a World Scale* (London: Zed Books).

A. Mohiddin (1977) 'Towards relevant culture and politics in Africa', *Africa Development*, 2.

J. Nyerere (1977) *The Arusha Declaration: Ten Years After* (Dar es Salaam: Government Printing Office).

R. Repetto (1978) 'The interaction of fertility and the size distribution of income', in G. Hawthorn (ed.) *Population and Development* (London: Frank Cass).

W. Rodney (1972) *How Europe Underdeveloped Africa* (Dar es Salaam: Tanzania Publishing House).

H. Singer (1970) 'Brief note on unemployment rates in developing countries', *Manpower and Unemployment Research in Africa*, vol. 8.

UNESCO (1986) *Statistical Digest* (Paris).

J. Van Allen (1974) 'Women in Africa: modernisation means more dependency', *The Center Magazine*, 123, pp. 60–7.

K. Watson (1982) *Education in the Third World* (London: Croom Helm).

P. Willis (1977) *Learning to Labour* (Farnborough: Saxon House).

P. Worsley (1984) *The Three Worlds* (London: Weidenfeld & Nicolson).

World Bank (1988) *World Development Report* (New York: Oxford University Press).

6 POLITICAL DEVELOPMENT AND SOCIAL CLASS

R. Abrahams (1987) 'Vigilantism in Tanzania'. Mimeo. Department of Anthropology, University of Cambridge.

P. Bachrach and M. S. Baratz (1962) 'The two faces of power', *American Political Science Review*, 56, pp. 947–52.

P. Cammack *et al.* (eds) (1988) *Third World Politics: A Comparative Introduction* (London: Macmillan).

N. Chomsky and E. Herman (1979) *The Washington Connection and Third World Fascism* (Boston: South End Press).

M. Crenson (1971) *The Un-Politics of Air Pollution: A Study of Non-Decision-Making in the Cities* (Baltimore: Johns Hopkins Press).

R. Dahl (1961) *Who Governs?* (New Haven: Yale University Press).

S. N. Eisenstadt (1966) *Modernisation, Protest and Change* (Englewood Cliffs, NJ: Prentice-Hall).

S. Finer (1974) *Comparative Government* (Harmondsworth: Penguin).

A. G. Frank (1971) *Capitalism and Underdevelopment in Latin America* (Harmondsworth: Penguin).

A. G. Frank (1981) *Crisis: In the Third World* (London: Heinemann).

A. G. Giddens (1981) *A Contemporary Critique of Historical Materialism* (London: Macmillan).

A. G. Giddens (1985) *The Nation State and Violence* (Cambridge: Polity Press).

S. Hall *et al.* (1978) *Policing the Crisis: Mugging, the State, and Law and Order* (London: Macmillan).

S. P. Huntingdon (1968) *Political Order in Changing Societies* (New Haven: Yale University Press).

G. Hyden (1984) *No Short Cuts to Progress* (London: Heinemann).

J. J. Johnson (ed.) (1962) *The Role of the Military in the Underdeveloped Societies* (Princeton University Press).

C. Kerr *et al.* (1960) *Industrialism and Industrial Man* (Harmondsworth: Penguin).

D. Kotz (1979) *Bank Control of Large Corporations in America* (University of California Press).

S. M. Lipset (1959) *Political Man* (London: Heinemann).

P. Lloyd (ed.) (1967) *The New Elites of Tropical Africa* (Oxford University Press).

S. Lukes (1974) *Power: A Radical View* (London: Macmillan).

A. Mafeje (1977) 'Neo-colonialism, state capitalism, or revolution?', in P. C. W. Gutkind and P. Waterman (eds) *African Social Studies* (London: Heinemann).

R. Miliband (1977) *Marxism and Politics* (Oxford University Press).

C. W. Mills (1959) *The Power Elite* (New York: Oxford University Press).

B. Moore (1966) *Social Origins of Dictatorship and Democracy* (Harmondsworth: Peregrine Books).

R. Murray (1977) 'The social roots and political nature of military regimes', in P. C. W. Gutkind and P. Waterman (eds) *African Social Studies* (London: Heinemann).

O. O. Odetola (1982) *Military Regimes and Development* (London: Allen & Unwin).

C. Offe and V. Ronge (1975) 'Theses on the theory of the state', *New German Critique*, 6, pp. 139–47.

B. Onimode (1988) *A Political Economy of the African Crisis* (London: Zed Books).

T. Parsons (1967) 'On the concept of political power', *Social Theory and Modern Society* (New York: Free Press).

J. Petras and M. Zeitlin (eds) (1968) *Latin America: Reform or Revolution?* (Greenwich, Conn: Fawcett).

G. Philip (1984) *The Rise and Fall of the Peruvian Military Radicals* (London: Athlone Press).

N. Poulantzas (1975) *Political Power and Social Class* (London: New Left Books).

D. Riesman (1961) *The Lonely Crowd* (New Haven: Yale University Press).

M. Rodinson (1974) *Islam and Capitalism* (Harmondsworth: Penguin).

I. Roxborough (1979) *Theories of Underdevelopment* (London: Macmillan).

B. R. Rubin (1985) 'Economic liberalisation and the Indian State', *Third World Quarterly*, October, pp. 942–57.

R. Sandbrook and R. Cohen (1975) *The Development of an African Working Class* (London: Longman).
P. Schlesinger (1978) 'On the shape and scope of counter-insurgency thought', in G. Littlejohn *et al.* (eds) *Power and State* (London: Croom Helm).
G. Therborn (1970) 'What does the ruling class do when it rules?', *Insurgent Sociologist*, 6, pp. 3–16.
C. Vogler (1985) *Nation State and Class* (Aldershot: Gower).
M. Zeitlin (1974) 'Corporate ownership and control: the large corporation and the capitalist class', *American Journal of Sociology*, 79, pp. 1073–1108.

7 DEVELOPMENT PLANNING AND AID

P. Bauer (1976) *Dissent on Development* (London: Weidenfeld & Nicolson).
P. Bauer (1981) *Equality, the Third World and Economic Delusion* (London: Weidenfeld & Nicolson).
W. Bello *et al.* (1982) *Development Debacle: The World Bank in the Phillipines* (London: Third World Publications).
A. Bhaduri (1983) *The Economic Structure of Backward Agriculture* (London: Academic Press).
Brandt Commission (1979) *North-South: a Programme for Survival* (London: Pan Books).
Brandt Commission (1983) *Common Crisis* (London: Pan Books).
R. C. Byrant and R. Portes (1988) (eds) *Global Macroeconomics, Policy Conflict and Cooperation* (London: Macmillan).
R. Chambers (1983) *Rural Development: Putting the Last First* (Harmondsworth: Penguin).
A. G. Frank (1971) *Capitalism and Underdevelopment in Latin America* (Harmondsworth: Penguin).
A. G. Frank (1981) *Crisis: In the Third World* (London: Heinemann).
S. George (1976) *How the Other Half Dies* (Harmondsworth: Penguin).
S. George (1988) *A Fate Worse Than Debt* (Harmondsworth: Penguin).
D. Gibbons (1981) *Agricultural Modernisation, Poverty and Inequality* (Farnborough: Gower).
K. Griffin (1976) *Land Concentration and Rural Poverty* (London: Macmillan).
P. Harrison (1981) *The Third World Tomorrow* (Harmondsworth: Penguin).
B. Hartmann and J. K. Boyce (1980) *Needless Hunger: Voices from a Bangladesh Village* (New York: Institute for Food and Development Policy).
T. Hayter (1971) *Aid as Imperialism* (Harmondsworth: Penguin).
T. Hayter (1981) *The Creation of World Poverty* (London: Pluto Press).
R. van der Hoeven (1988) *Planning for Basic Needs: A Soft Option or a Solid Policy?* (Aldershot: Avebury).

K. King (1975) 'Boomerang aid', *New Internationalist*, October.
B. H. Kinsey (1987) *Agribusiness and Rural Enterprise* (London: Croom Helm).
G. Kitching (1982) *Development and Underdevelopment in Historical Perspective* (Milton Keynes: Open University Press).
G. Lanning and H. Mueller (1979) *Africa Undermined* (Harmondsworth: Penguin).
D. Lerner (1964) *The Passing of Traditional Society* (New York: Free Press).
M. Lipton (1977) *Why Poor People Stay Poor* (London: Temple Smith).
J. S. Mann (1969) 'The impact of Public Law 480 on prices and domestic supply of cereals in India', *Journal of Farm Economics*, 49.
D. McClelland (1961) *The Achieving Society* (New York: van Nostrand).
S. R. Mehta (1984) *Rural Development Policies and Programmes* (London: Sage).
C. Payer (1974) *The Debt Trap: The IMF and the Third World* (Harmondsworth: Penguin).
R. C. Riddell (1987) *Foreign Aid Reconsidered* (New York: ODI and Johns Hopkins University Press).
W. W. Rostow (1960) *The Stages of Economic Growth* (Cambridge University Press).
B. Warren (1981) *Imperialism: Pioneer of Capitalism* (London: New Left Books).
G. Williams (1981) 'The World Bank and the peasant problem', in J. Heyer *et al.* (eds) *Rural Development in Tropical Africa* (London: Macmillan).
J. Williamson (ed.) (1983) *IMF Conditionality* (Washington: Institute for International Economics).

8 CRITIQUE OF INDUSTRIALISATION

N. Clarke (1985) *The Political Economy of Science and Technology* (London: Blackwell).
N. Girvan (1976) *Corporate Imperialism: Conflict and Expropriation* (New York: Monthly Review Press).
P. Harrison (1980) *The Third World Tomorrow* (Harmondsworth: Penguin).
G. Kitching (1982) *Development and Underdevelopment in Historical Perspective* (Milton Keynes: Open University Press).
D. Meadows (1972) *Limits to Growth* (New York: Universe Books).
R. Mellor (1982) *The Urban Perspective* (Milton Keynes: Open University Press).
R. McCutcheon (1979) *Limits of a Modern World* (London: Butterworth).
G. McRobie (1980) *Small is Possible* (New York: Harper & Row).
J. K. Nyerere (1968) 'Socialism and rural development', *Freedom and Socialism* (Dar es Salaam, 1967; Oxford University Press).

C. Reich (1970) *The Greening of America* (New York: Random House).
J. Saul (1977) 'Nationalism, socialism and Tanzanian history', in P. C. W. Gutkind and P. Waterman (eds), *African Social Studies* (London: Heinemann).
E. F. Schumacher (1973) *Small is Beautiful. Economics as if People Mattered* (New York: Harper & Row).
C. Sweet (1983) *The Price of Nuclear Power* (London: Heinemann).
R. H. Tawney (1966) *The Radical Tradition* (Harmondsworth: Pelican Books).
The Ecologist (1972) *A Blueprint for Survival* (Harmondsworth: Penguin).
H. Wainwright and D. Elliott (1983) *The Lucas Plan* (London: Allison & Busby).
P. Worsley (1984) *The Three Worlds* (London: Weidenfeld & Nicolson).

9 CONCLUSION

P. Baran (1973) *The Political Economy of Growth* (Harmondsworth: Penguin).
P. Bauer (1981) *Equality, the Third World and Economic Delusion* (London: Weidenfeld & Nicolson).
Brandt Commission (1979) *North-South: a Programme for Survival* (London: Pan Books).
M. Caldwell (1977) *The Wealth of Some Nations* (London: Zed Press).
F. H. Cardoso and E. Faletto (1979) *Dependency and Development in Latin America* (Berkeley: University of California Press).
R. Cohen *et al.* (eds) (1979) *Peasants and Proletarians* (London: Hutchinson).
A. De Vylde (1976) *Allende's Chile* (Cambridge University Press).
P. Dicken (1986) *Global Shift* (London: Harper and Row).
S. C. Dube (1988) *Modernisation and Development* (London: Zed Books).
S. N. Eisenstadt (1966) *Modernisation: Protest and Change* (Englewood Cliffs; NJ: Prentice-Hall).
A. G. Frank (1971) *Capitalism and Underdevelopment in Latin America* (Harmondsworth: Penguin).
A. G. Frank (1980) 'North–South and East–West Keynesian paradoxes in the Brandt Commission', *Third World Quarterly*, 2, 4.
S. George (1988) *A Fate Worse Than Debt* (Harmondsworth: Penguin).
D. Gordon (1988) 'The global economy: new edifice or crumbling foundations?', *New Left Review*, 168, March–April.
G. Kitching (1982) *Development and Underdevelopment in Historical Perspective* (Milton Keynes: Open University Press).
D. Lerner (1964) *The Passing of Traditional Society* (New York: Free Press).
B. Moore (1966) *Social Origins of Dictatorship and Democracy* (Harmondsworth: Penguin).

T. Parsons (1966) *Societies* (Englewood Cliffs, NJ: Prentice-Hall).

J. Petras (1969) *Politics and Social Forces in Chilean Development* (University of California Press).

J. Petras *et al.* (1974) 'Industry in the Third World', *New Left Review*, 85, May–June.

I. Roxborough *et al.* (1977) *Chile: The State and Revolution* (London: Macmillan).

E. F. Schumacher (1973) *Small is Beautiful. Economics as if People Mattered* (New York: Harper & Row).

M. S. Singh (1988) 'The Changing Role of the Periphery in the International Industrial Arena Exemplified by Malaysia and Singapore', in G. R. Linge (ed.) *Peripheralisation and Industrial Change* (London: Croom Helm).

J. G. Taylor (1979) *From Modernisation to Modes of Production* (London: Macmillan).

W. Warren (1980) *Imperialism, Pioneer of Capitalism* (London: New Left Books).

Author Index

Subject Index

Printed in the United States
94055LV00002B/72/A

9 780333 495087